I0901058

IMAGES
of America

ROCK CREEK VALLEY

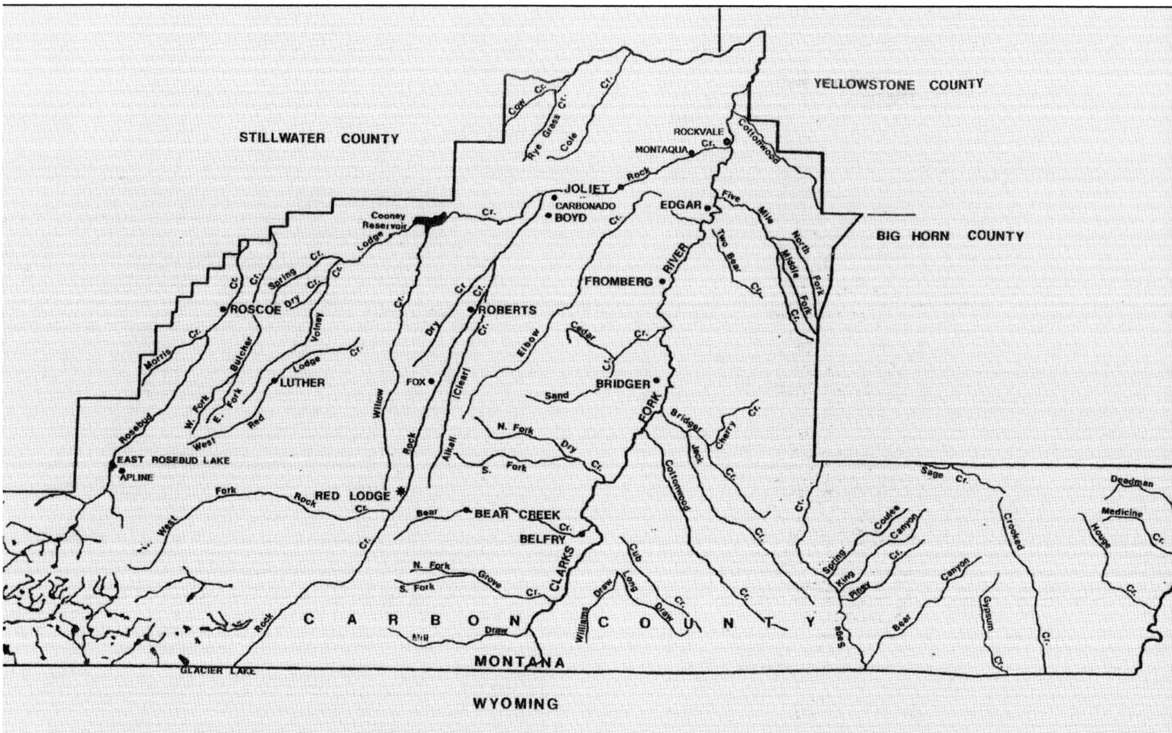

Rock Creek begins in the southwestern corner of Carbon County, its valley weaving a fertile floodplain north-northeast for 68 miles until it empties into the Clark's Fork of the Yellowstone River. The emphasis of this book will be the communities of the Rock Creek Valley and western Carbon County. (Courtesy of the Carbon County Historical Society.)

On the Cover: Roberts locals pause in the sunshine for an afternoon beer in 1934 outside the New Deal Bar on First Street. Built by Batt Bertolino Sr., it was run by Batt Bertolino Jr., seen in the doorway at far right. The family also operated a café next door for several years. (Courtesy of the Carbon County Historical Society.)

IMAGES
of America

ROCK CREEK VALLEY

Bob Wallace and
the Carbon County Historical Society

ARCADIA
PUBLISHING

ISBN 978-0-7385-9999-1

Published by Arcadia Publishing
Charleston, South Carolina

Printed in the United States of America

Library of Congress Control Number: 2012954816

For all general information, please contact Arcadia Publishing:
Telephone 843-853-2070
Fax 843-853-0044
E-mail sales@arcadiapublishing.com
For customer service and orders:
Toll-Free 1-888-313-2665

Visit us on the Internet at www.arcadiapublishing.com

To all who have lived, labored, and loved in the Rock Creek Valley,
to those who have worked to preserve its history,
and to my parents, who kindled my love of history

Contents

ACKNOWLEDGMENTS

To my family, friends, and neighbors, new and old, I owe you an unfathomable debt for your help and support in assembling this work.

For working to preserve Carbon County historical heritage, I would like to thank Carbon County Historical Society (CCHS) executive director Donna Madson; past and present CCHS employees Dana Wahlquist, Debbi Brown, Joan Guralnick, Cathy Wiltgren, and Scot Lauf; Deb Hronek, executive director of the Joliet Public Library; Jodie Moore, executive director of the Red Lodge Carnegie Public Library; Krystal Zentner, executive director of the Bridger Public Library; Shirley Smith, owner of the Little Cowboy Bar and Museum in Fromberg, Montana; and Penny Redli (Redli), executive director of the Museum of the Beartooths in Columbus, Montana.

The photographs in this book that are courtesy of the CCHS are from the Craig-Worth, Puutio, Lampi, Luoma, Collins (Collins), Johnson, Greenough, Tolman-Dilworth, Linley-Pogue (Linley-Pogue), Lahti, Bertolino, Koski, Kivikangas, Gardner, Pat Twomey, M.E. Hawkes, Gibson, Tolman, Zupan, Hatten, Spaulding, Golden, Whitcher, Siegfriedt, and Durst-Indreland collections.

Photographs from Joliet Public Library (JPL) include photographs from the Spaulding, Arthun, Whitcher, Talmage, Stender, Bell, Hull, Golden, Stene, and Blain collections.

For sharing photographs from their private collections, I would like to thank Norm and Margaret Dewell (Dewell), Todd Bell (Bell), Terry and Teena Kennedy (Kennedy), Mary Allen (Allen), Joel Bertolino (Bertolino), Elta Ayre (Ayre), Bob Jensen (Jensen), Bill and Deb Hogan (Hogan), Richard Thayer (Thayer), Ron and Thelma Woody (Woody), Bob and Jeanne Wakenshaw (Wakenshaw), Ken and Mike Hoines (Hoines), Jim and Beverly Charleton (Charleton), Annette Anderson (Anderson), Isabel Monaco (Monaco), Barbara Herbert (Herbert), and Joan Johnston (Johnston). Contemporary photographs were taken by the author (Wallace).

I would also like to thank David Davidson, Albert Brown, Mike Manweiler, Stanley Antilla, Marj Oliver, Patrick Buckingham, Don Lorash, Diana Dunn, Preston Sweeney, Mike and Bridget Firehammer, Alastair Baker, Christie Krook, and fellow Arcadia authors Jeff McNeish, John Clayton, and Patty Hooker.

For their help in researching historical information, I would like to thank historians Karen Hergenrider and Leona Lampi-Hassen; Jim Domino of the Montana Department of Natural Resources and Conservation (DNRC); Earl Radonski of the Montana Department of Fish, Wildlife & Parks; and Tom and Sherry Egenes of Flash's Photography (Flash).

INTRODUCTION

Rock Creek begins high on the Beartooth Plateau, a mountainous area in southwestern Carbon County, in south-central Montana, where peaks rise to over 12,000 feet above sea level, including Montana's highest: the 12,799-foot Granite Peak. The area, one of the most remote in the lower 48 states, is home to thousands of lakes fed by glacial runoff and heavy snowfall. From Glacier Lake, Rock Creek's headwaters on the Montana-Wyoming state line, the waterway winds 68 miles in a north-northeasterly direction to its confluence with the Clark's Fork of the Yellowstone River near Rockvale.

Rockvale, a small unincorporated community, is named for the vale of rock that lies along the east bank of the Clark's Fork River and into which Rock Creek runs perpendicularly. The rock formation is the northern end of the Pryor Uplift, which created the Pryor Mountains and Beartooth Plateau during the mid-Tertiary period, 30 to 40 million years ago. Over ages, materials eroded from the Beartooths were carried downstream and, during various stages of drainage, were deposited to form gravel terraces known locally as "benches." These benches lining Rock Creek rise up to 200 feet near Red Lodge and vary from 7 feet to 115 feet farther down Rock Creek Valley, stretching as far as 30 miles from the base of the Beartooths and defining Rock Creek's floodplain.

Human habitation in the Rock Creek Valley dates back to 10,000 BC, when Paleo-Indians followed animal migration routes up the valley into the Beartooth Mountains and the area that would one day become Yellowstone National Park. Evidence that these Paleo-Indians wintered in the valley and summered in the mountains is supported by projectile points, atlatls, and other artifacts discovered in the valley as well as high in the ice fields of the Beartooths. Pressure by other Plains Indians such as the Sioux and Blackfoot forced the Apsàalooke—the predecessors of the Crow Indians—to migrate westward from their native range in the Midwest. Petroglyphs found near Joliet bearing impressions of a shield-bearing warrior, a woman dancing, and two large bears date from between the 1620s and 1880s.

The Lewis and Clark Expedition did not quite make it to Rock Creek; they camped about 15 miles away near the confluence of the Clark's Fork and Yellowstone Rivers in 1806. Trappers, including Joe Meek and John Colter from the Rocky Mountain Fur Company, are known to have camped near the confluence of Rock Creek, then known as Rocky Fork, in the 1830s.

In 1864, Jim Bridger surveyed the Bozeman Trail, but he did not like the original route it took east of the Big Horn Mountains because it was susceptible to Sioux attack. The next year, Bridger charted the trail west of the Big Horns up the Clark's Fork River Valley, then up Rock Creek to a crossing just below where the town of Joliet now stands. From there, the trail continued north to the Yellowstone River Valley before turning westward. Using this trail, Myron Jeffers brought cattle from Texas to the Rock Creek Valley, near Red Lodge, in 1869.

From the 1860s to the 1890s, the Rock Creek Valley served as a wide, smooth passage for early stagecoach lines. The main stage line of the time linked the Union Pacific Railroad in Rawlins, Wyoming, to the Northern Pacific Railway in Billings. The stage stops of Coulee Creek and Rocky Crossing were predecessors to the towns of Roberts and Joliet, respectively.

Montana Territory was established in 1864, and the following year, it was divided into nine counties. Most of what is now Carbon County was originally part of the Crow Indian Reservation. Montana was granted statehood on November 8, 1889. In 1895, Carbon County was created out of parts of Gallatin and Big Horn Counties. Later that year, voters selected Red Lodge as the county seat over Joliet, 687 votes to 307.

In 1866, prospector James "Yankee Jim" George first found coal deposits near Red Lodge. Ownership of George's claim eventually passed into the hands of L.J. Platt. An energetic developer, Platt set up a small mining camp near the confluence of Rock Creek and its west branch, just south of Red Lodge; however, he faced challenges in getting coal to market, with the nearest rail line 47 miles away in Laurel. With a tacit agreement that the Northern Pacific Railway and the Anaconda Copper Company would be lucrative customers for Red Lodge coal, Platt formed the Rocky Fork & Cooke City Railroad, which completed a line from Red Lodge to Laurel in 1889. Regular service began on May 20, 1889. In 1890, the Northern Pacific purchased the Rocky Fork & Cooke City Railroad and named it the Rocky Fork Branch. By 1891, Red Lodge had become Montana's largest coal producer. Completion of the rail line opened the length of Rock Creek Valley for settlement.

The opening of the Red Lodge mines brought an influx of European immigrants, as well as pioneers from the East Coast and the Midwest, to the Rock Creek Valley around 1900. Through the 1920s and into the 1930s, labor unrest, diminishing deposits, and decreased demand for coal led to the decline and eventual extinction of Red Lodge's coal industry. Meanwhile, many families who had come to the region to mine moved out of the mines onto homesteads and took up farming or raising livestock. Early settlers found Rock Creek Valley a picturesque place as cruel as it could be bountiful, a place of wildflowers and wildfires, bright sun and blinding blizzards, where neighborliness was borne out of necessity.

In 1936, the Beartooth Highway was completed, linking Red Lodge with Cooke City and the northeast entrance to Yellowstone National Park. The scenic highway, which climbs switchbacks up the steep, narrow walls of Rock Creek Canyon, was the product of years of lobbying on the part of prominent Carbon County businessmen. Their efforts resulted in the Park Approach Act and Amendment to the Federal Highway Act in 1931, making financing and construction of the highway possible. Red Lodge quickly established itself as a traveler's gateway to the unspoiled wilderness of the Beartooth Mountains and Yellowstone.

Downstream, on the fruitful fields along Rock Creek, agriculture continued to prosper. In Roberts, Fox, Luther, and Roscoe, cattle, sheep, poultry, grain, beans, peas, and hay were bumper crops. In 1936, Cooney Reservoir was completed eight miles west of Boyd, making a water impoundment at the junction of two of Rock Creek's main tributaries, Red Lodge Creek and Willow Creek. The project brought irrigation to an additional 20,000 acres of land in the Rock Creek Valley between Boyd and Rockvale to compliment already fertile bottomland. Today, the Rock Creek Valley flourishes on the agricultural foundation that took root in the last century, and it continues to serve as a gateway for tourists to the pristine high country of the Beartooth Mountains and Yellowstone National Park.

One

Rockvale and Poverty Flat

Rockvale got its start as a flag stop on the Rocky Fork Branch of the Northern Pacific Railway. It was first settled in 1893 and had a post office from 1894 to 1914. About a mile south of Rockvale, Rock Creek empties into the Clark's Fork River. The Lewis and Clark Expedition did not quite make it to Rock Creek, camping about 15 miles away near the confluence of the Clark's Fork and Yellowstone Rivers in 1806.

Trappers from the Rocky Mountain Fur Company, including Joe Meek and John Colter, are known to have camped near the confluence of Rock Creek in the 1830s. Independent trapper Osborne Russell, in his *Journal of a Trapper*, recounts camping with Meek and about 60 others near the confluence of Rock Creek (then known as Rocky Fork) and the Clark's Fork River. In September 1837, Russell wrote of trappers and their Delaware Indian scouts coming under attack from Blackfoot Indians. After a trapper named Howell was killed in a skirmish with Blackfoot the following spring, he was buried under a large tree near the confluence, and the site was dubbed Howell's Encampment.

For years afterward, natives, trappers, and mountain men would rendezvous in the area, trading, communicating, and recreating together. In recent years, the site has played host to several mountain man rendezvous reenactments. Although the Wilsey railroad depot, store, and section house were located about a mile northeast of Joliet, the Wilsey school was near Rockvale, about a mile and a half to the southwest in a farming area known as Poverty Flat, where the Rock Creek Valley and Clark's Fork Valley floodplains intersect. The floodplains make for especially fertile bottomland, which flanks the southern bank of Rock Creek from Rockvale upstream to Joliet.

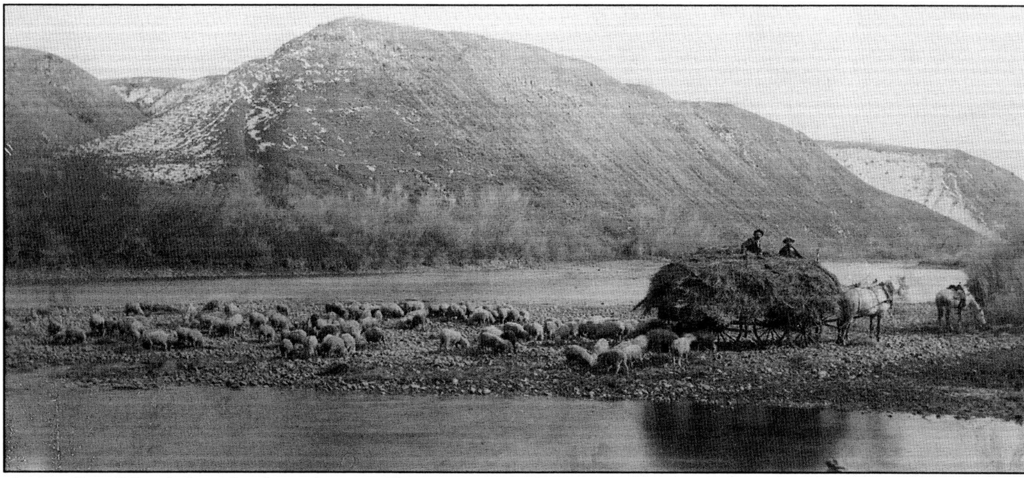

A shepherd feeds his flock at the confluence of Rock Creek and the Clark's Fork of the Yellowstone River in the 1890s. The confluence marks a centuries-old crossroads. Native Americans used it to migrate from prairie to mountain. Trappers camped here in the 1830s. Nearby, the Northern Pacific Railway's Rocky Fork Branch met the Chicago, Burlington & Quincy Railroad's Casper Subdivision. Today, Highways 212 and 310 meet at Rockvale. (CCHS.)

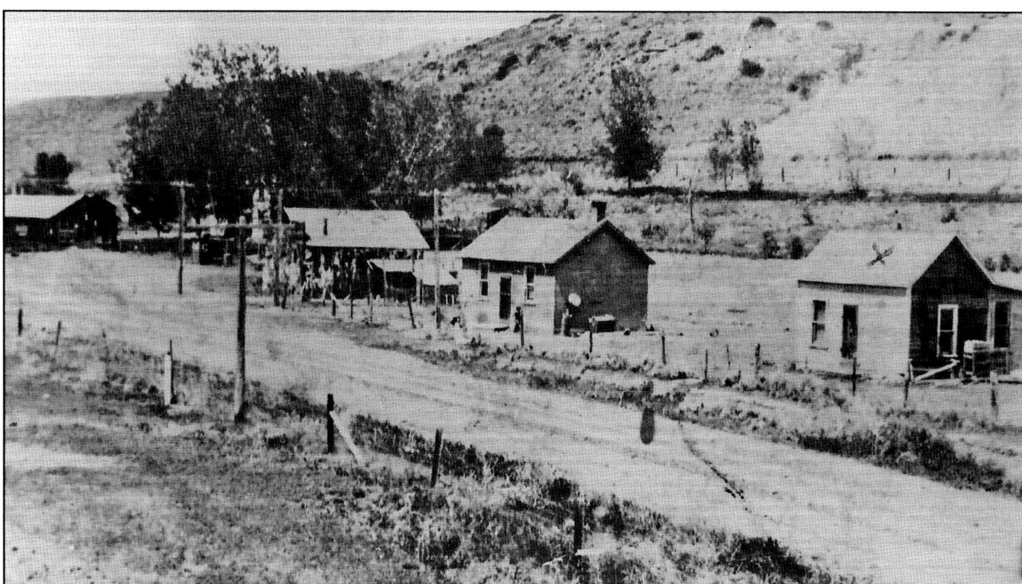

Despite its natural position as a crossroads, Rockvale never amounted to more than a shipping point for stock and produce and as a place for locals to get mail, supplies, and send their children to school. This 1917 photograph shows the first Rockvale school (second from the right), which was built in 1899. To its right is the teacherage. To the far left is the blacksmith shop. (CCHS.)

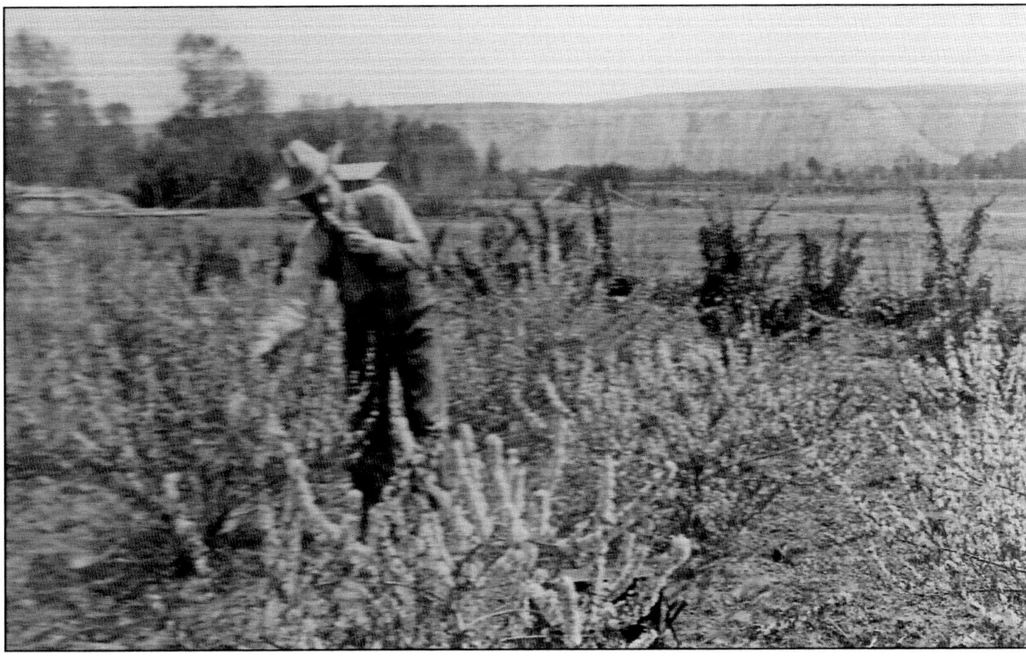

Above, Arthur Pierce checks the fragrance of cherry blossoms on the Nutting Bush Farm, north of Rockvale. Early agricultural endeavors in this part of the Rock Creek Valley centered around fruit production, with cherries, strawberries, and apples flourishing in the fertile soil in this part of the valley. Nutting's chief competitor was the Yellowstone Nursery Company, owned by Rockvale's Oliver Chilcott, which raised apples, cherries, plums, currants, pears, and strawberries. Below, workers sow young plants in one of Chilcott's fields. By 1907, Chilcott's orchards had 20,000 three-year-old trees and 50,000 two-year-old trees. The farmhouse in the background still stands in Rockvale. (Both, CCHS.)

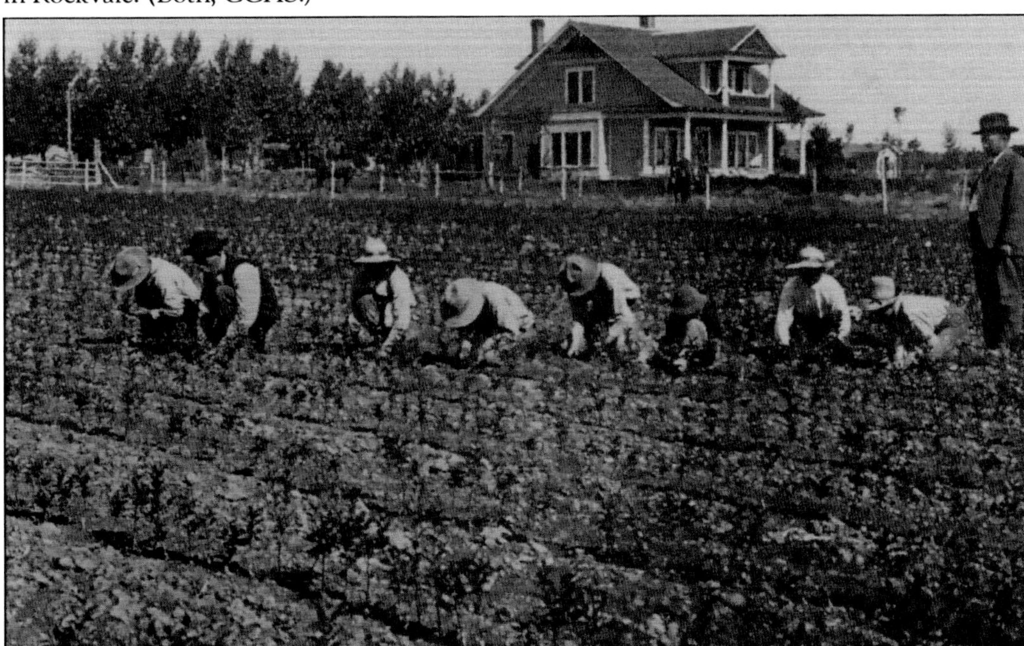

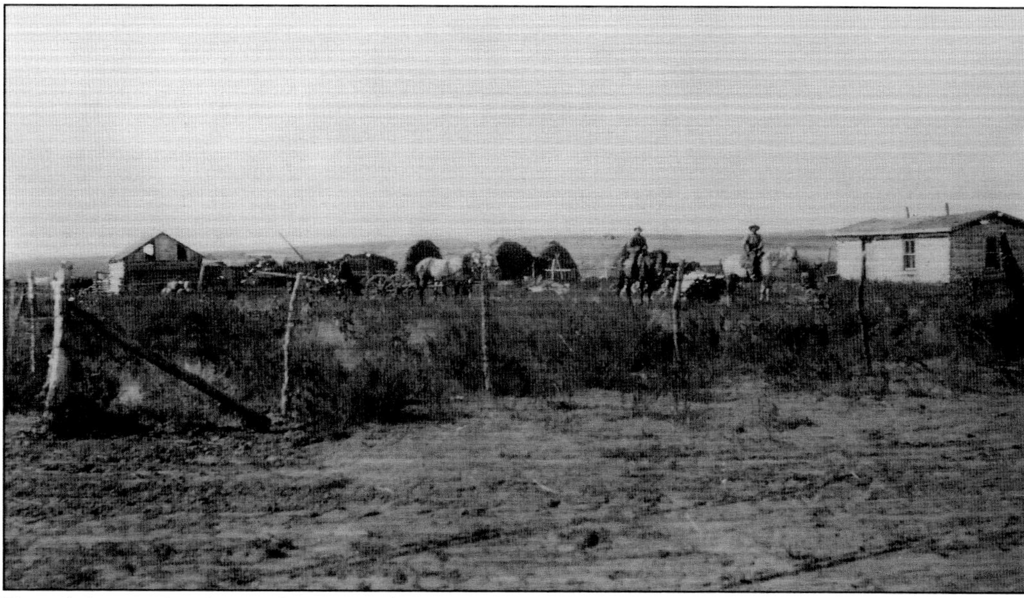

From left to right, Anton Jensen, Bob Duncan, and John Clawson prepare for a trip to the Pryor Mountains in 1898 to harvest timber with which to build the Jensen homestead, about a mile south of Rockvale in the Poverty Flat area. Duncan and his wife, Lillie, had seven children. Around 1900, Jensen and some neighbors founded the Rockvale Cemetery. (Jensen.)

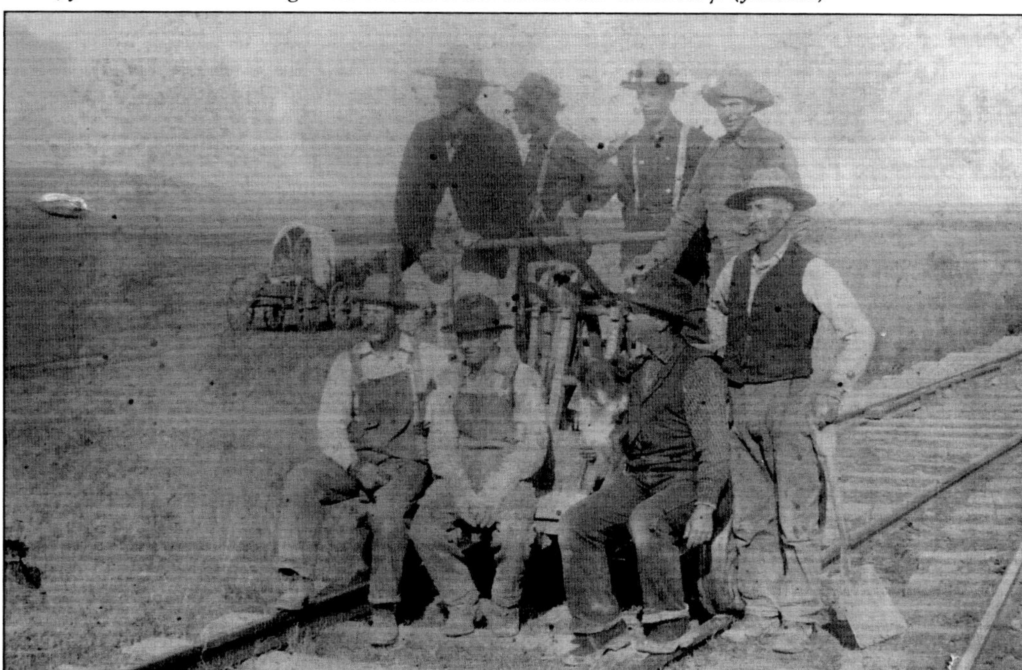

Wear and tear of heavy coal trains, extreme weather, and regular mishaps kept railroad section crews busy during the early years of the Rock Fork Branch. Here, members of the Rockvale section team ride the handcar around 1895. They are, from left to right, (first row) Ed Enochs, ? Smith, Frank Craig, and unidentified; (second row) Till Webber, John Craig, Wayman Dix, and unidentified. (CCHS.)

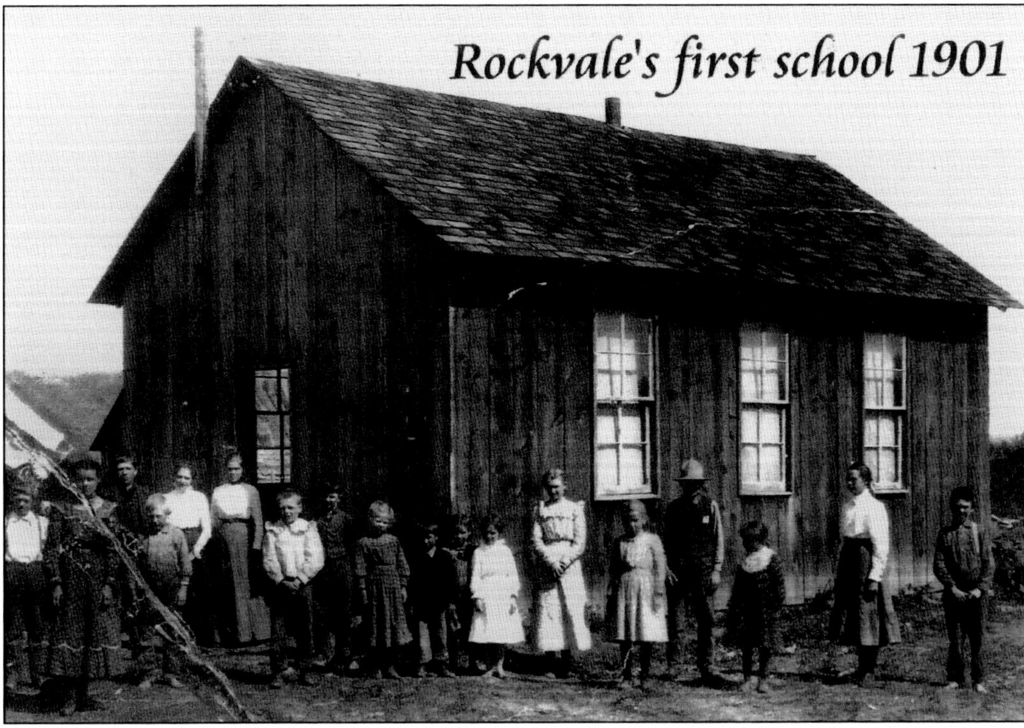

Above, students from grades one through eight stand outside the first Rockvale school in 1901. They are, from left to right, Harry Luke, Pearl Simpson, Willie Henry, Jim James, Ethel Luke, teacher Martha Holland, Paul Simpson, Earl Clawson, Mary McClintock, Carl Henry, Bertha Nelson, Becca James, Dallis James, Druzilla Craig, Ray James, Minnie Craig, Laura Craig, and Clarence Baldwin. The second Rockvale school (below) opened west of town in 1907 but burned in 1963. (Above, JPL; below, CCHS.)

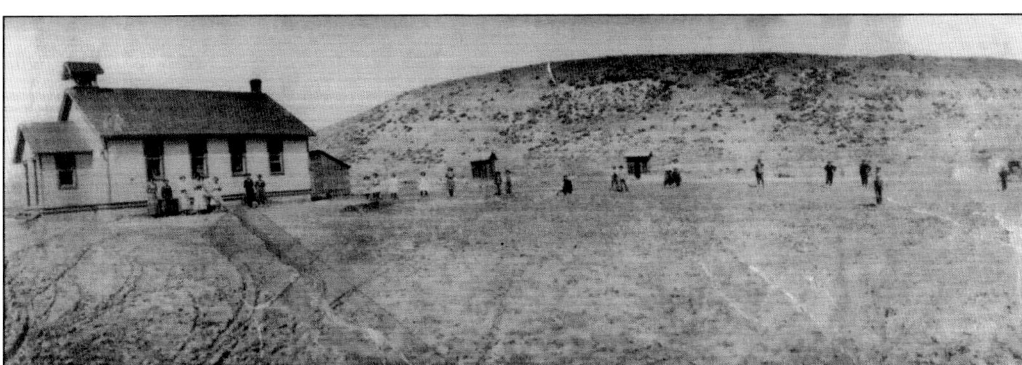

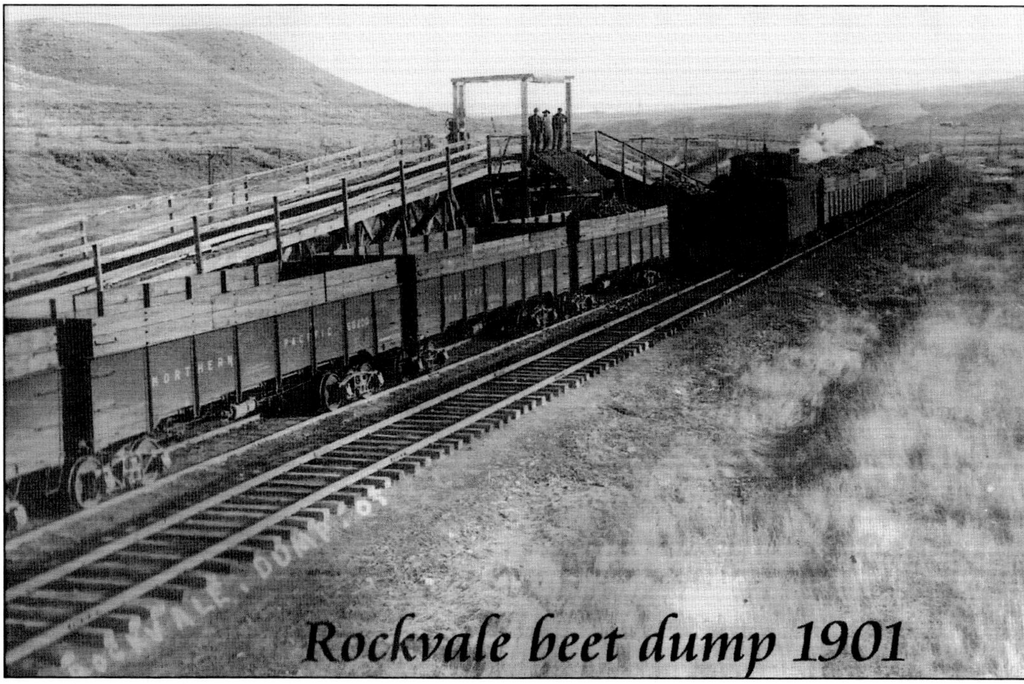

Sugar beets were first introduced to the Rock Creek Valley around 1905 and quickly became a staple crop that remains so today. To facilitate the sugar beet boom, the Northern Pacific Railway set up several beet dumps, like the one in Rockvale seen in these photographs. The railroad constructed a siding track (above) and built a platform and dumping mechanism to quickly unload wagons of beets into waiting gondolas. Wagons were fastened to the platform and turned sideways, tipping the platform and wagon on its side (below) to spill the beets into the gondola. (Both, JPL.)

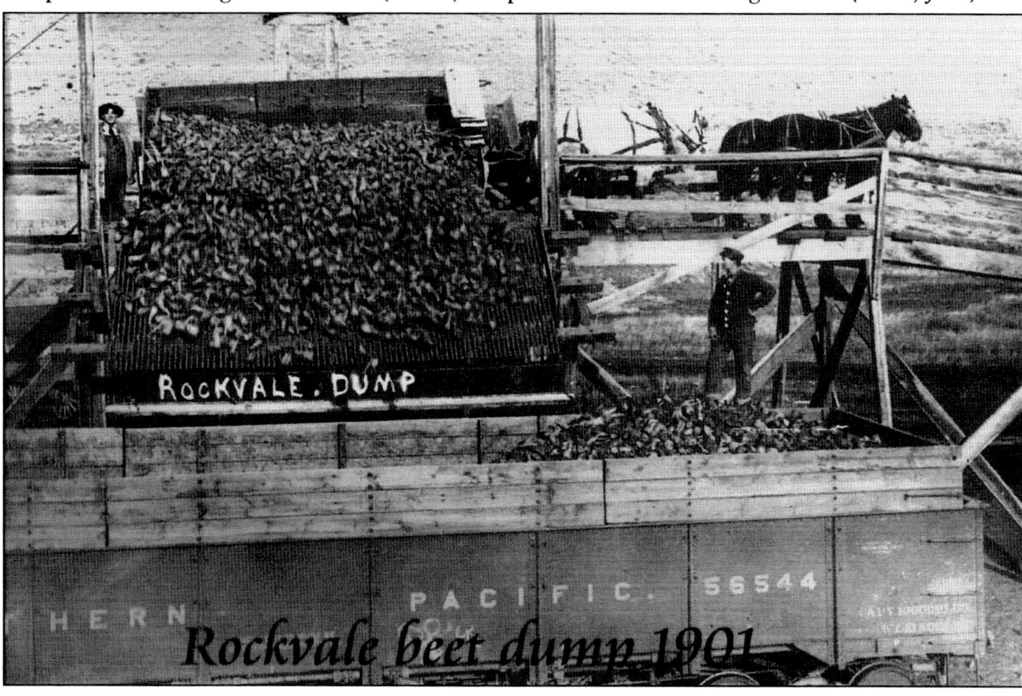

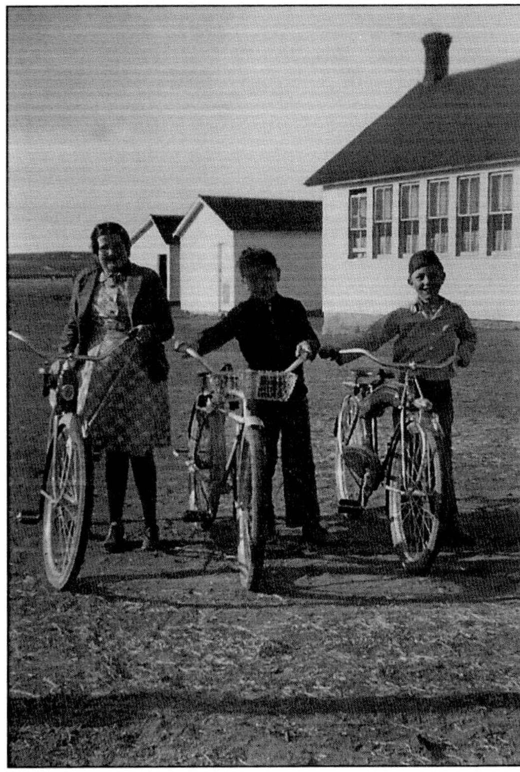

The Wilsey school was located on Young Road, about a mile west of the Rockvale Cemetery in an area known as Poverty Flat. Opened in 1885, it operated until 1957, when it was consolidated into the Edgar School District. These photographs from around 1940 show that, while more students were riding bicycles to school, some were still taking the family horse (below). David Stark is seen on his bicycle on the far right. Fruit trees and orchards dotted Poverty Flat in the early years. Later, sugar beets would come to dominate Poverty Flat farms. Other early homesteading families on Poverty Flat included the Youngs, Serights, Jensens, and Stenders. (Both, CCHS.)

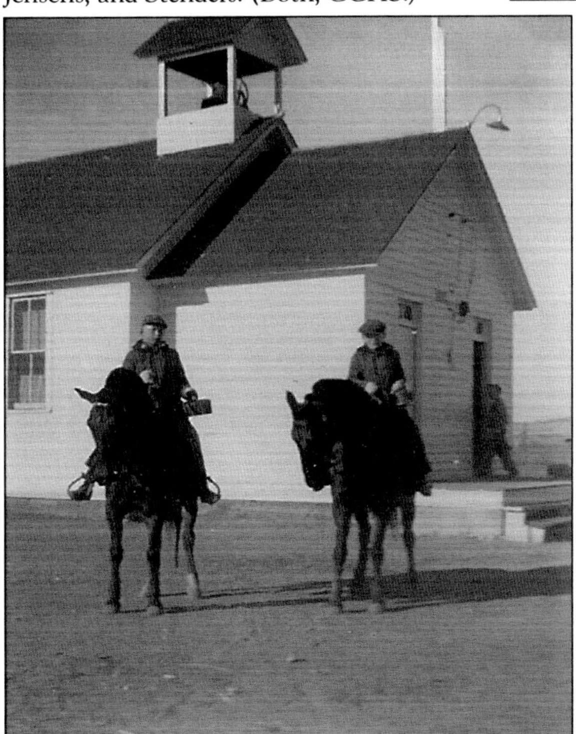

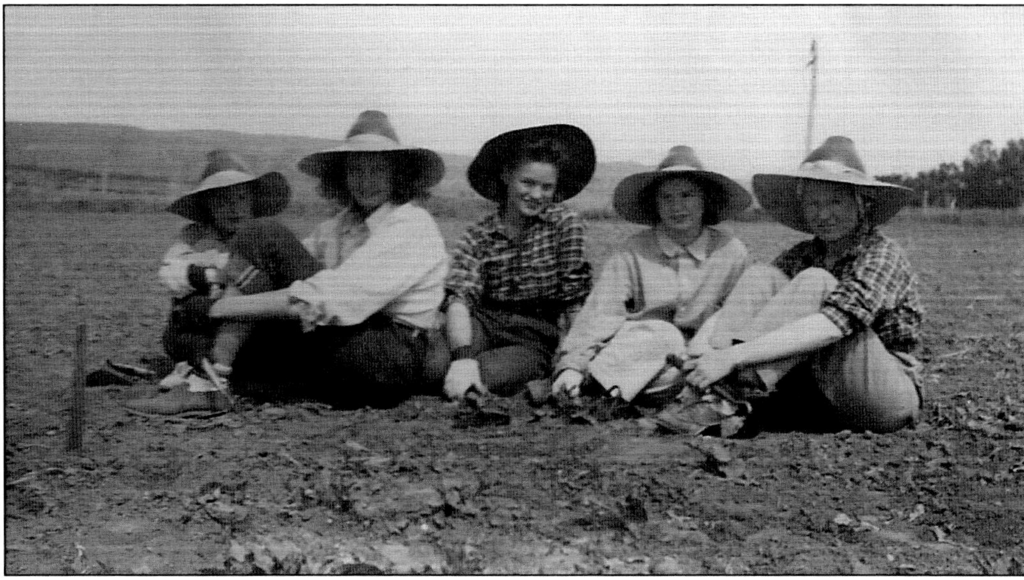

Above, from left to right, Mary Ducksberry, Annabelle Talmage, two unidentified, and Jo Hatten pause while sowing seeds (below) on Poverty Flat around 1940. Little is known of how Poverty Flat earned its name, as its bottomlands are some of the most fertile in the county. Orchards once lined the banks of Rock Creek on Poverty Flat, but as early as 1905, production switched over to grains, hay, and sugar beets. It has been suggested that, since many of the first homesteaders were Scandinavian, the name may have been a classic misidentification, similar to the verdant island named Iceland and the barren ice mass named Greenland. (Both, CCHS.)

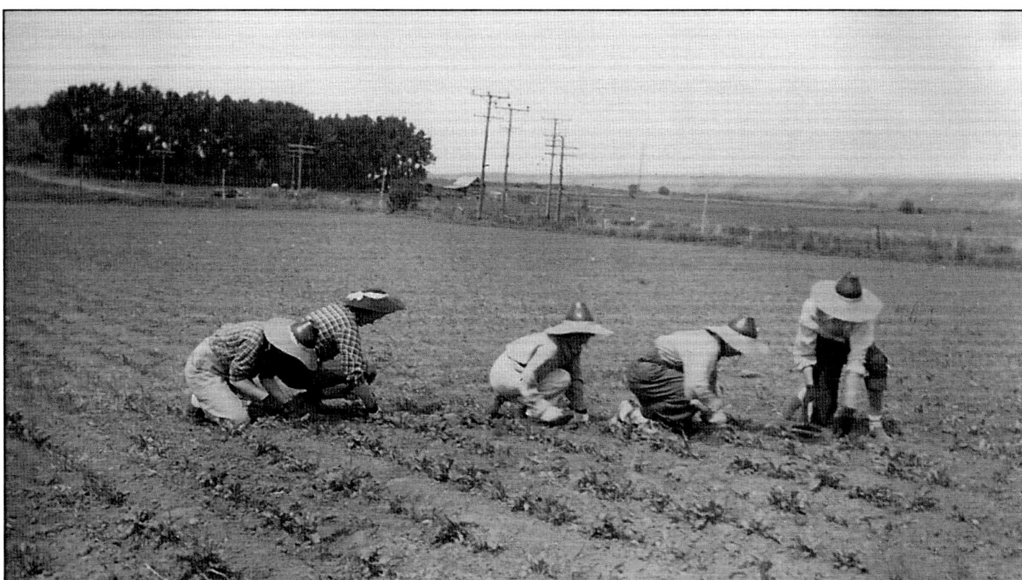

Two

Montaqua

Montaqua is a small settlement along Rock Creek about two miles southwest of Rockvale. It was the home of the Mont-Aqua Mineral Wells Company, a hot springs resort that once attracted visitors from as far away as North Dakota. Eventually, the two words were joined into one word: Montaqua. The resort featured a pool, a plunge, blanket sweats, showers, a restaurant, a hotel, a lunch counter, guest cabins, a dining room, and a dance hall. But the original vision for Montaqua started quite differently.

The site began as a beet dump named Dutton after early homesteader Martin Dutton. In 1911, Frank W. Craig homesteaded 160 acres on Rock Creek southwest of the Dutton homestead. Northern Pacific employees referred to the siding at Dutton as Keown, named for a veteran railroad detective. In 1918, a man named Hoyt sank a well on the Craig homestead and named his company Hoosier Oil Company of Montana. Drilling continued for several years. The severe depth of the well and funding shortages slowed progress. After drilling to a depth of over 4,000 feet, the well struck a reservoir of 111-degree mineral water, rather than the oil or gas that had been expected.

In 1927, James West purchased the well from Hoyt, renamed it Mont-Aqua Mineral Well Company, and started the resort. The hot springs became a popular destination in the 1930s, but its popularity waned in the 1940s and 1950s. The water shut off suddenly on August 17, 1959, when a 7.3-magnitude earthquake struck Hebgen Lake, west of Yellowstone National Park about 125 miles from Montaqua as the crow flies. The seismic shift collapsed the well for good, shut off the hot water, and opened a seam of odorless, colorless natural gas that went undetected until the bathhouse exploded days later. All that remains today are the concrete ruins of the bathhouse and the main house. A pipe protruding from the bathhouse ruins still spurts water every few minutes or so, but the water is cool, as it comes from higher in the water table.

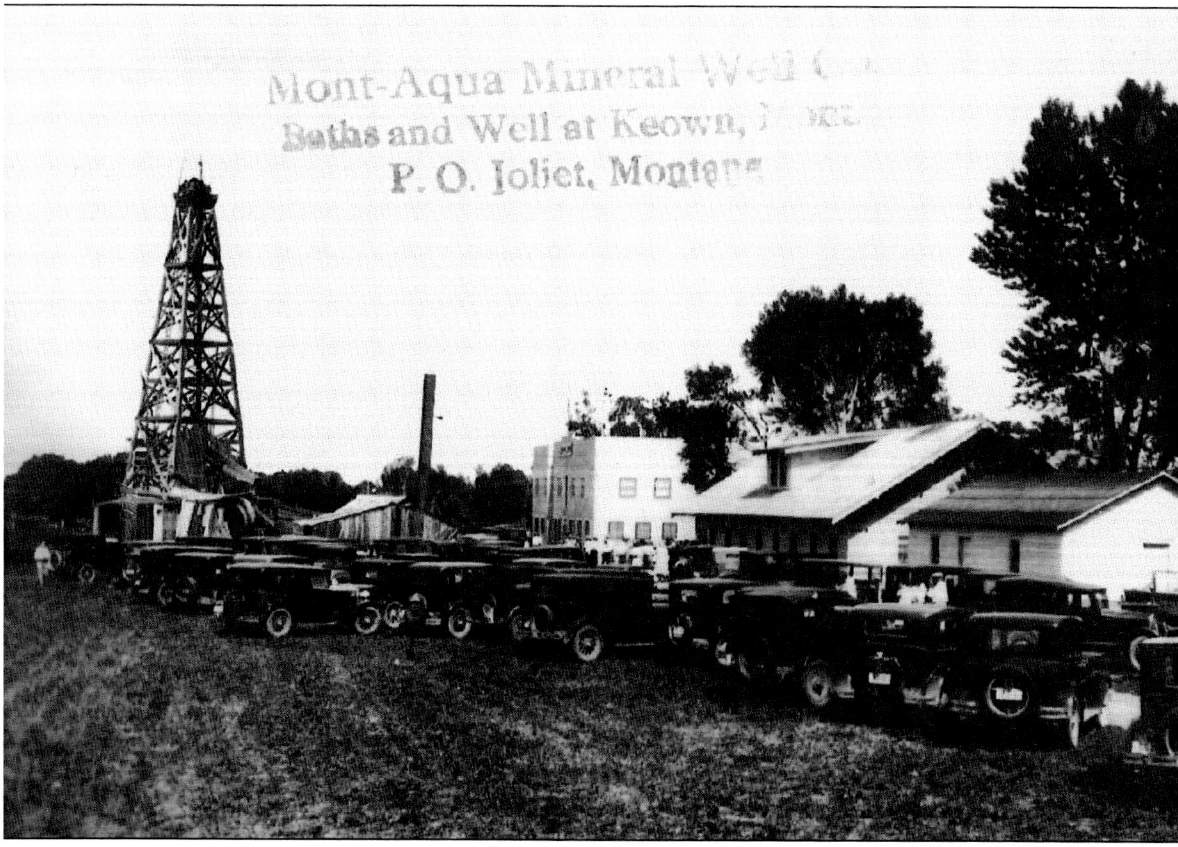

Large crowds attended Mont-Aqua Mineral Wells Company's resort in its heyday, as seen in this 1930s photograph. Notice the large number of sporty sedans, hinting at the racy affluence of its patrons. The *Fromberg Herald* reported that between 2,500 and 3,000 people attended the opening ceremonies on Saturday, June 29, 1929. A chicken dinner was served, followed by a dance with music from the Montana Ambassadors. The article continued, "The dining hall is equipped with a powerful radio set with Victrola attachment which is sure to prove enticing for dancing by small parties at any time. Mont-Aqua is destined to become a community center that will attract from great distances." The largest revenue-earner for Montaqua, however, did not come from resort visitors; instead, it came from bottling and exporting Mont-Aqua mineral water to over 20 states at a cost of $1.25 a gallon—about $14.50 a gallon in today's dollars. The slogan on its five-gallon glass jugs read, "Nature's Gift to Suffering Humanity." (Bell.)

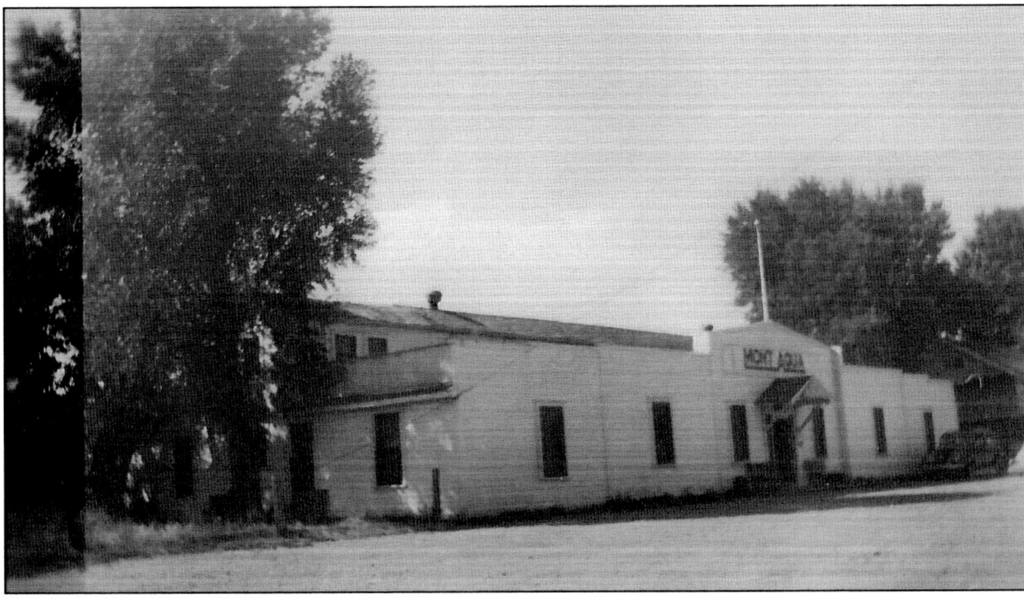

The main bathhouse at Montaqua, seen here in the 1930s, contained a plunge, a large swimming pool, soaking tubs, showers, and sweat blankets. A physician was available to guests from 1:00 p.m. to 2:00 p.m. each Tuesday, Thursday, and Saturday. One reviewer predicted that Montaqua would soon be as popular as resorts such as Hot Springs, Arkansas, and French Lick Springs, Indiana. (Charleton.)

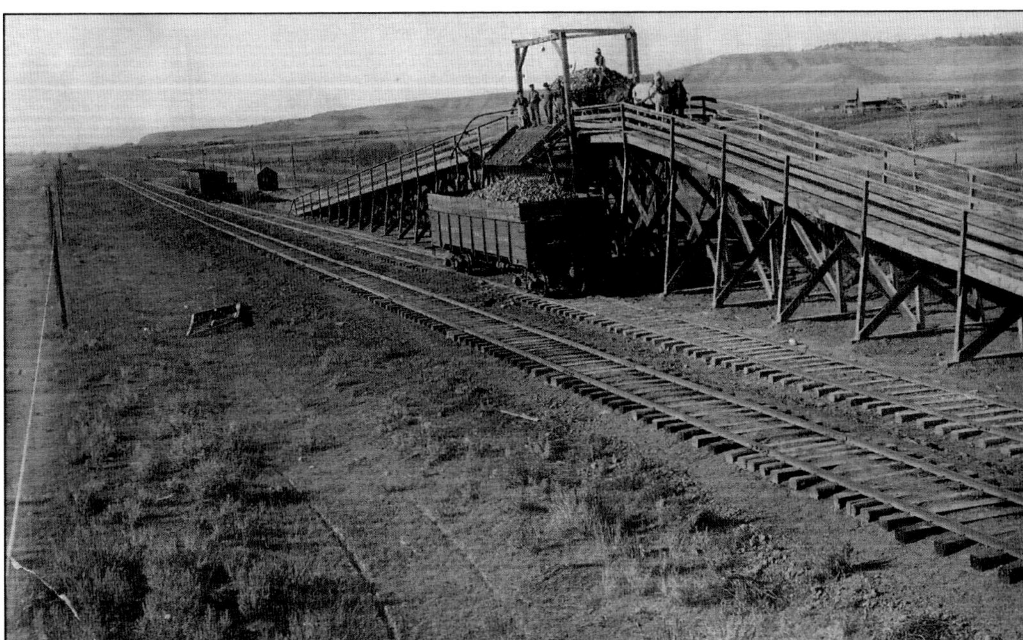

This photograph of the Dutton beet dump, near Montaqua on the Northern Pacific's Rocky Fork Branch, shows sugar beets being loaded onto gondola cars. The beet dump was named for Martin B. Dutton, who homesteaded just north of the siding. Visible in the right background is the homestead of Bill Daum, another early pioneer. (Bell.)

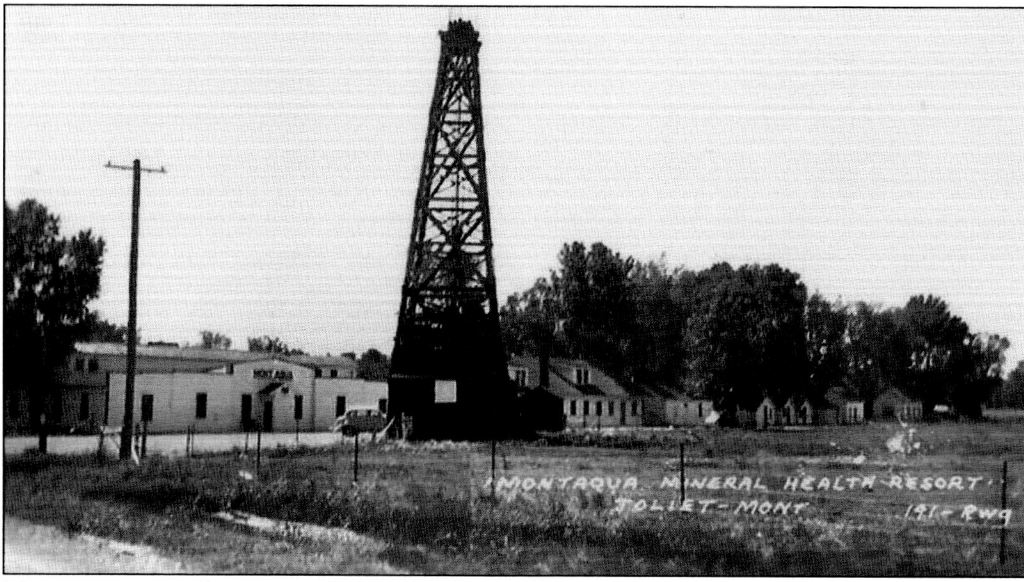

This 1930s view of Montaqua shows the derrick, the bathhouse, the guesthouse, and the guest cottages strung down the lane. Aside from its therapeutic waters, guests visited Montaqua for its famous fried chicken dinners and strawberry shortcake, made with strawberries grown in Montaqua's garden. Schoolchildren from as far as Joliet helped pick strawberries to earn extra money. (CCHS.)

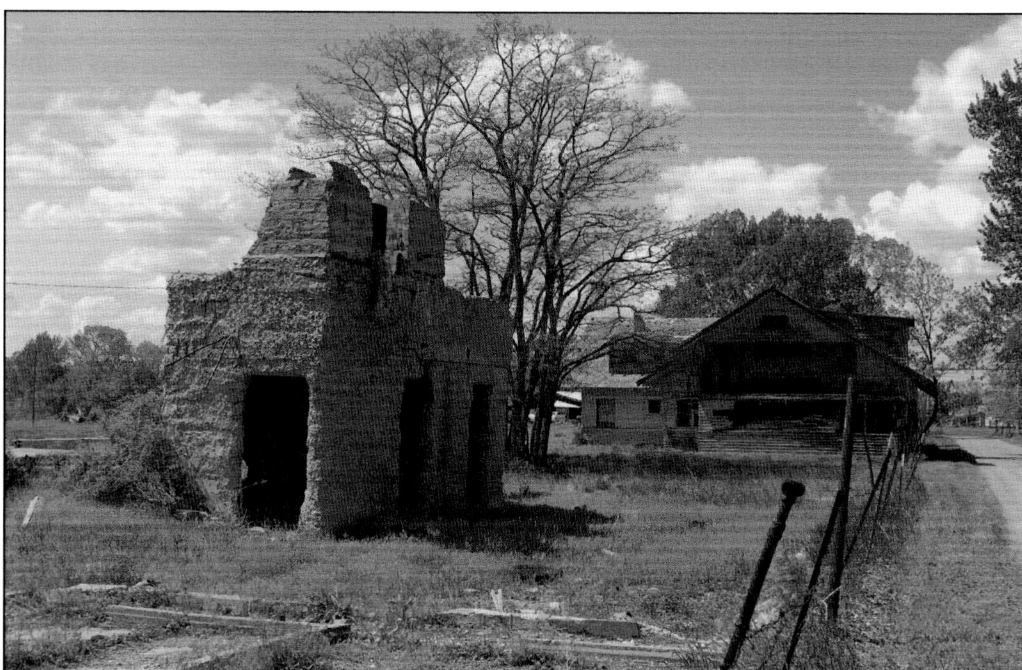

Montaqua is now a ruin, as seen in this contemporary photograph, with the remains of the bathhouse in the foreground and the main lodge in the background. The dark drum visible on the second floor of the bathhouse, between crumbling concrete, is a skimmer, which removed trace amounts of crude oil from the water that was later sold as Mont-Aqua healing salve. (Wallace.)

MONTAQUA

JOLIET, MONTANA

DR. HENRY J. PFAFF

CHIROPRACTOR

WED, THURS. FRI. SAT. SUN.

PHONE JOLIET 2435. HOURS 10 A. M. TO 10 P. M.

Dr. Henry J. Pfaff was a Joliet chiropractor who treated guests at Montaqua in the 1940s and died tragically at the age of 39 on January 1, 1950. The back of his business card (right) displayed the mineral breakdown of Montaqua water. Classified as "a typical Sulphate Mineral Water," it contained high levels of calcium sulfate and magnesium sulfate, but according to former patrons, the water did not smell strongly of sulfur. Total solids in the water were 255.295 grains per gallon, or about 4,340 parts per million. Testimonials in Montaqua advertisements praised its benefits for treating everything from diabetes and rheumatism to Saint Vitus' dance and tuberculosis. (Both, CCHS.)

ANALYSIS OF MONT-AQUA WATER

Excerpts from Report by
Herman Harms, Ph. G.,
Utah State Chemist

Solids in Solution	Grains Per Gallon
Calcium Carbonate	.187
Magnesium Carbonate	1.400
Calcium Sulphate	128.353
Magnesium Sulphate	56.438
Sodium Sulphate	2.888
Potassium Sulphate	4.539
Sodium Chloride	3.273
Silica-Acid Insoluble	1.307
Iron Oxide	.099
Alumina	.029
Water of Crystal'ization (Including Other Volatile and Organic Matter.)	56.356
Undetermined and Loss	.426
Total Solids	255.295

NOTE: One Grain per Gallon equals approximately 17 parts per million.

Classification: A typical Sulphate Mineral Water. Contains in Solution an exceedingly large amount of mineral solids. Objectionable constituents entirely absent.

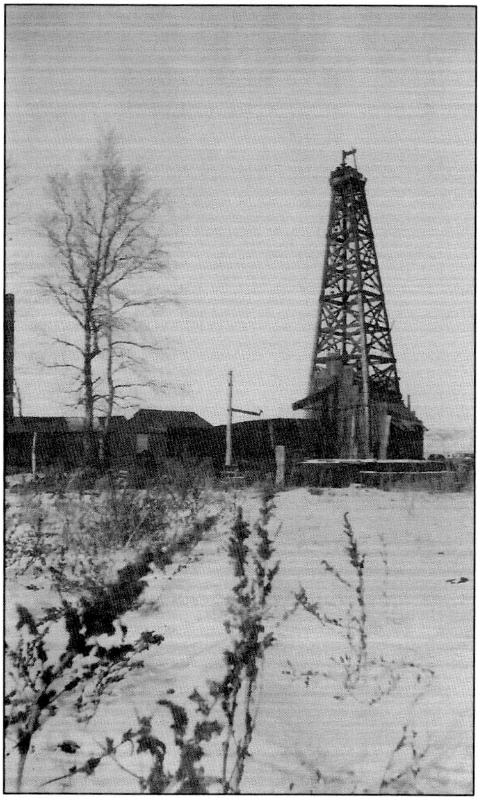

Normally, after a well is tapped, it is capped and the derrick is taken down. But at Montaqua, the derrick (left and below) was left in place because, twice a year, mineral buildup known as "scale" had to be cleaned from the well casing. A veteran oil driller from Casper, Wyoming, was hired for this task. He would fire up the boiler, and the pulley works would turn an eccentric, which would lift the drill bit up and down to clear the blockage, letting out a little more of the cable as the bit worked its way down the casing. The process took three or four days. After a cleaning, both the temperature and the water pressure greatly increased. (Both, Charleton.)

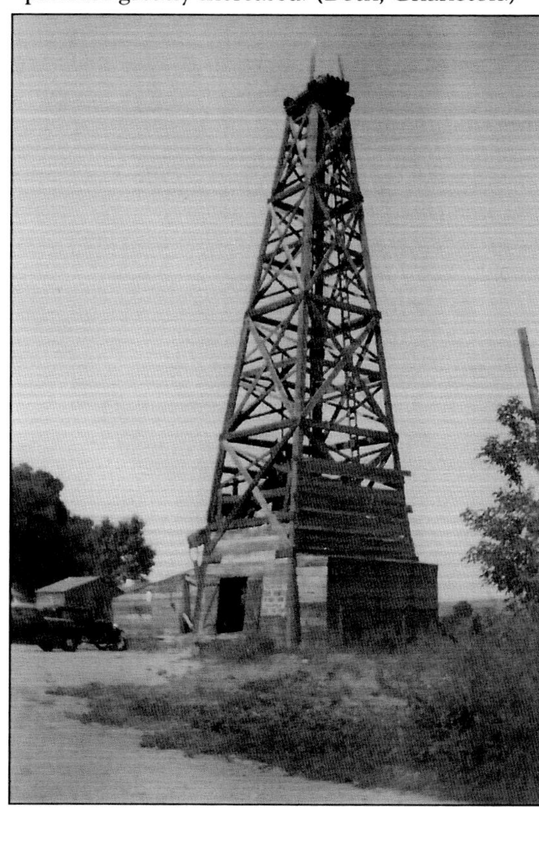

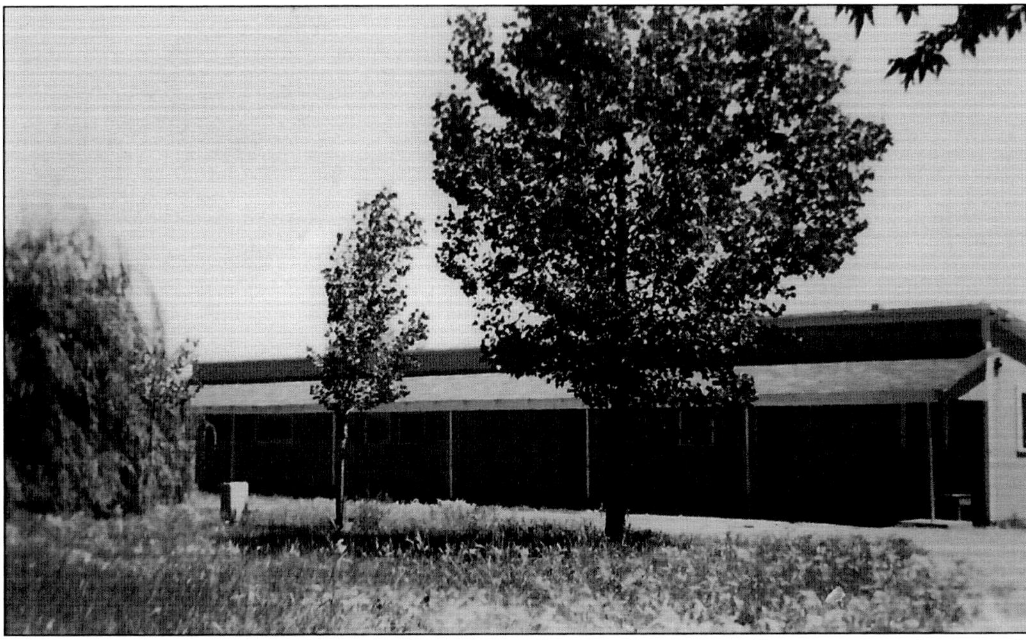

Business at Montaqua was always brisk in the early years, but especially in winter, when people from as far away as North Dakota and Minnesota came to warm aching bodies and soothe tired bones. To handle the overflow, the Rock Creek cabins (above) were built across the road from the bathhouse in 1930. Herman Salveson and his wife, Francis (below), purchased the cabins in 1959, just months before the Hebgen Lake earthquake closed the hot springs for good. Since that time, the motor court and the cabin next to it have been private residences. (Both, Kennedy.)

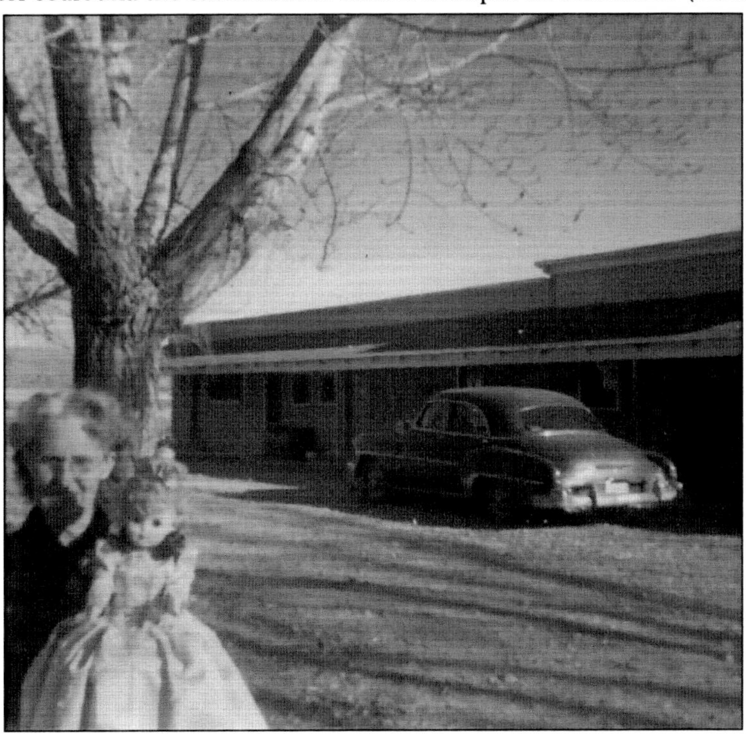

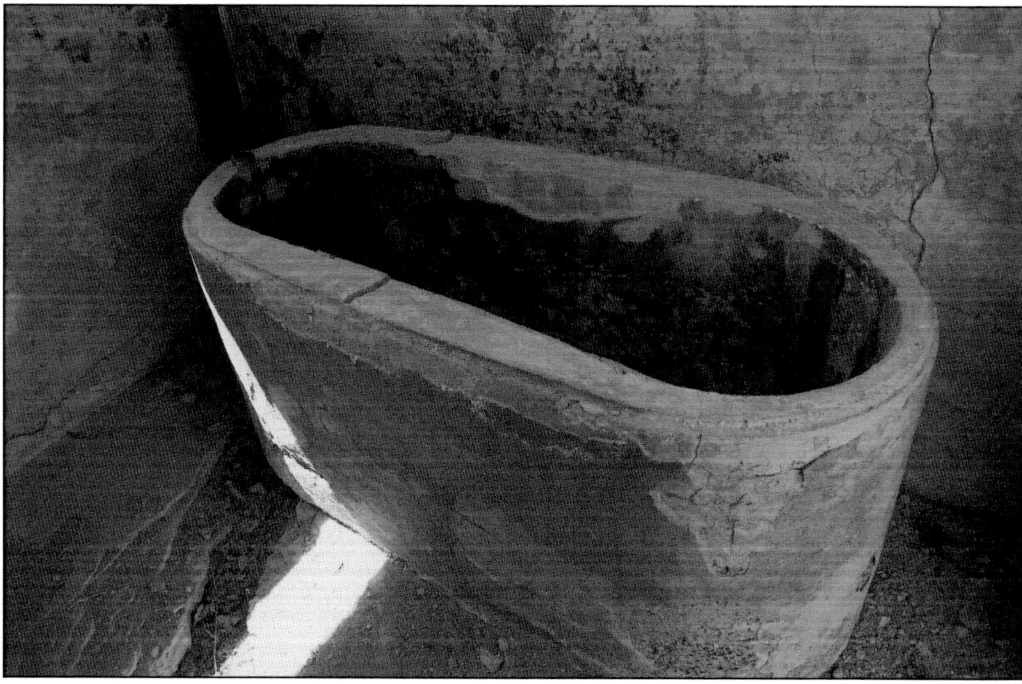

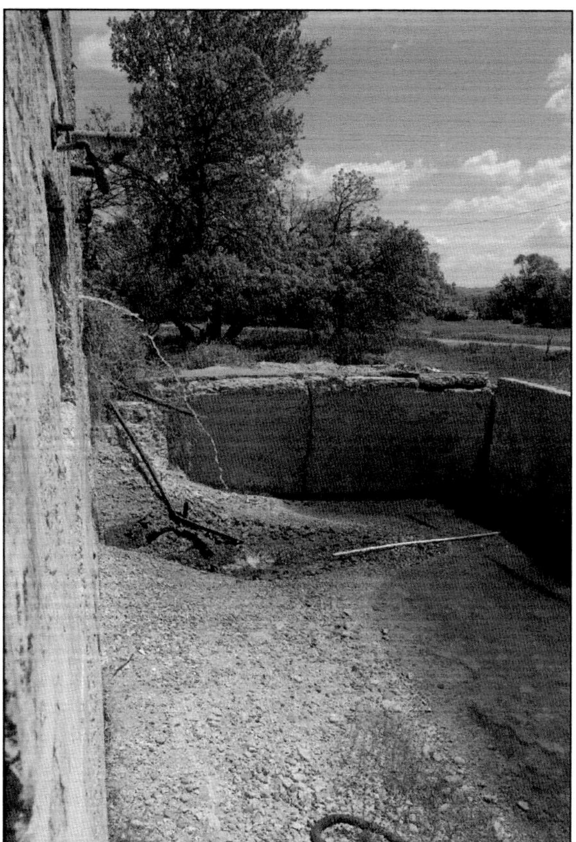

The contemporary photograph above shows one of the large clay tubs in which Montaqua guests once soaked. The photograph at left shows the plunge today. Water does still spurt from a pipe coming out of the bathhouse ruins every 20 minutes or so, but it is not hot. It is water that seeps into the well casing from above the blockage that cut off the hot water in 1959. The ruins are located on private property and trespassers are not welcome, but good views of the former Mont-Aqua Mineral Wells Company can be seen from Montaqua Road. (Both, Wallace.)

Three

Joliet

The town of Joliet was once part of the Crow Indian Reservation. A group of 25 early settlers, including Harry Duffield, Thomas W. Smith, and John McMonigal, bought a tract of land from a Crow chief named Long Bear for $1,000 down with another $1,000 due the following spring. Each received homestead rights in 1898, and in 1899, the Joliet Townsite Improvement Company, with Duffield as president, began platting the town of Joliet. Several additions between 1905 and 1909 followed. But Joliet had been a town for almost a decade before it was formally platted.

The Rock Fork & Cooke City Railroad's line from Laurel to Red Lodge was completed in 1889. According to one account, the first structure in Joliet, a tent that served as a saloon, was erected on July 4, 1893. In 1896, the small town grew to include a post office, four stores, three saloons, two hotels, and several residences. When the Carbonado mine, two miles southwest of Joliet, closed in 1901, many of its residents and business owners moved to Joliet. Many brought their shops and houses along, moving them across the frozen Rock Creek in winter. The town incorporated in 1906 in order to initiate electrification and build a modern water system.

By 1907, Joliet featured several new brick and stone buildings and a population of over 500, making it the second largest town in Carbon County. Surrounded by the fertile fields of the Rock Creek Valley floodplain, Joliet became an essential trading hub for a substantial farming district. Hay, grains, alfalfa, sugar beets, and fruits were popular crops.

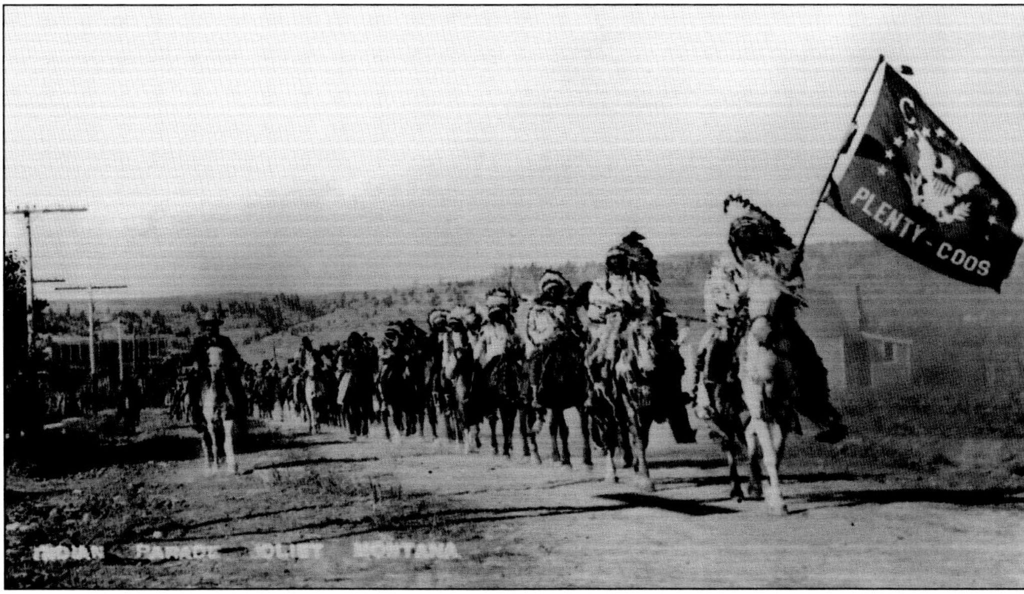

A procession of Crow Indians led by Chief Plenty Coos parades through Joliet in the late 1890s. All of the land on which Joliet now sits was part of the Second Crow Agency until it was opened for homesteading in 1892. In the left background is a rare view of the grandstands of the Joliet horse racing track. (JPL.)

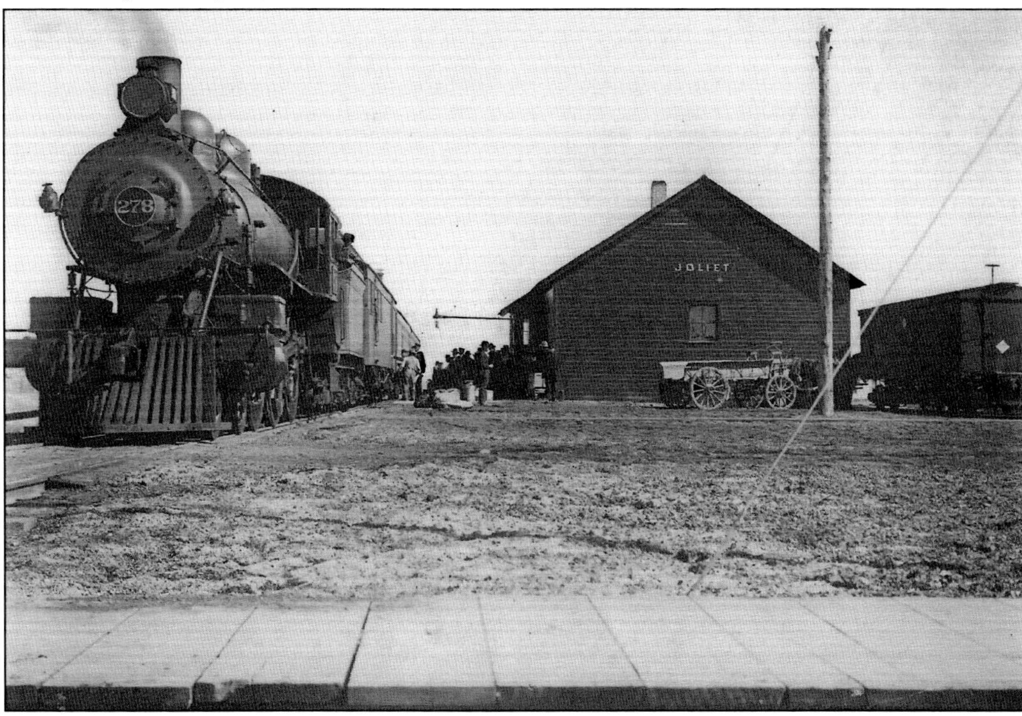

Northern Pacific Railway 4-6-0 locomotive No. 278 takes on passengers at Joliet around 1920. The Rocky Fork & Cooke City Railway completed its 47-mile branch line from the Northern Pacific Railway mainline at Laurel to the coal mines at Red Lodge in 1889. The Joliet depot was built in 1909, replacing a stop a mile north of town at Wilsey. (JPL.)

One of Joliet's earliest settlers was Harry Duffield (right), who homesteaded in the Joliet area in 1894. He organized the Joliet Township Improvement Corporation, which first platted Joliet. Duffield served as the town's first constable in 1895, when Carbon County was created. He served as a county commissioner from 1898 to 1901 and served as Joliet mayor in 1912. He also ran the Duffield Cash Grocery and Meat Market on Main Street and was a leading supporter of the Episcopal church. In 1881, Duffield married Mary Elizabeth Hobbs (below), originally from Wisconsin. They raised four children: William Albert, Elva, Ethel, and Elizabeth. (Both, JPL.)

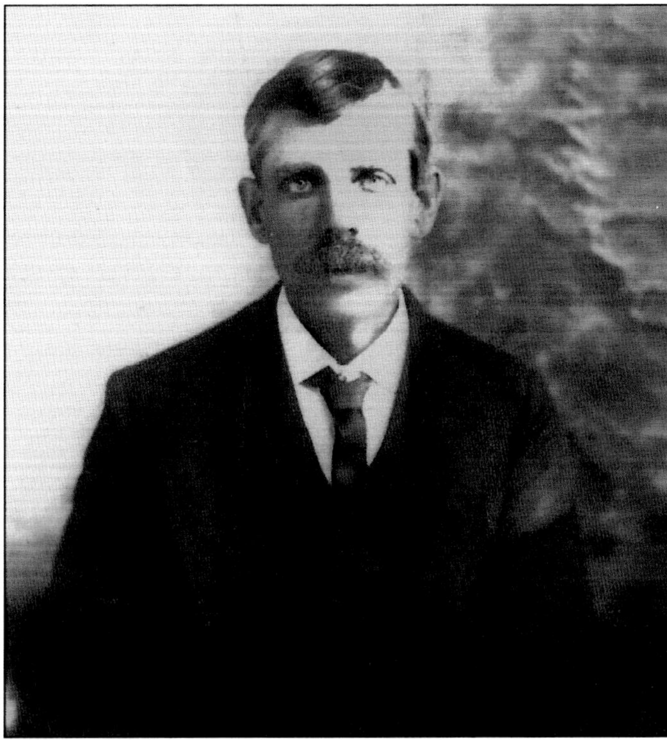

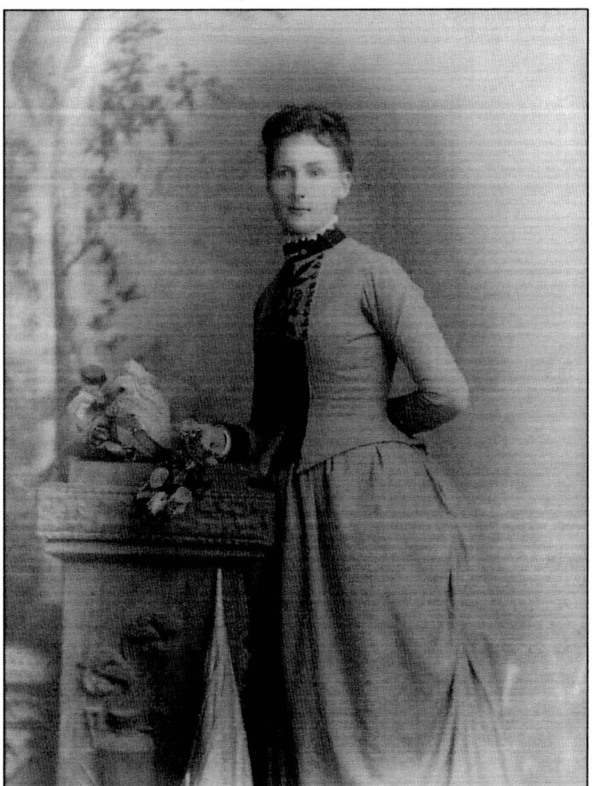

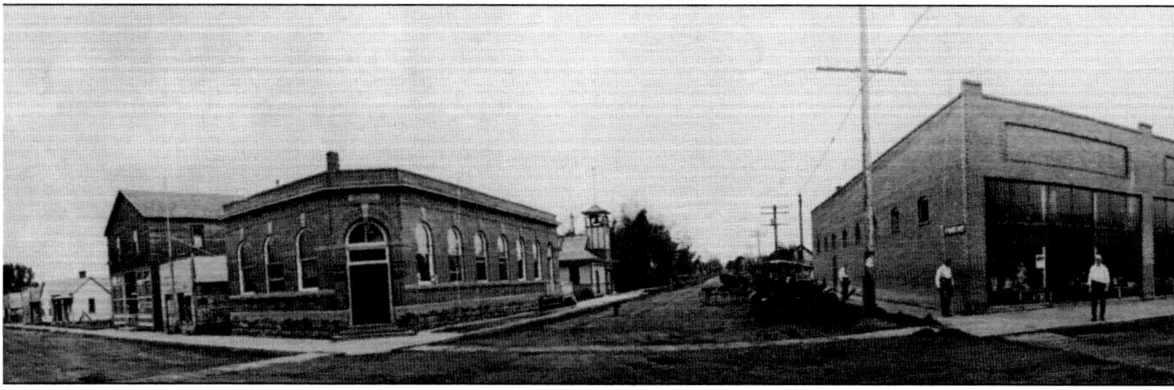

This panoramic photograph of Main Street in Joliet from around 1910 shows how much the town had grown in its first decade. The two-story building at the far left was once a meat market that held boxing matches and dances upstairs. On the corner is Rock Creek State Bank, erected in 1909. The building with the bell tower on Central Avenue (left), behind the bank, is the city hall. Across Central Avenue sits the Houda Building, which housed the Talmage-Sayer Hardware

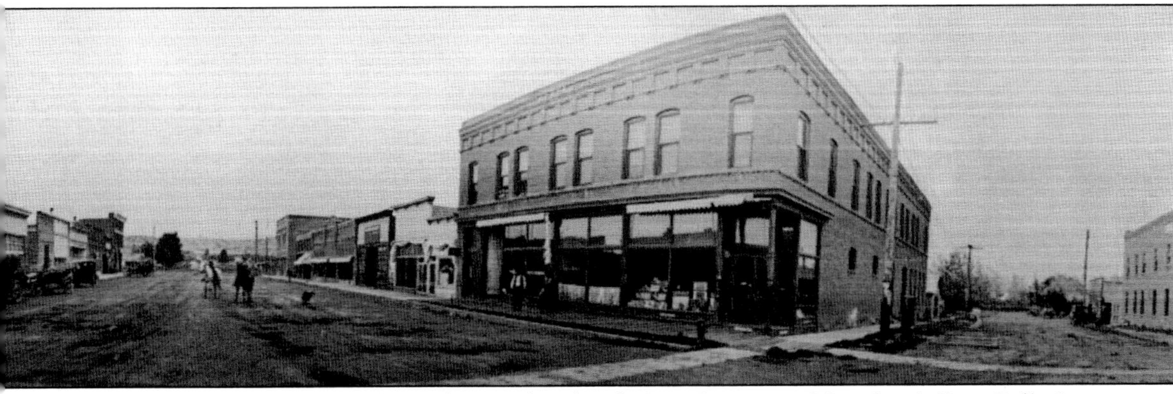

& Lumber Company. Farther down the south side of Main Street are Monahan's Bar, Collin's Saloon, a dry goods store, the Porter Café, and Whitney's Store. The Masonic hall sat on the southeast corner of Front and Main Streets, beside the Baker & Lovering general merchandise store. The Meyer Block contained the Kozy Korner drugstore and also held community gatherings in its second-floor Eagle's Hall. (Dewell.)

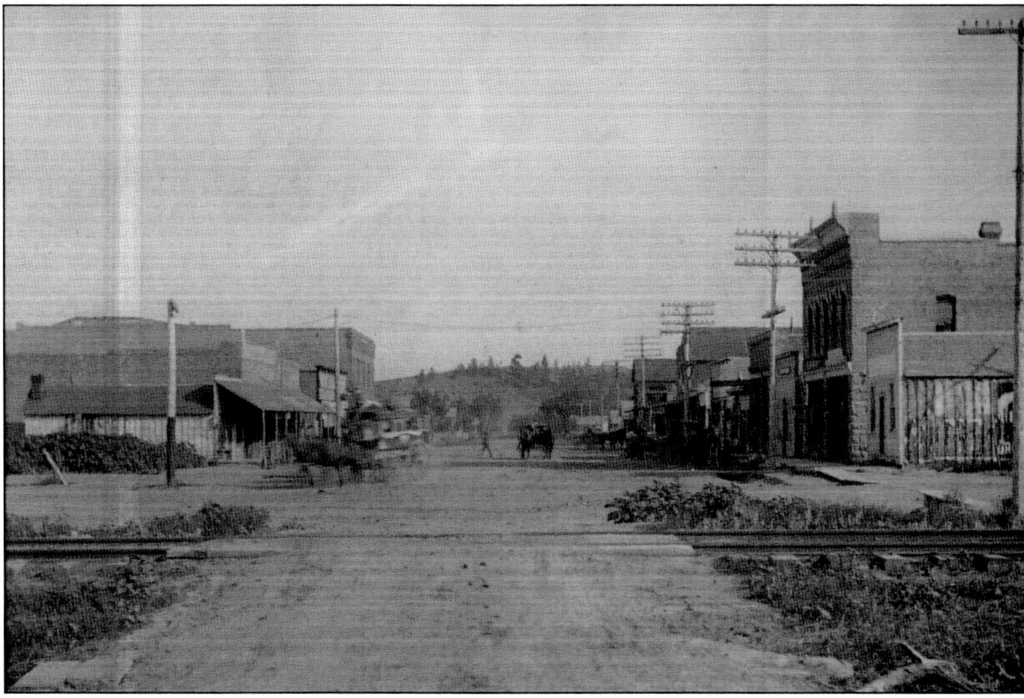

Above, a blurred stagecoach hurries northward in 1906. Joliet was a stop on the stagecoach line between Billings and Meeteetse, Wyoming, before a rail line linked Billings to Cody, Wyoming, in 1912. The Pat Henry Saloon (left) sat on one corner of Main and Front Streets, while the brick and stone Joliet post office sat on the opposite corner. Below, the "Virtue" stagecoach heads down the Meeteetse Trail. Less affluent passengers often rode on top of the carriage, while a scout (far right) rode ahead of the team, keeping an eye out for hazards. (Above, JPL; below, CCHS.)

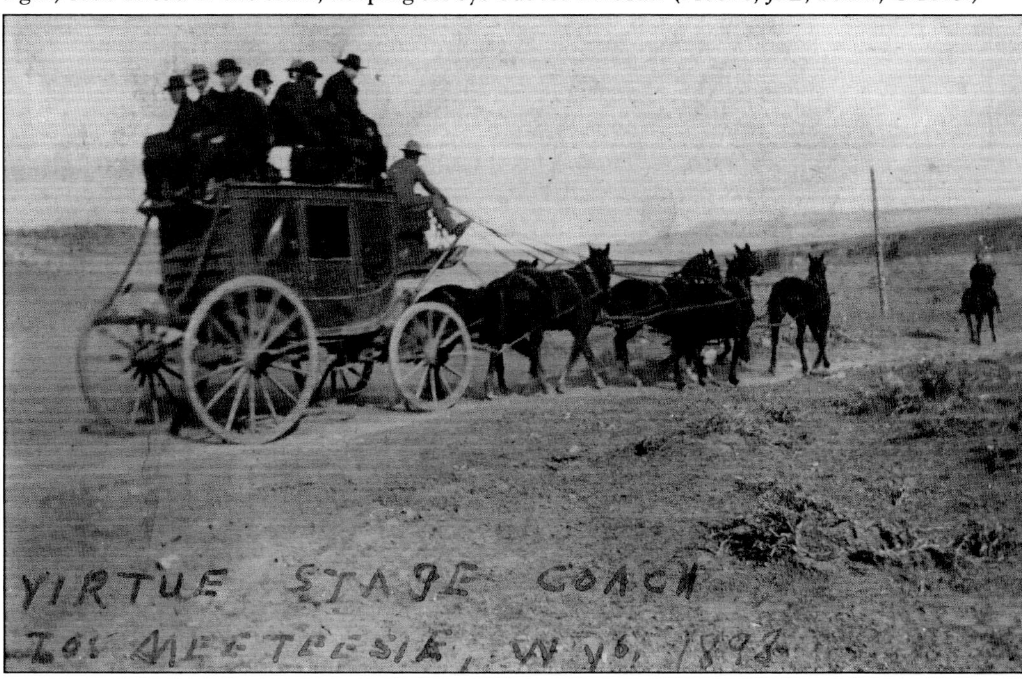

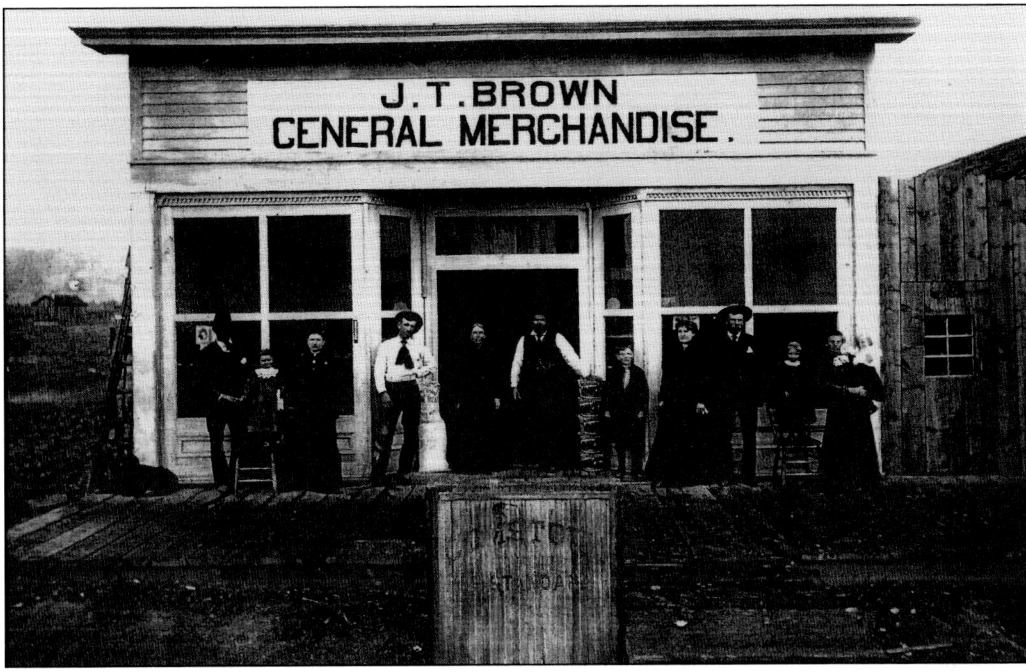

The Wilsey store, the first in the area, was started by Thomas W. Smith, who was stationed there as a section foreman for the Rocky Fork & Cooke City Railroad when the rail line from Laurel to Red Lodge was built in 1889. His wife, Maude, served as the first postmistress in the Joliet area. (JPL.)

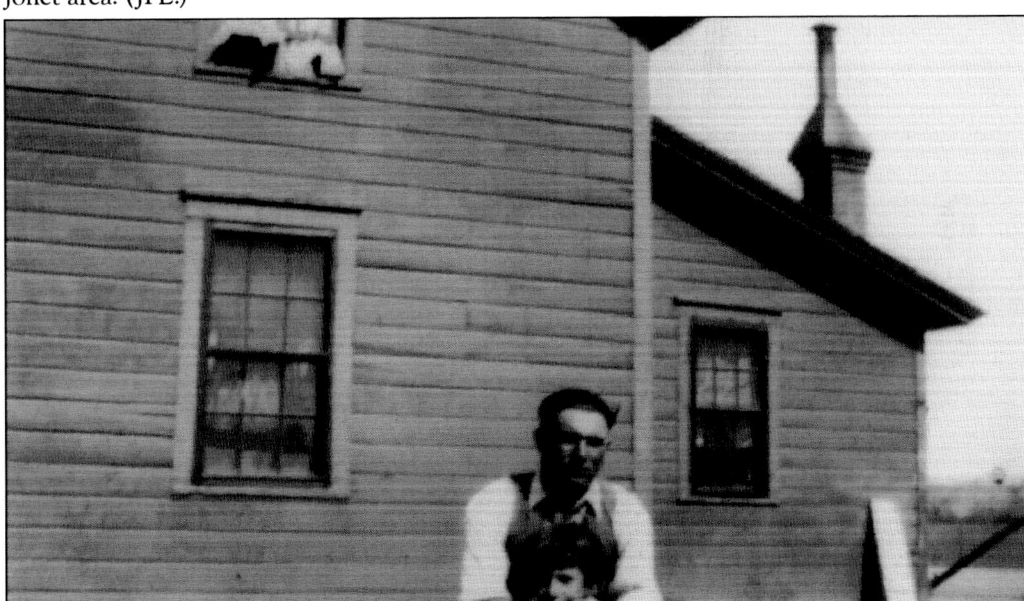

John Monaco and his sister Isabel sit outside the Wilsey section house of the Northern Pacific Railway in 1928, where they lived while their father, Gaeteno, worked as a section foreman for the railroad from 1908 until his retirement in 1936. John followed in his father's footsteps, working for the Northern Pacific in Billings. The section house was located near Wilsey, about a mile north of Joliet. (Monaco.)

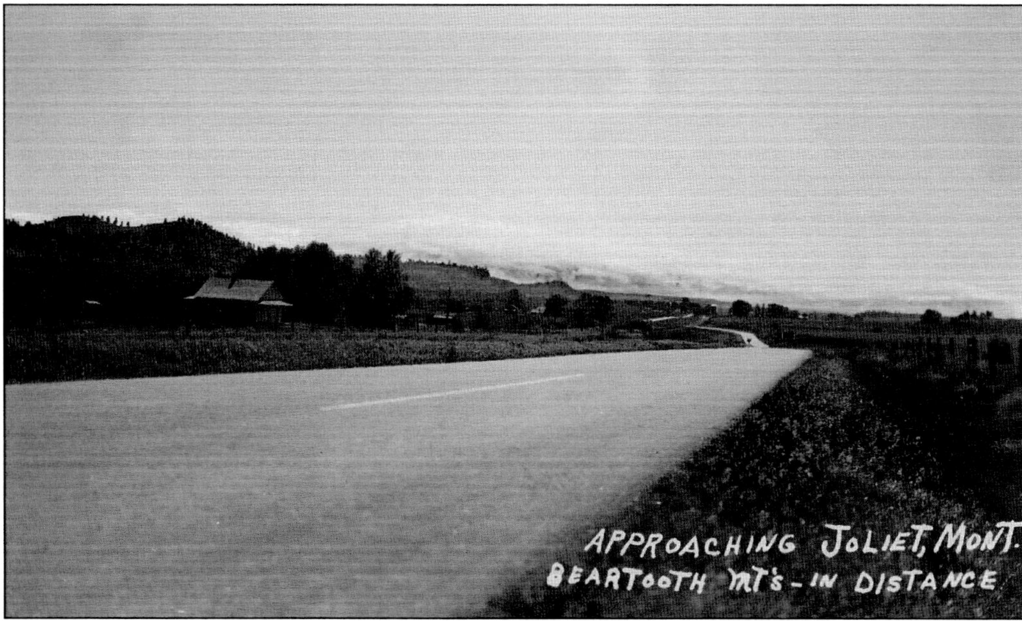

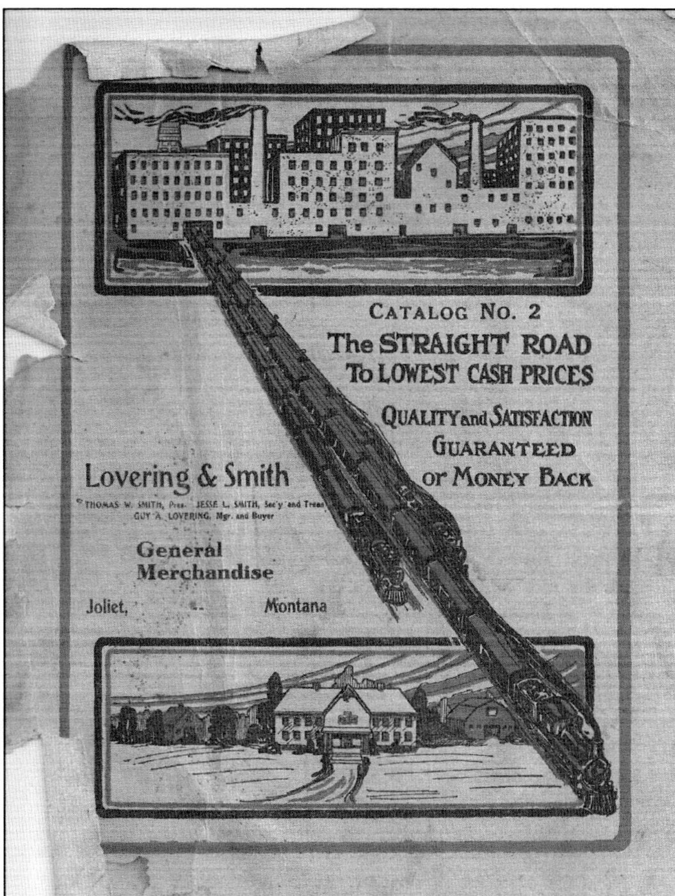

The photograph above of the approach to Joliet from Rockvale was taken near the site of the Wilsey flag stop and section house, where the first store in the area, the Wilsey store, was set up by Thomas W. Smith around 1890. In 1904, Smith went into a partnership with his son-in-law Guy Lovering to open the Lovering-Smith mercantile store on Main Street in Joliet. Smith's son Jesse worked at the store as the secretary and treasurer. The advertisement at left depicts a sleek train making a straight line from modern factory to farm, demonstrating the store's ability to procure cosmopolitan items quickly from distant cities. (Above, Flash; left, CCHS.)

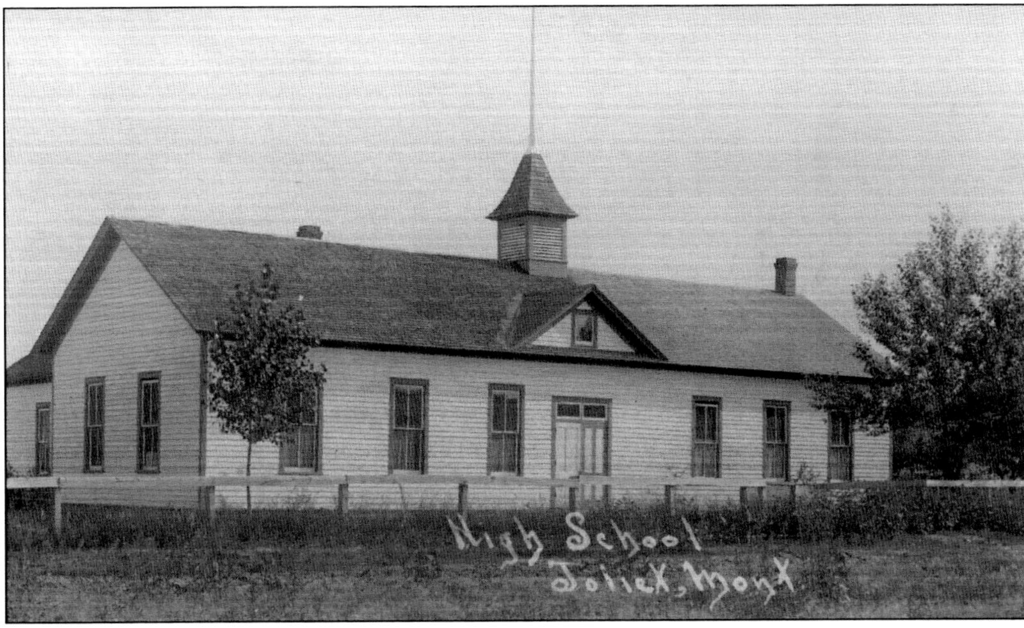

The first Joliet High School (above) was built near the corner of Front and State Streets for the start of the 1907–1908 term. In 1910, Prof. Arthur O. Nelson graduated the first high school class from what was a three-year high school program at the time. The inaugural graduating class consisted of Hazel Goff, Margaret Gallagher, Stella Nerlin, and Carl Morgan. By 1911, faced with a blossoming population and overcrowded schools, the school board selected a site on Main Street, north of the railroad tracks, to erect a new school (below), which housed both elementary and high schools in one building. (Above, Anderson; below, JPL.)

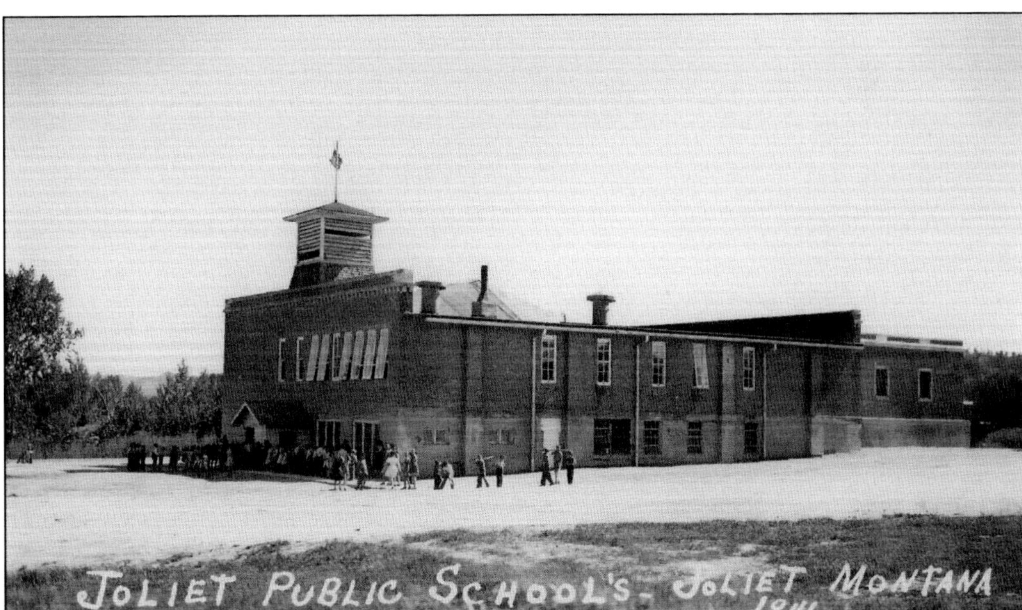

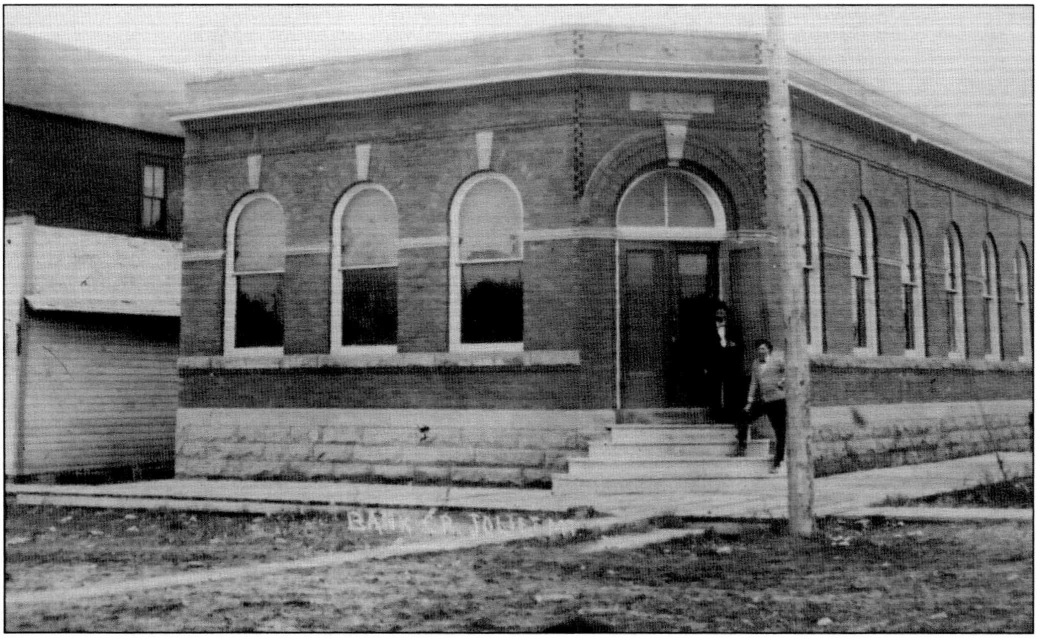

Seen here just after its opening in 1907, the Rock Creek State Bank's Romanesque architecture was touted in the *Joliet Journal* as possessing "both beauty and strength, thus adding materially to the appearance of . . . our rapidly-growing little city." Drought and low commodity prices caused the bank to close in 1923. The building, however, was added to the National Register of Historic Places in 1986 and still stands today. (JPL.)

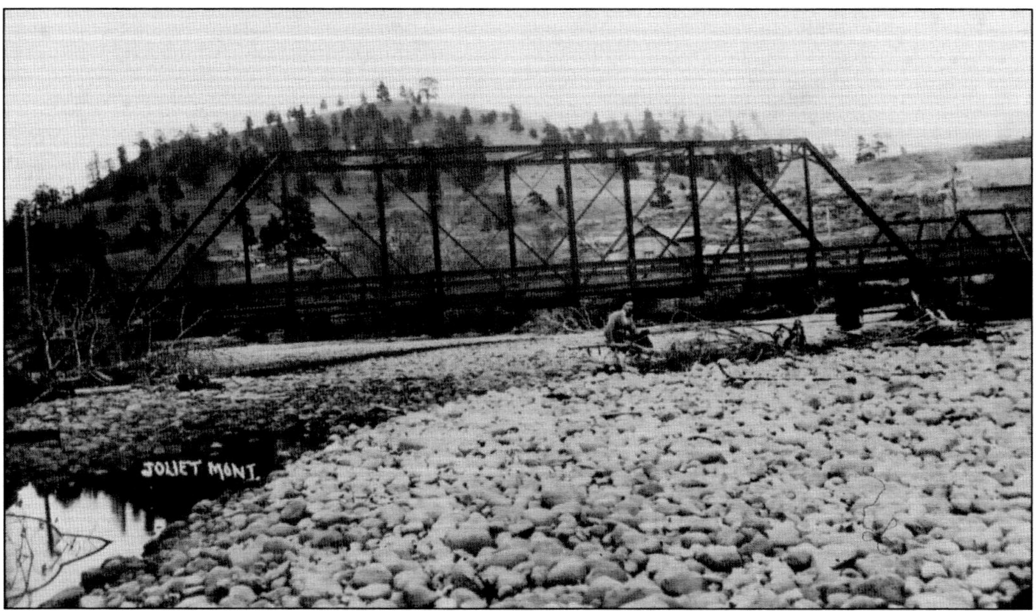

A man sits on the rocks of a low-flowing Rock Creek in front of the Joliet Bridge. Built in 1901, it was Carbon County's first steel-truss bridge. Built by William S. Hewitt of Minneapolis, its location crossing Rock Creek was critical to the growth and development of Joliet. The bridge was added to the National Register of Historic Places in 1986. (JPL.)

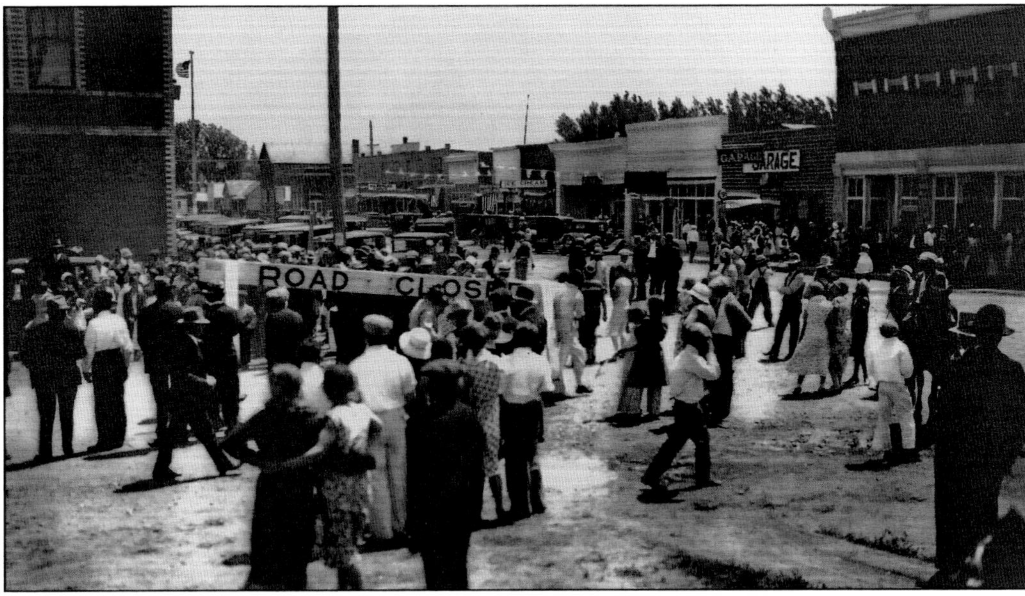

Joliet residents prepare for a Memorial Day parade followed by a street dance in this 1937 photograph. Because of the hardscrabble existence of early life in the Rock Creek Valley, the people of Joliet's ranches and farms jumped at every opportunity to relax and take a break from the chores of their homesteads. (JPL.)

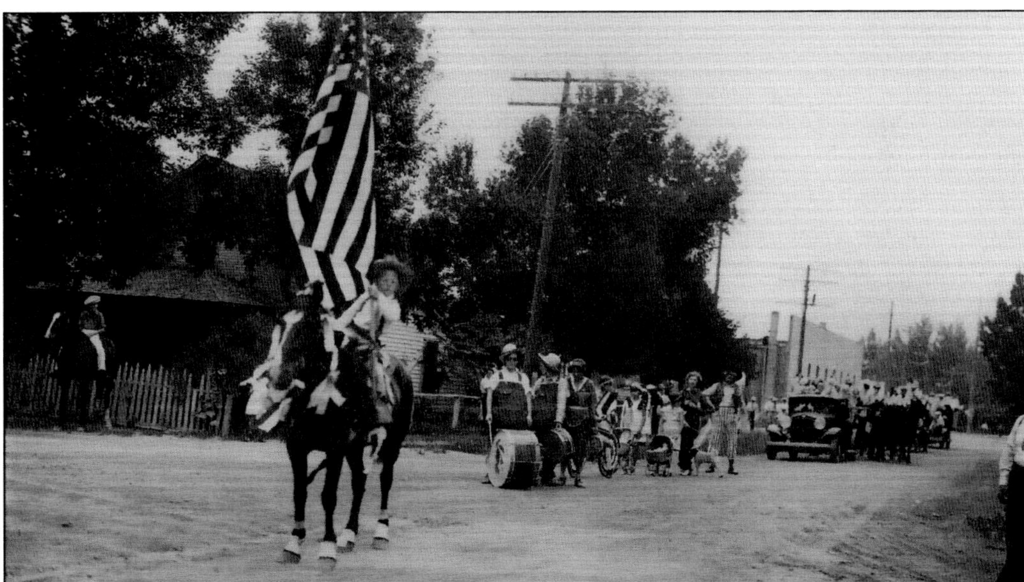

A young boy in cowboy garb carries a large flag as he leads Joliet townsfolk into position on Carbon Avenue prior to a holiday parade down Front and Main Streets in the late 1930s. An eccentric band forms the next group in line, followed by groups riding on automobiles. (JPL.)

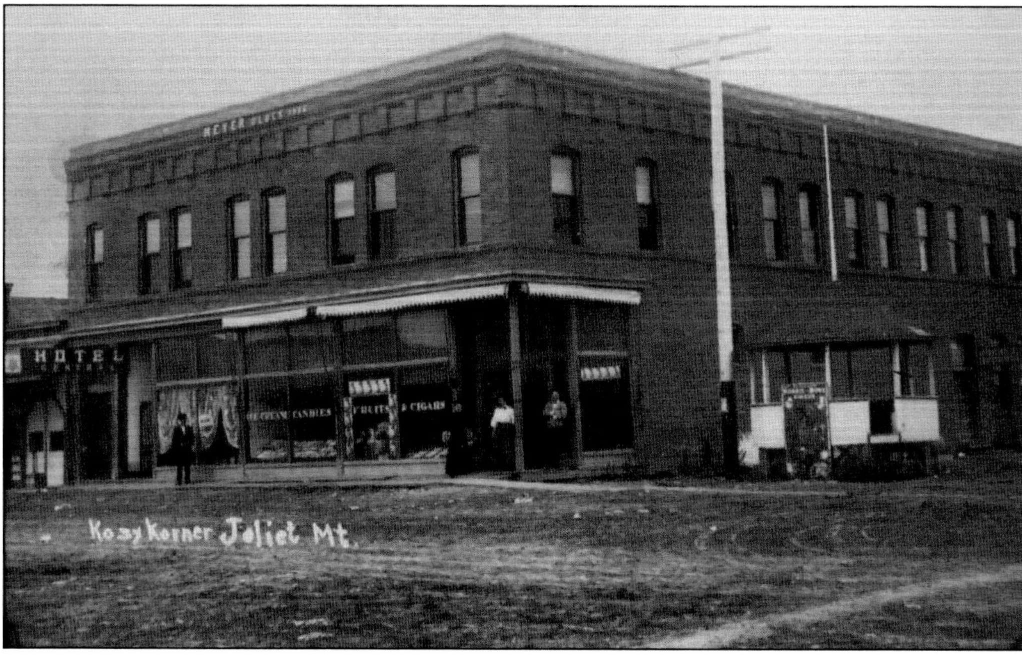

The Meyer Block (above) was one of the first major brick business blocks in Joliet. Built in 1906 by Ehler "Ed" John Meyer, it housed the Central Hotel, the Eagles Nest Saloon, the post office, the *Joliet Journal* offices, and the Kozy Korner drugstore. Eagle's Hall (below) occupied the second floor, with a compact stage and expansive dance floor where plays, operas, dances, basketball games, and most other community events took place until the building burned in 1922. Meyer was born in Bremen, Germany, in 1868 and married Helen Clara Klein in Butte in 1898 before moving to Joliet in 1900. (Both, JPL.)

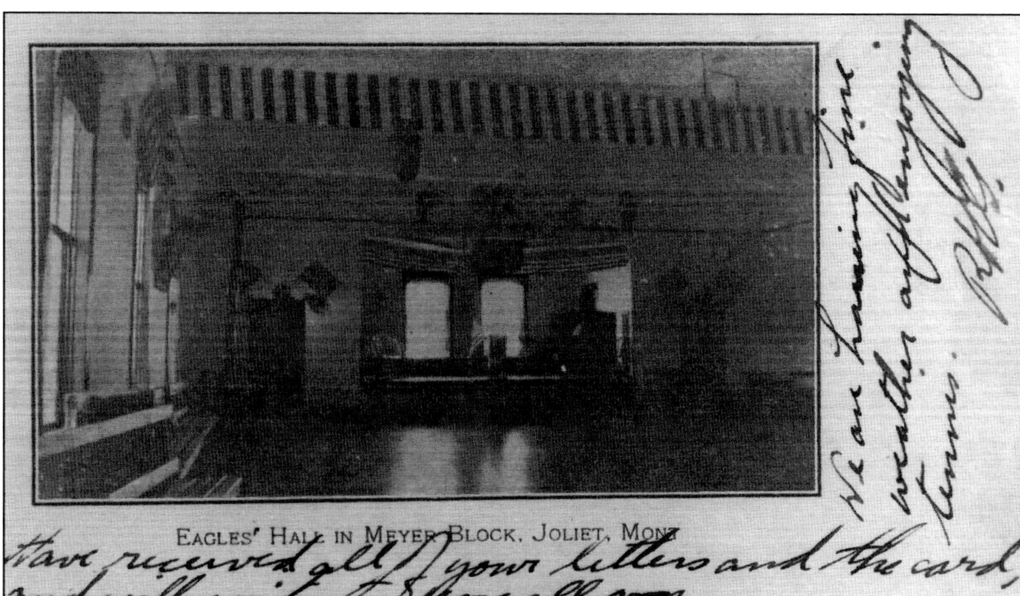

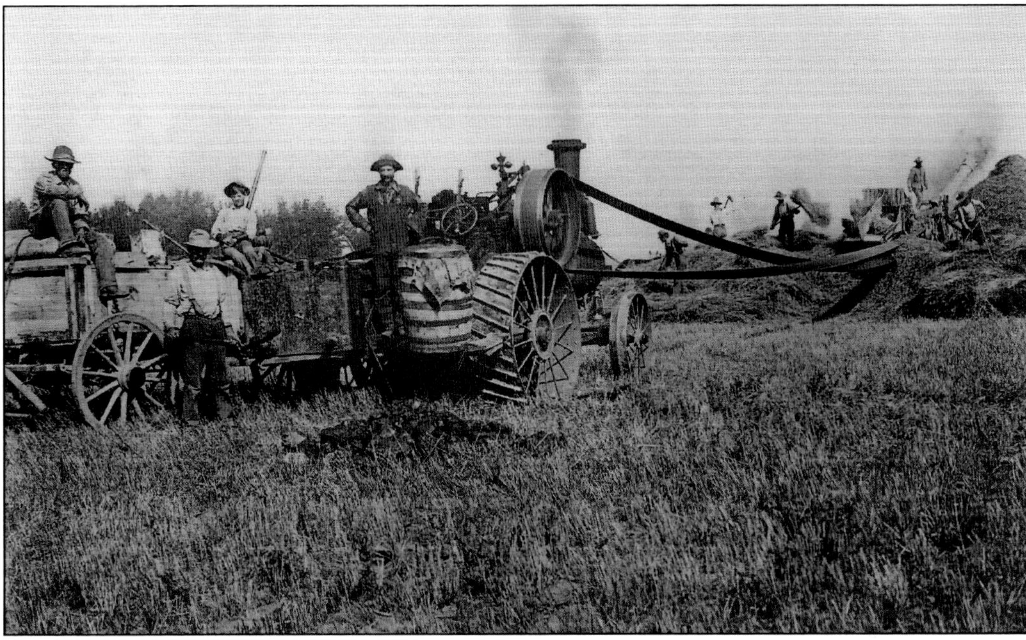

Steam power had brought increased output and efficiency to farming by the time this photograph was taken of the Engelbert threshing crew around 1910. Because of the potentially volatile pressure that builds up in steam boilers, a license was required to operate a steam-powered tractor like the one on the left, which is running the thresher via an external drive belt. (JPL.)

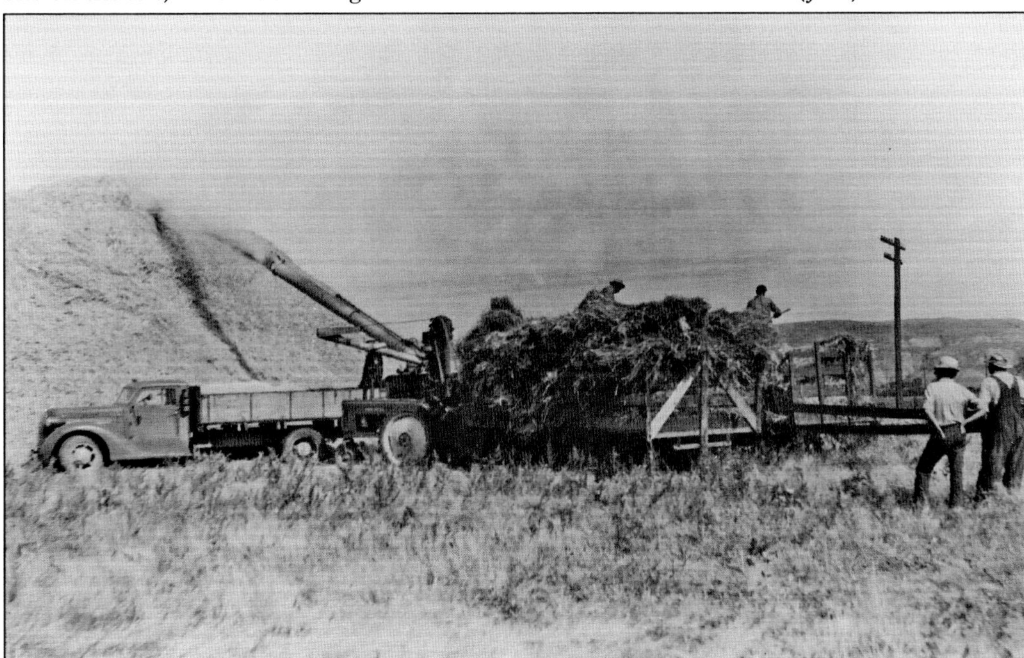

Hay has always been an important agricultural product in the Rock Creek Valley, sustaining many of the county's cattle and sheep ranches. Here, in the 1950s, Bud Jensen and Gene Stender (far right) use a Diamond-T truck and a John Deere tractor powered by a Rumley engine to cut and pile hay on the Jensen ranch, near Joliet. (JPL.)

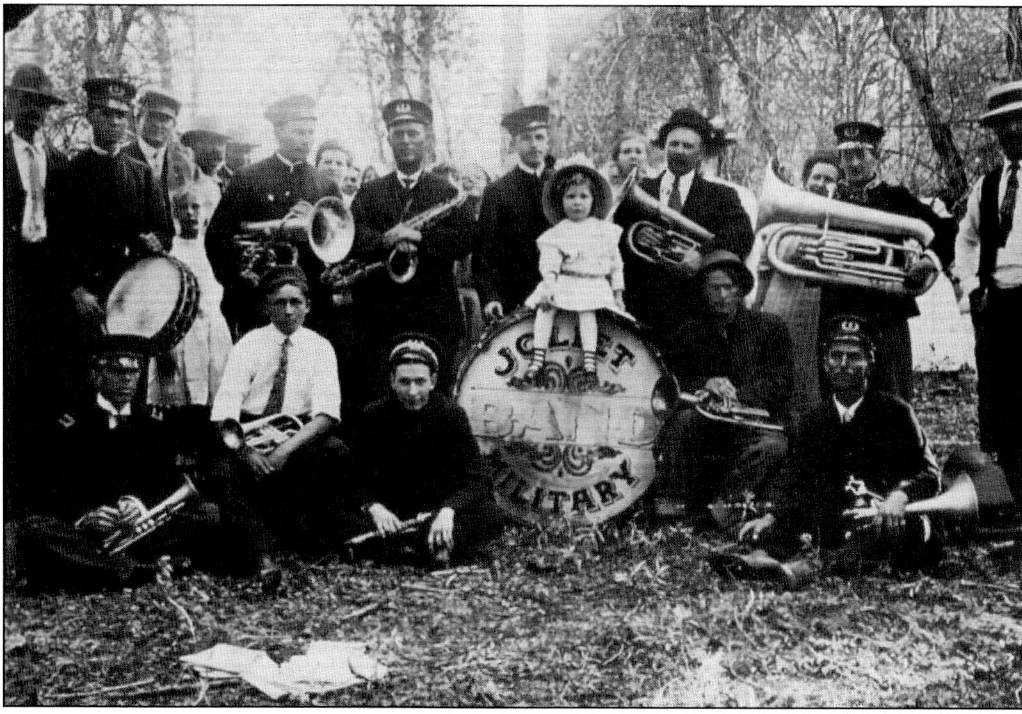

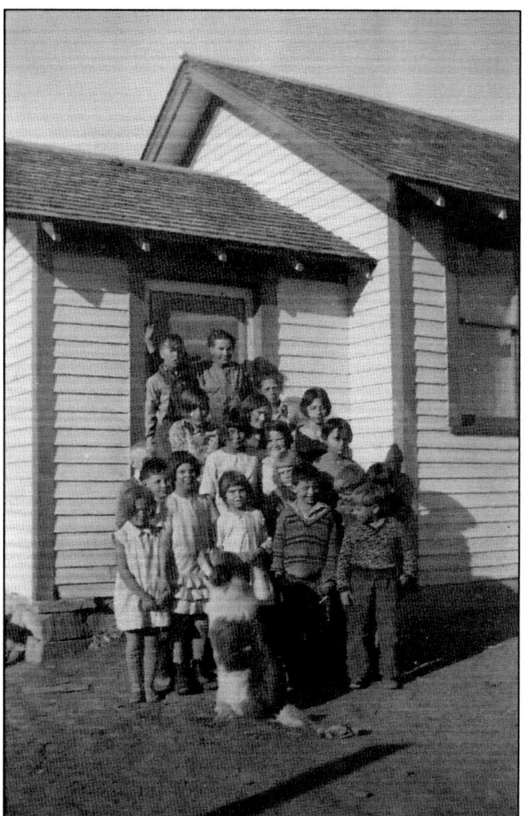

Joliet druggist J.P. Gibhart first organized the town's leading musicians into a band in 1903. By the time of the 1910 photograph above, Claude Hudson directed the band. Bands from small towns all along Rock Creek played at almost every community function. The rivalry between community bands ran high when they shared the stage at countywide events. (JPL.)

The Chapell school, located on Cole Creek in the hills north of Joliet, operated from 1914 to 1940. The school had an enrollment of 34 students between the ages of 6 and 18 in this 1929 photograph. Margaret Murray was the teacher. The school was near the corner of Bellion Creek Road and Cole Creek Drive. (JPL.)

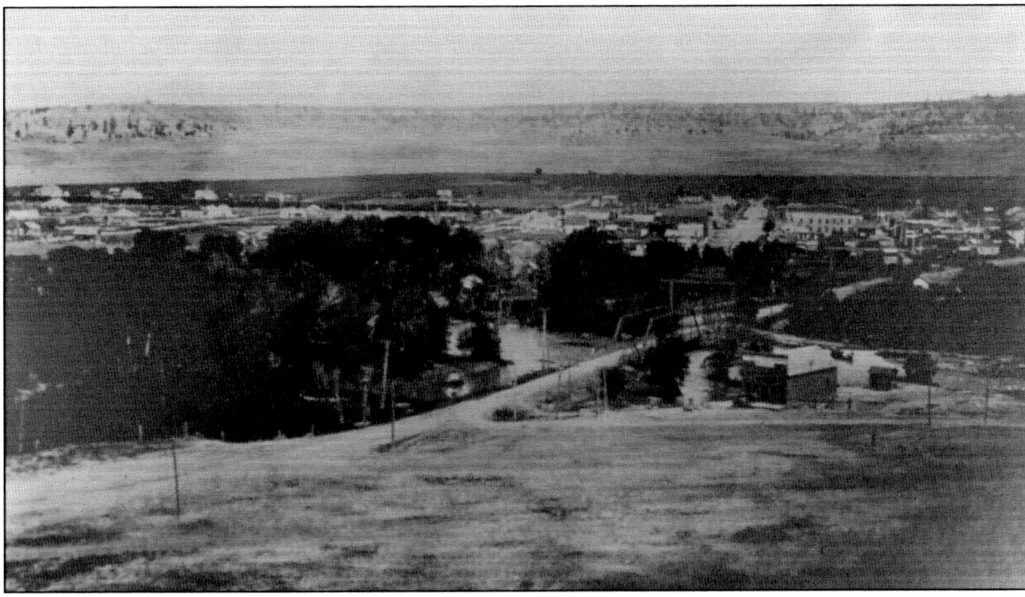

The Joliet Bridge and Last Chance Saloon are seen in the foreground of this 1906 photograph, which looks northwest over Joliet. By 1905, Joliet had two merchandise stores, a bank, two livery barns, a mill, a meat market, a confectionery store, an opera house, a brick factory, a creamery, seven saloons, and 47 dwellings, 36 of which were still standing as late as 1993. (JPL.)

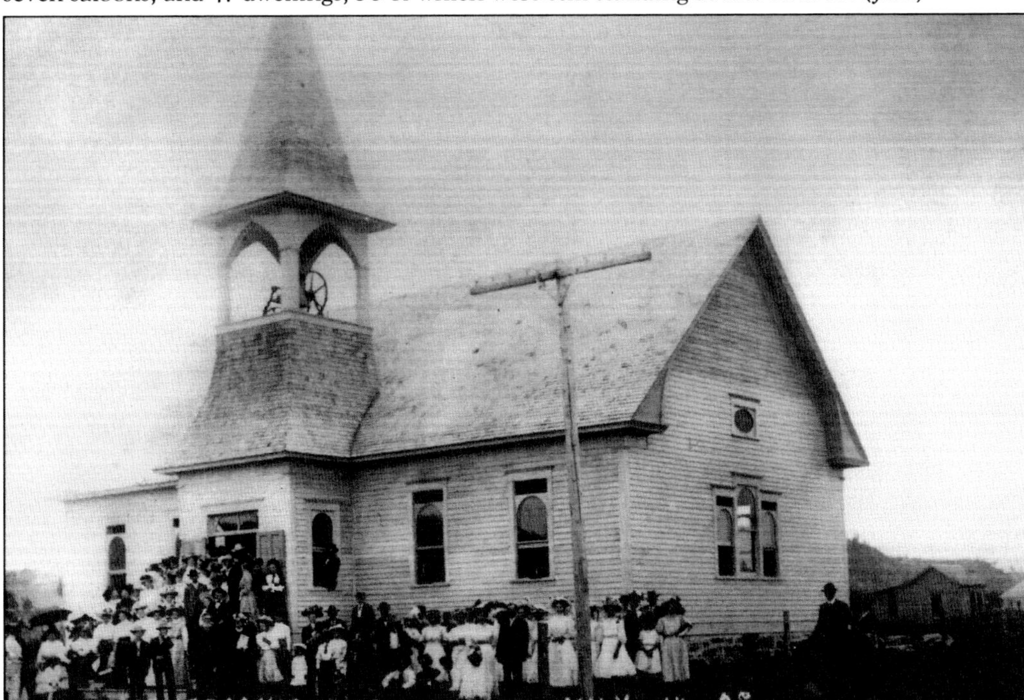

The congregation assembles outside the Joliet Christian Church just weeks after the building's dedication in June 1909. With the help of famed evangelist Walter Jordan, Rev. Oliver G. Shanklin organized the church in 1908. Prior to the completion of the church building, revival meetings were held in the upstairs of the meat market or the opera house, both filled to capacity. (JPL.)

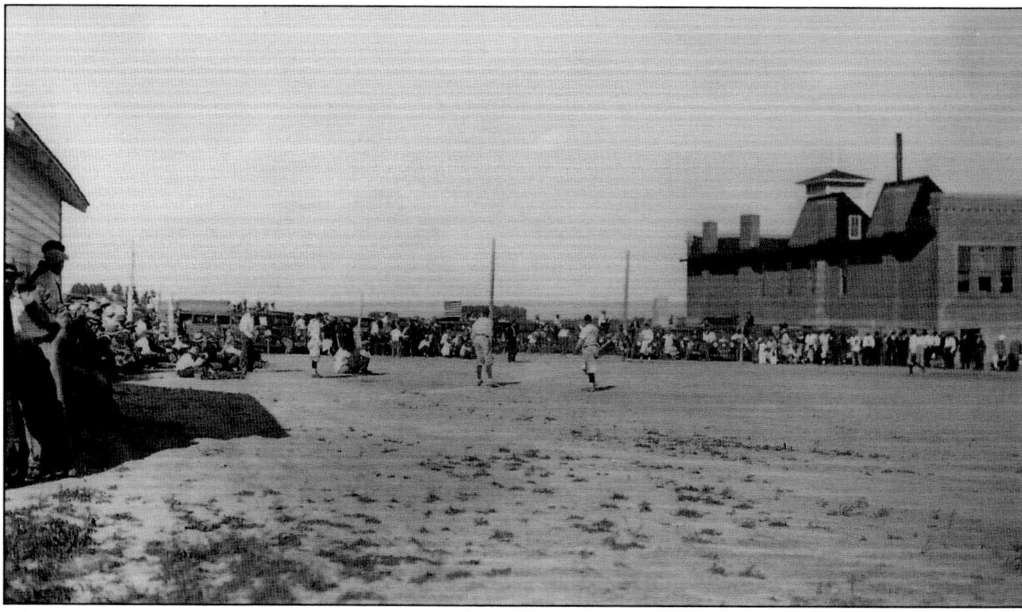

Many a summer afternoon was spent out behind Joliet High School, where an empty lot doubled as a baseball diamond, as seen here in the 1930s. Joliet played in a league against teams from other Carbon County communities such as Red Lodge, Bearcreek, and Fromberg, but it had an especially heated rivalry with Roberts. (JPL.)

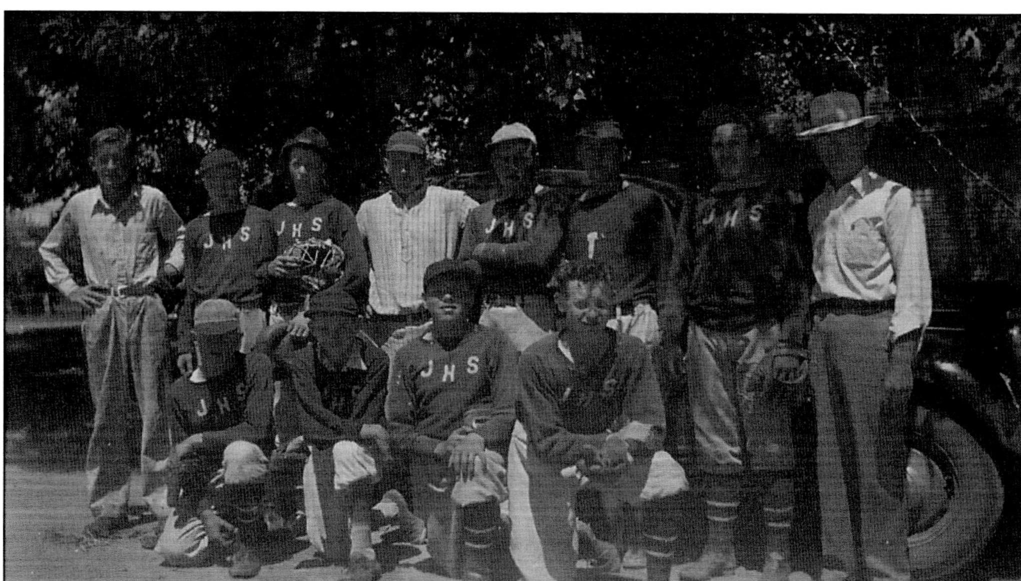

Coach Charles Johnson (far right) and his 1941 Joliet American Legion baseball team were named cochampions of the Carbon County league that summer. Their triumphs included a 42-7 victory over Belfry. Joliet fell to Fromberg 7-4 in the league championship game. This team included, in no particular order, Jim Hatten, Burton Wilcox, Reuben Steinmetz, and Jerry Murray. (CCHS.)

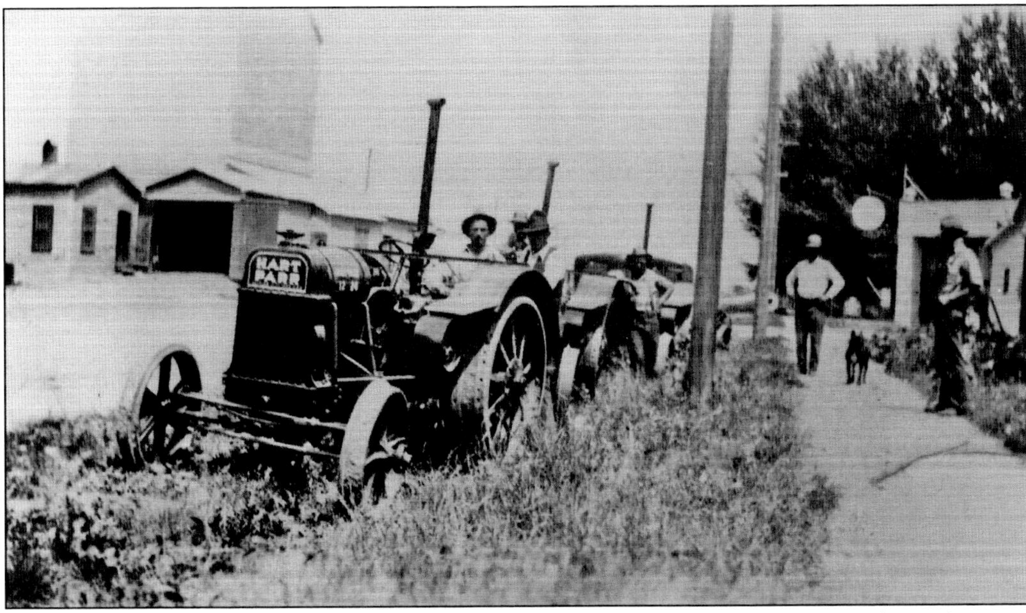

A trio of Hart-Parr 12-24H tractors lines up along Front Street in Joliet across from the grain elevator. Built between 1927 and 1930, the 4,400-pound 12-24H was a favorite of Western farmers for its durability and because it was relatively easy to maintain. Notice the tractor's distinctive winged radiator cap. (CCHS.)

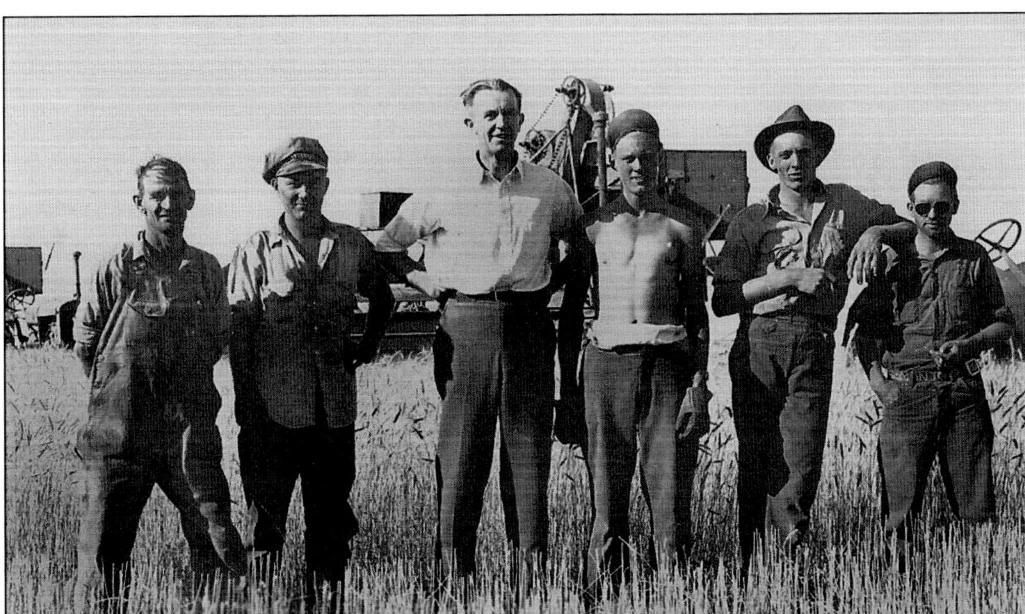

Elmer Talmage (third from left) stands tall with this haying crew on his Cole Creek ranch in the 1930s. In addition to managing his family's hardware store in Joliet, Talmage was one of the first to homestead on Cole Creek in the hills north of Joliet in the 1920s. (JPL.)

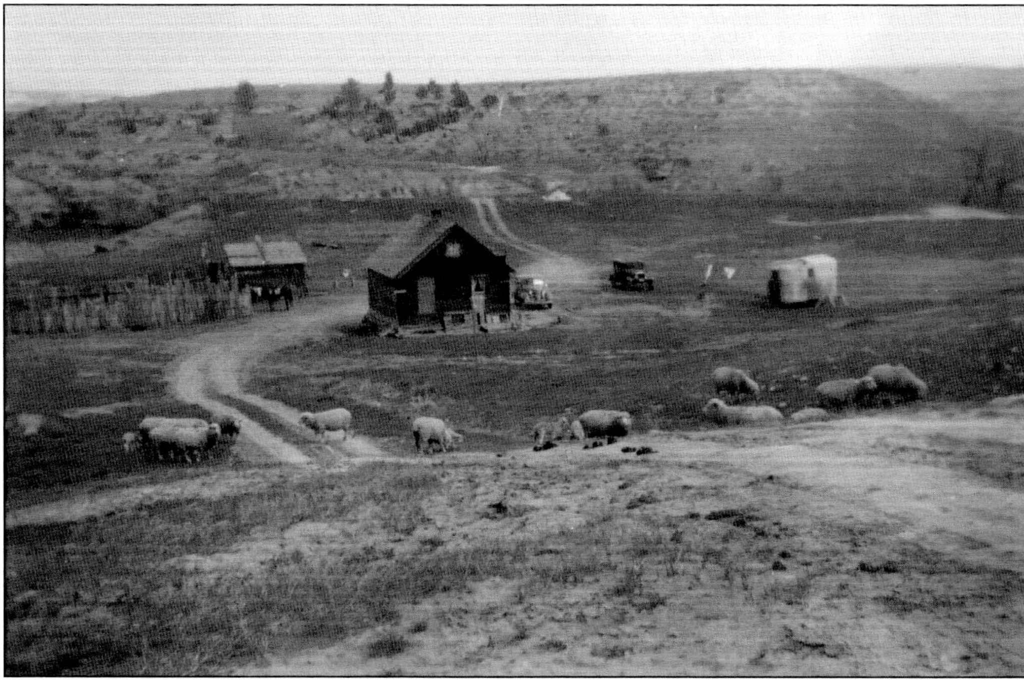

Sheep nibble in the front yard of Melvin Stene's ranch in the hills northwest of Joliet around 1940. Stene had 1,500 sheep on his range. In summer, the sheep were driven to the high country near Nye in Stillwater County or to the Dryhead region of the Pryor Mountains. While grazing their sheep away from the homestead, Stene and his wife, Lillian, would live in the sheep wagon (below). Once, in 1938–1939, they lived in it for over a year in the Dryhead. The wagon was built entirely by hand by Stene's uncle Reinhard in 1927. (Both, JPL.)

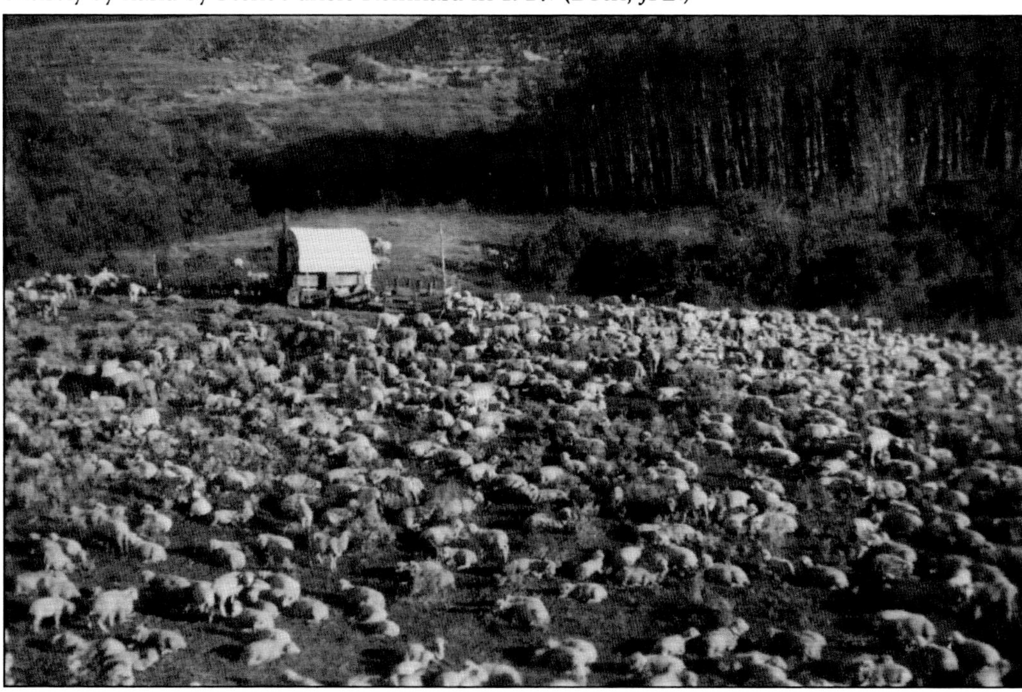

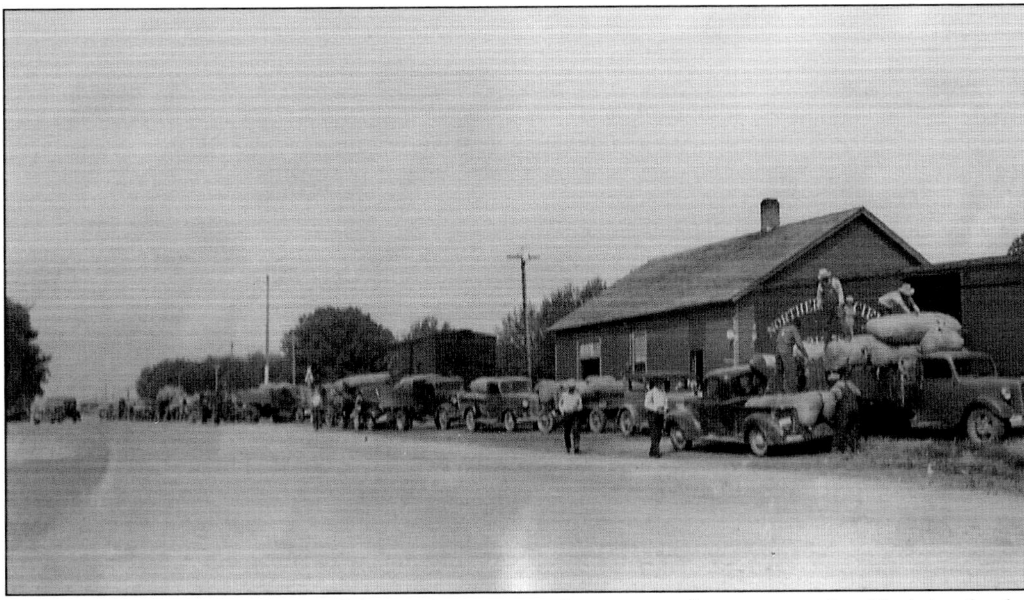

Trucks loaded with wool bound for markets across the country line up to unload bulging burlap sacks weighing as much as 400 pounds into Northern Pacific Railway boxcars at the Joliet train depot around 1940. For the remote ranches ringing the Rock Creek Valley, Joliet was an important shipping point for both sheep and cattle. (CCHS.)

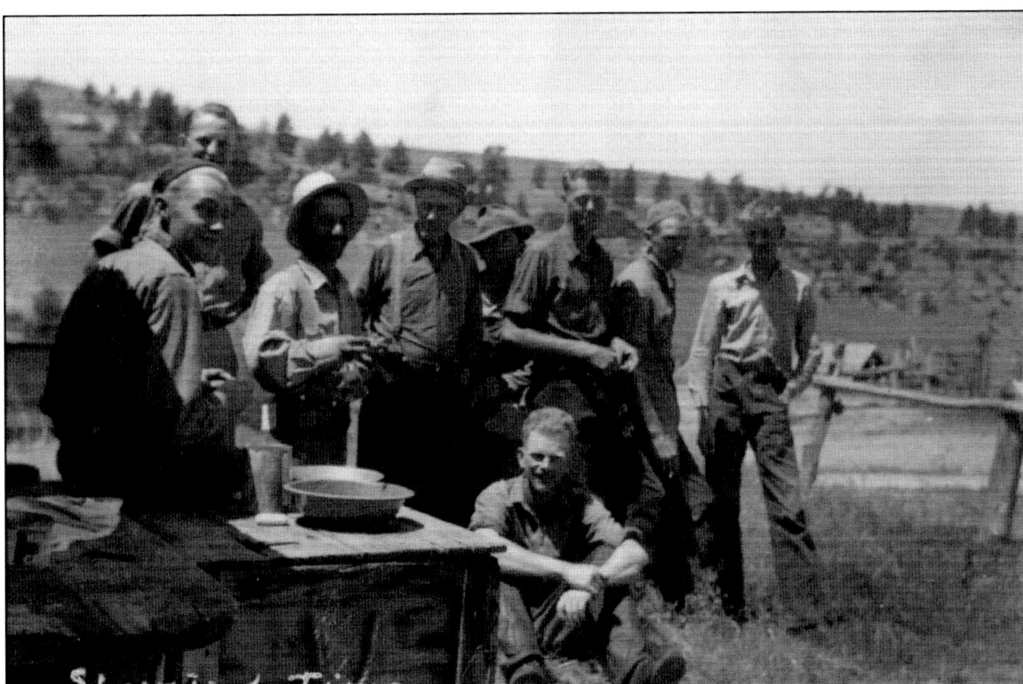

Sheepshearers take a break on the Ole Arthun ranch. Nobody in the photograph is identified, as sheepshearers often led a transient existence, moving from ranch to ranch across wide swaths of the West during sheering season. Arthun emigrated from Norway in 1905 and eventually built his ranching interest to several thousand acres by the time of his death in 1945. (JPL.)

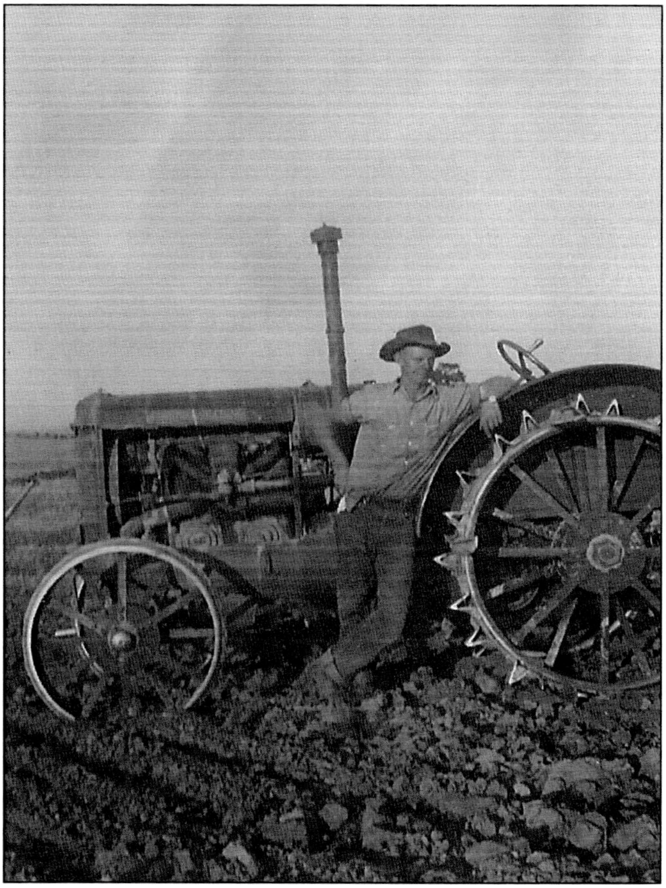

A Joliet farmer stands next to one of his most valuable assets, his McCormick Deering International Harvester 22-36 tractor. Made between 1929 and 1934, it was powered by a seven-liter, in-line four-cylinder, 30-horsepower kerosene engine and weighed 6,500 pounds. It was a favorite among dryland farmers, whose future depended on their ability to deeply till hard-packed soil. (CCHS.)

Joliet's first business, a saloon, is said to have started in a tent on July 4, 1893. By the time of the 1930s photograph below, Joliet had established itself a solid brick-and-mortar footprint, as the Masonic lodge building, across Front Street from the train depot, attests. Jay Spaulding's Carter gas station (left) was behind the lodge. (CCHS.)

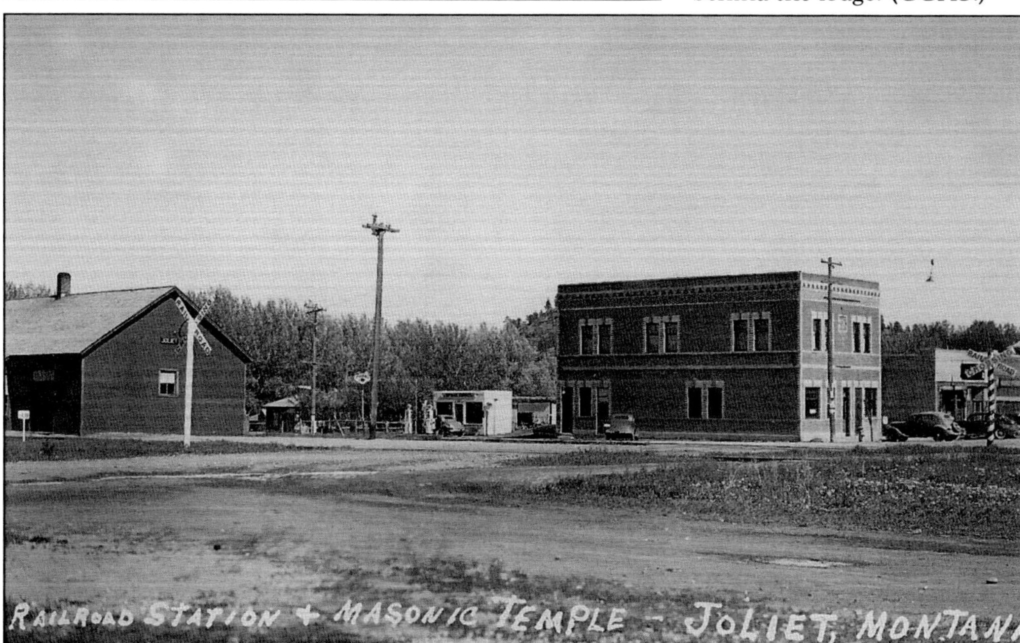

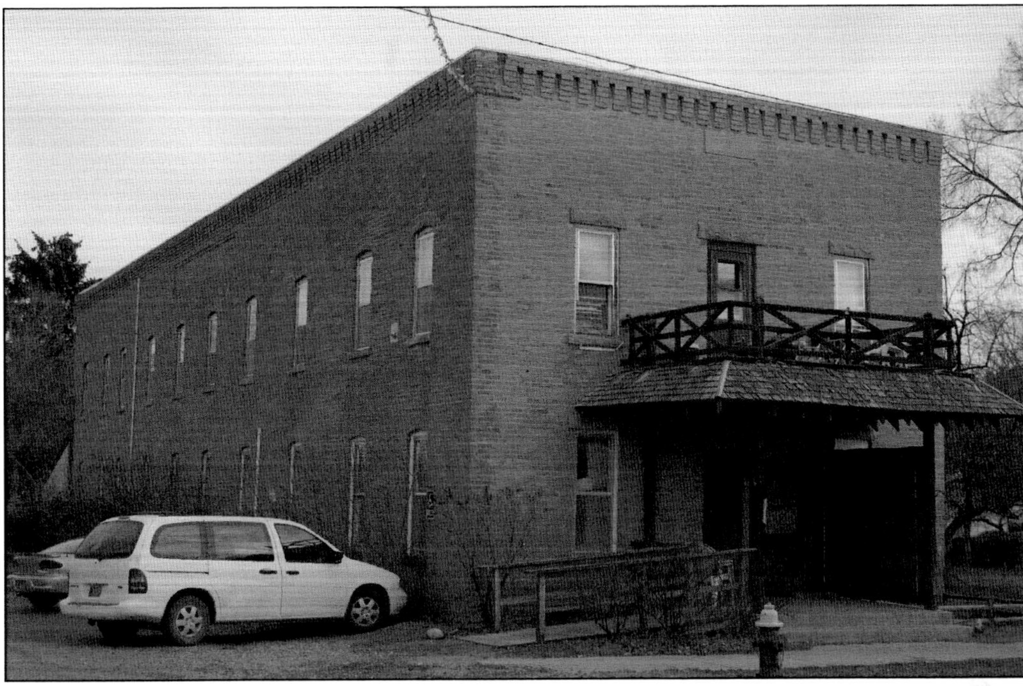

Built from local brick in 1906, the two-story Hotel Southern was once the most substantial commercial building in Joliet. It was built by Luther Symington. His wife, Agnes, handled day-to-day operations. She was well known for her cleanliness and fine food. The building, seen in the contemporary photograph above, was added to the National Register of Historic Places in 1986 and is now an apartment building. (Wallace.)

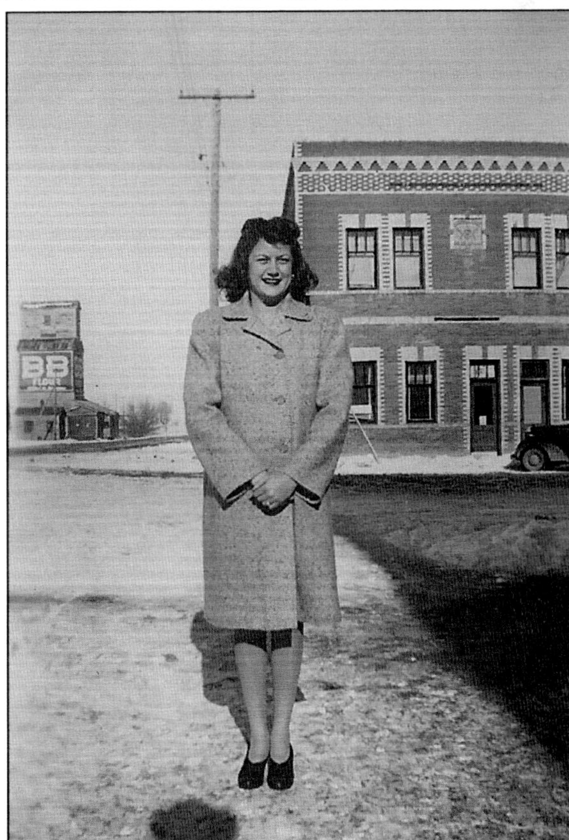

Annabelle (Talmage) Golden stands in front of the Joliet Masonic lodge in the 1950s. Visible in the background is the grain elevator, one of two that served the town through the years. While the Rocky Fork Branch of the Northern Pacific Railway started as a coal-hauling line, by the 1950s, it had become a "granger road," gleaning most of its tonnage from grains and sugar beets. (CCHS.)

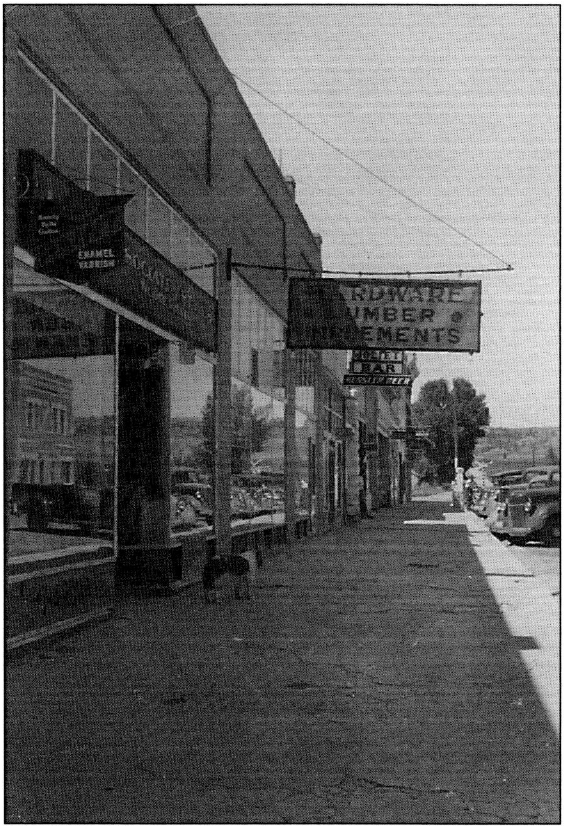

After opening a successful mercantile store in Red Lodge in 1891, William A. Talmage went into a partnership with Albert Sayer and established the Talmage-Sayer Hardware & Lumber Company in Joliet in 1912. He ran the business with his sons Elmer and Earl until his death in 1927, when Elmer took over management. (JPL.)

Elmer Talmage (center) is seen below in the store around 1935 among household staples and fabrics as well as luxury items such as washing machines and bicycles. A tall man, Talmage gave his height as "five-foot, 19 inches." He was also one of the first homesteaders on Cole Creek in the hills north of Joliet. (JPL.)

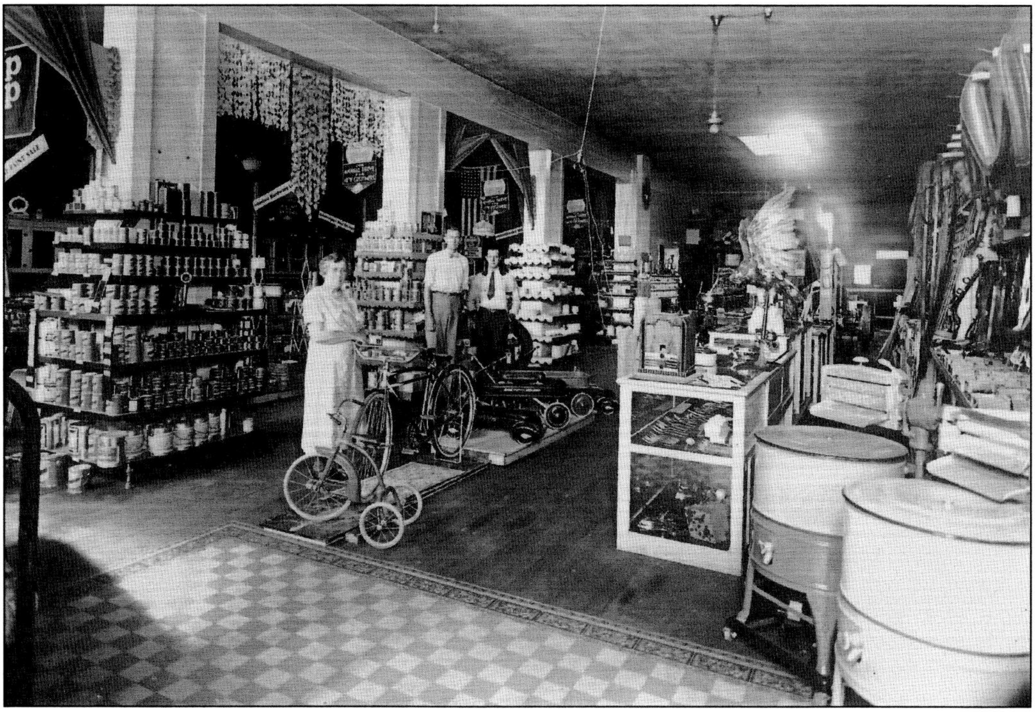

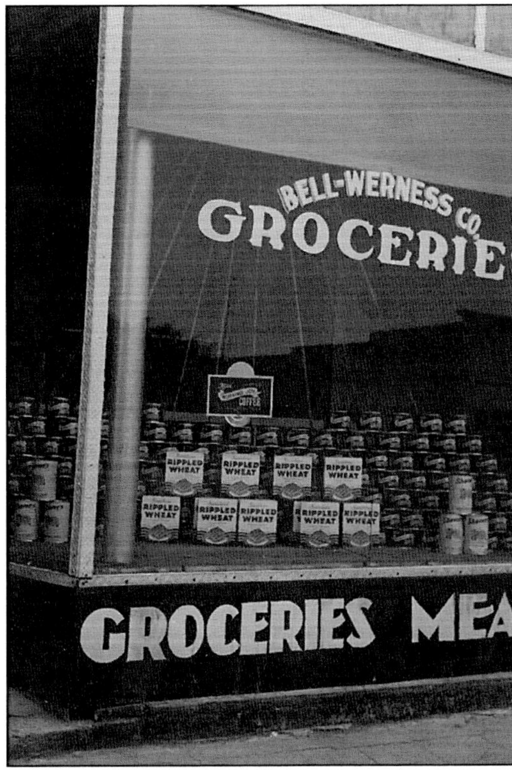

In 1941, George M. Bell bought the hardware and merchandise store from Elmer Talmage and combined it (right) with his dry goods and grocery store. In 1942, Talmage raised the building's rent from $75 to $100 a month. Refusing to pay, Bell and his son Buck instead built a new store. George M. Bell's son George D. Bell married Josephine Feldman in 1941, and the two operated the store together until 1966. In later years, competition forced the Bells to sell off the hardware section and concentrate on selling groceries. Below, Josephine Bell is seen behind the grocery counter leaning on a carton of Ripley's Root-Aid soft drinks. (Both, JPL.)

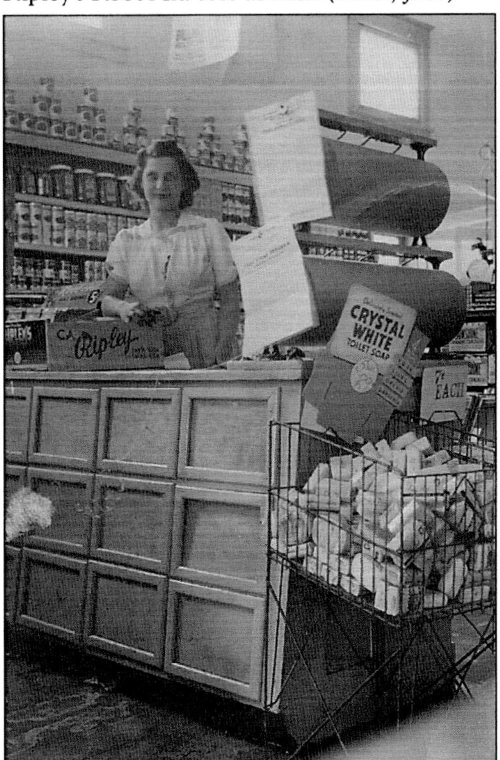

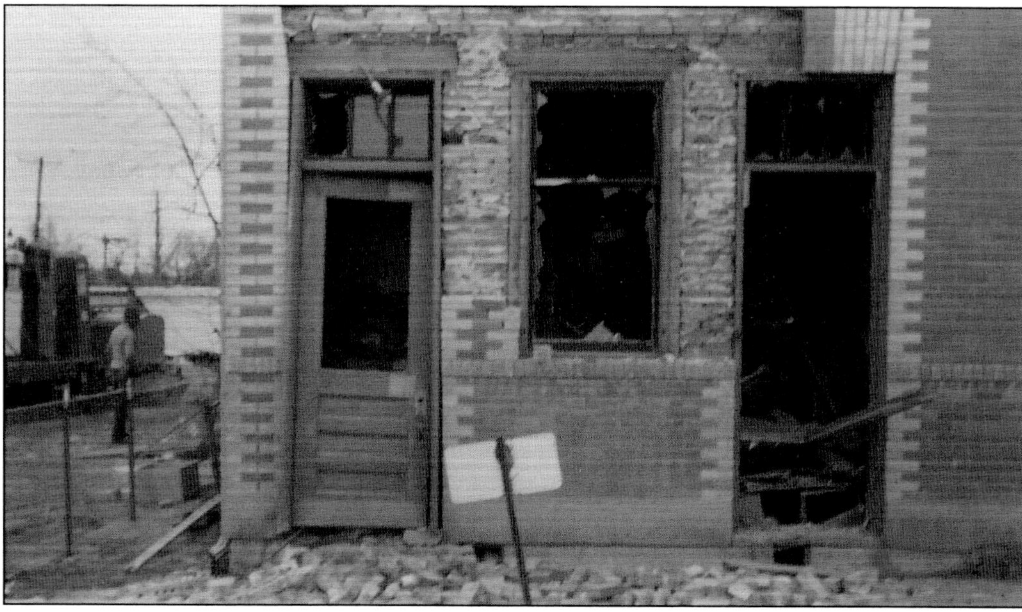

On April 1, 1964, a gas explosion (above) destroyed the Masonic lodge building, which also housed the Joliet State Bank and the Agricultural Stabilization and Conservation (ASC) office on the first floor. Miraculously, despite the blast cracking the building's foundation, blowing out all the windows, and scattering glass and venetian blinds across the street, the four women working in the ASC offices at the time of the explosion escaped unharmed. Josephine Hatten, one of the women, took the photograph below of debris strewn where her desk once sat. The building had to be torn down due to irreparable damage to its foundation. (Both, CCHS.)

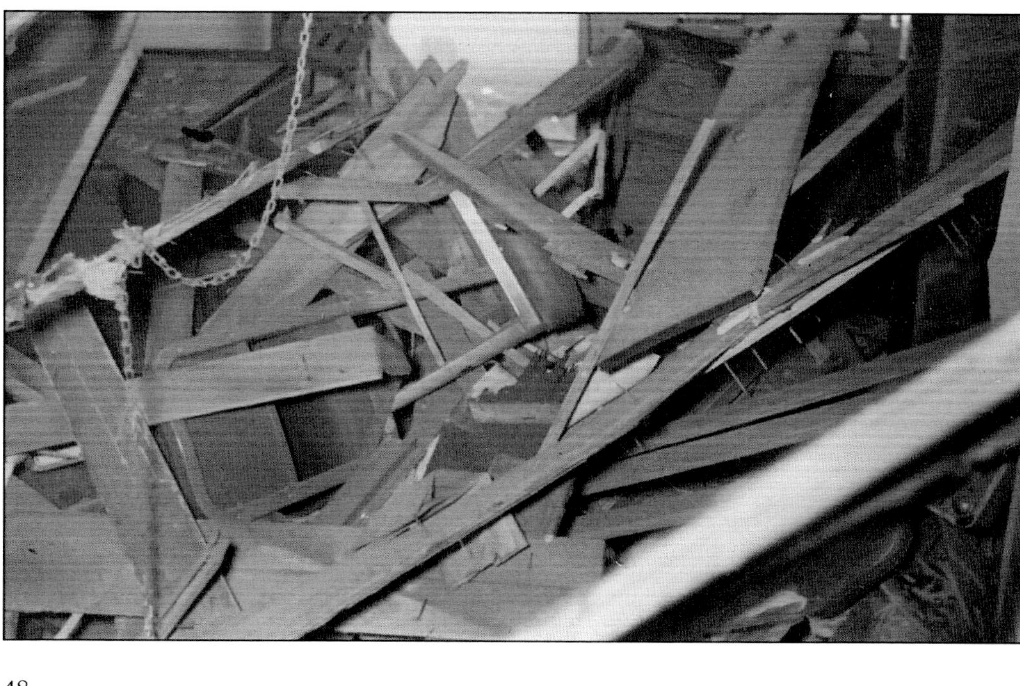

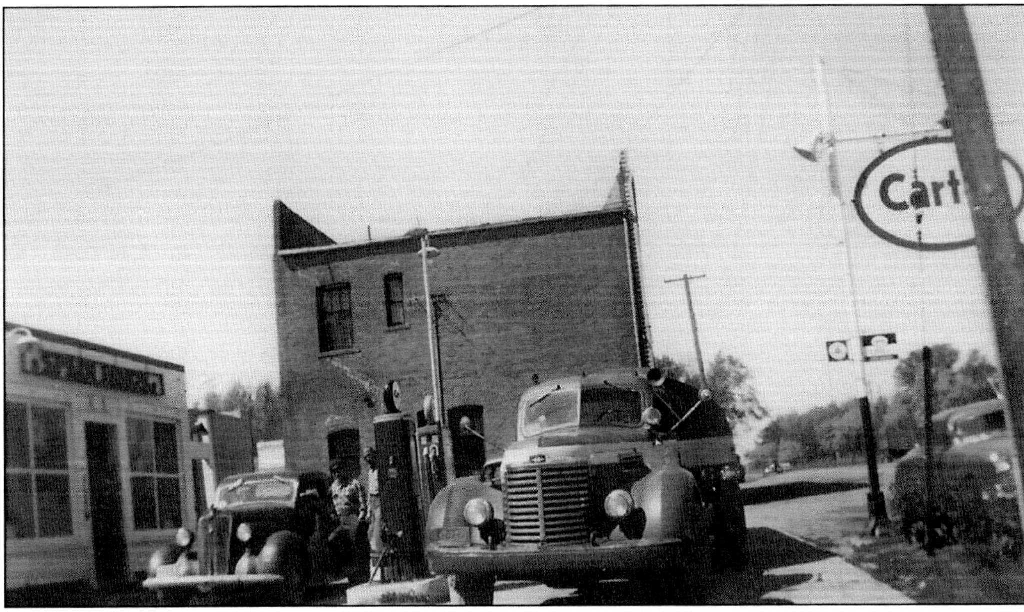

Above, Jay Spaulding chats while filling up a customer's automobile at his Carter gas station, located just behind the Masonic building. He was fortunate that the natural gas explosion next door did not ignite his underground gasoline tanks, which would have set off a conflagration that could have leveled the whole town. Below, Spaulding's daughters Lynda (left) and Kathy are dressed in spring outfits in front of their father's Ford pickup. Note the tank in the truck bed for fuel delivery to area farms and ranches. The Joliet depot and section house are in the background. (Both, JPL.)

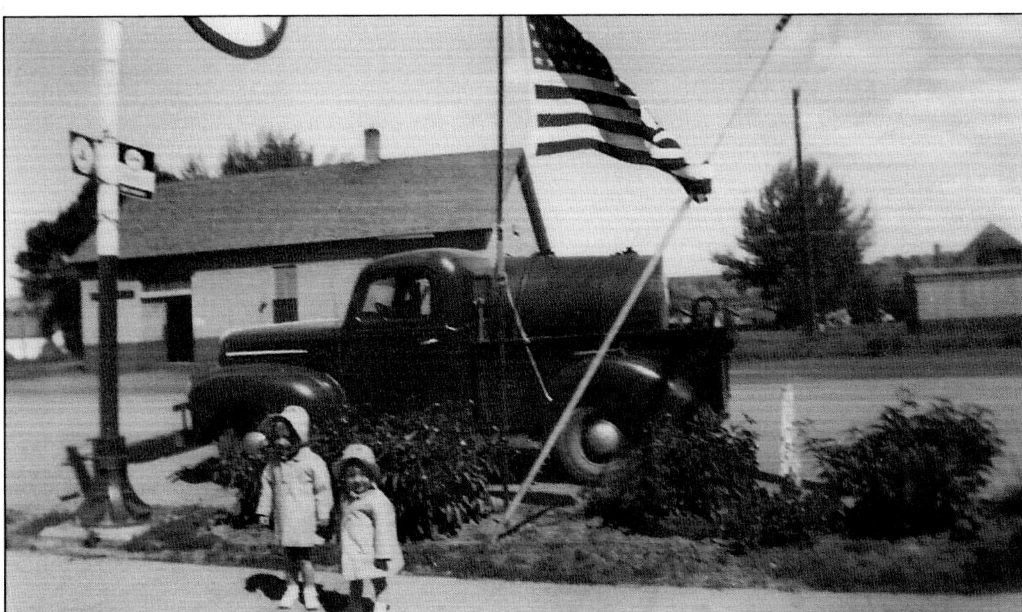

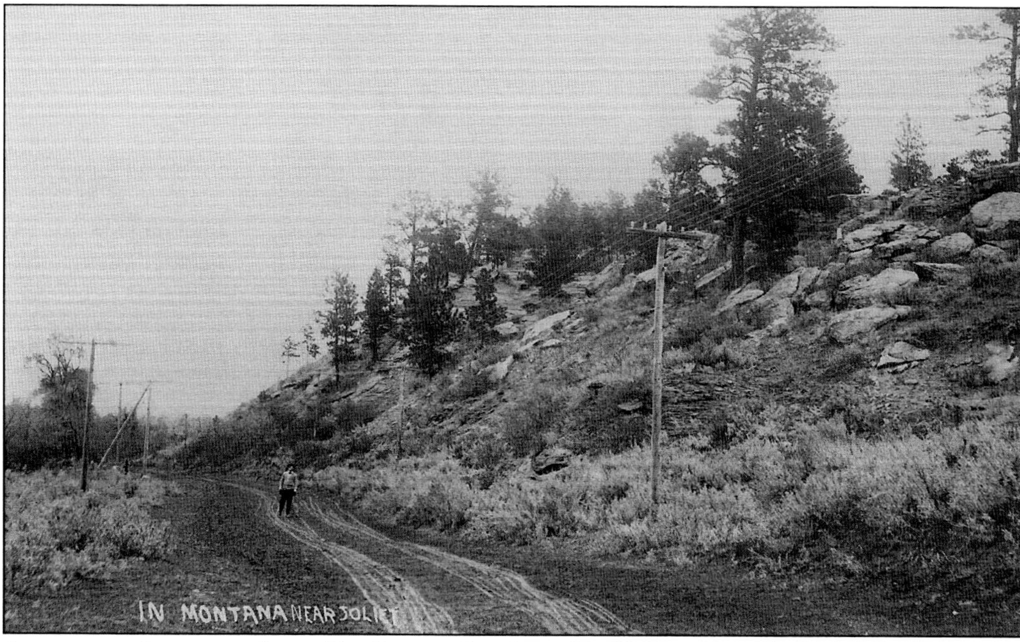

A man stands on rutted, muddy Granite Road south of Joliet near where the Bozeman Trail traversed Rock Creek, immediately downstream from the Joliet Bridge as the trail turned from the Clark's Fork Valley west into the Rock Creek Valley. Granite Road leads down the southern bank of Rock Creek to the Poverty Flat agricultural area. (CCHS.)

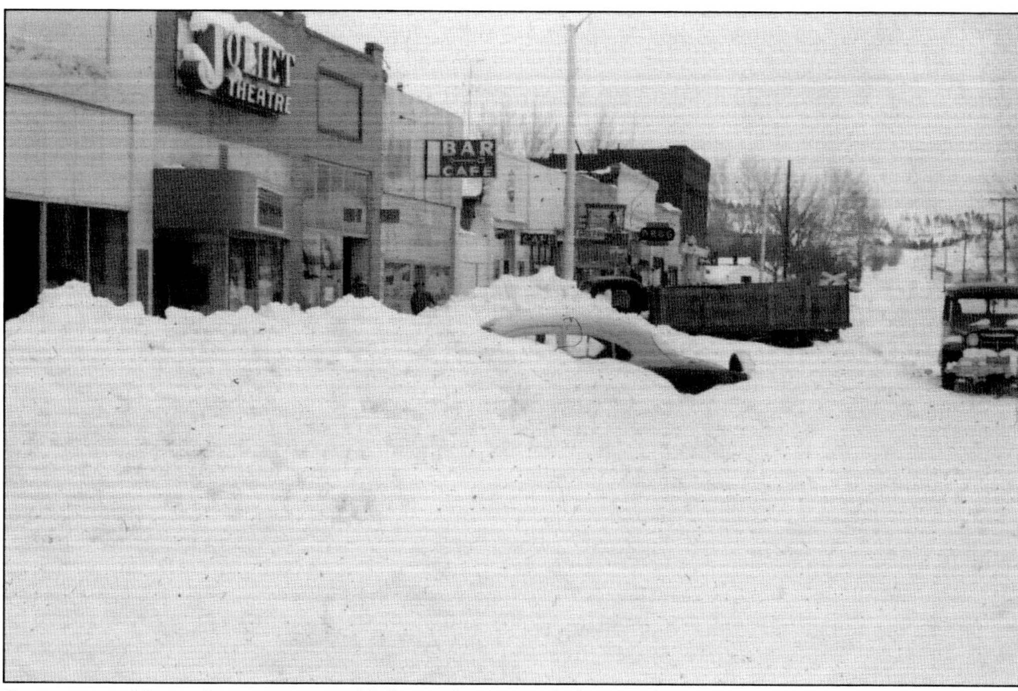

Springtime blizzards are a way of life at the foot of the Rocky Mountains. But the April 1955 blizzard along Rock Creek was exceptional, dumping 42 inches of snow in a little over 12 hours, creating snowdrifts that nearly buried these cars parked on the west side of Main Street. (JPL.)

Four

Carbonado and Boyd

Carbonado is a former townsite in the Rock Creek Valley about two miles southwest of Joliet. The town came and went in only five years, rising and falling with the fortunes of its coal mine. The town was started in 1897 by the Anaconda Copper Company to supply coal for its hungry smelters in Butte. During its brief heyday, Carbonado had a population of around 700 and consisted of a two-room schoolhouse, a hotel, a saloon, a post office, a general store, a confectionery, a brick factory, two rooming houses, and a clothing store.

The mine employed 150 miners. Its shaft went down 980 feet and produced 450 tons of lignite per day, according to a 1900 report from the Montana inspector of mines. Major water seepage, combined with the coal's low quality, finally made it cost-prohibitive to continue, and the mine closed in 1902. Businesses and houses from Carbonado were moved to Joliet in winter, when they could be slid across a frozen Rock Creek, or they were moved to Boyd. All that remains of Carbonado today is the cemetery and a small slag pile.

Named after John Boyd, a Canadian who homesteaded the area in 1894, the town of Boyd began as a necessity when Carbonado ceased to be, as there were no stores between Joliet and Roberts, a distance of 13 miles. In 1906, a patent for Boyd was granted by Pres. Teddy Roosevelt, and two years later, a railroad stop, a store, and a post office were built. Many homes and buildings from Carbonado were moved to Boyd.

By the 1920s, there was a grade school, a saloon, a dance hall, a pool hall, a bank, two grain elevators, a confectionery, a creamery station, a beet dump, a barbershop, and a Methodist Episcopal church. At its peak, the town had over 50 residents, as well as others homesteading in the nearby Cow Creek area. As roads improved and more people were driving cars by the 1930s, the town slowly waned. Today, there are still several homes, a community center, and a self-service post office. Its only store closed in the 2000s, but the building still stands.

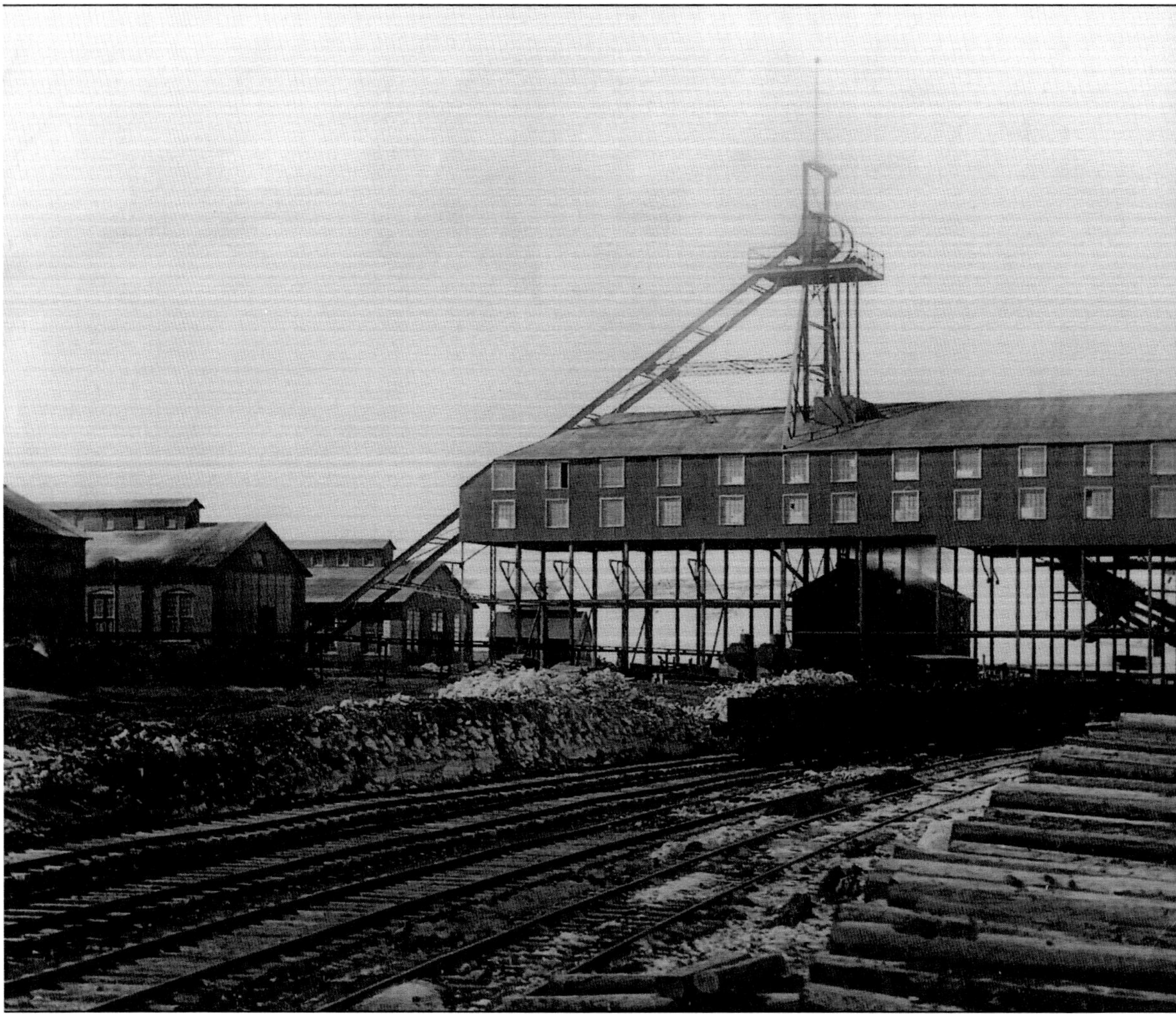

At its peak in 1901, shortly before its demise, the Carbonado mine produced 700 tons of coal per day. The mine was owned by the Anaconda Copper Company of Butte, and its coal went to fuel copper smelters there. Mining operations ended abruptly in 1901, when the Anaconda president, "Copper King" Marcus Daly, took a quick trip down the mine shaft, emerged, and ordered the mine closed within a few hours. During its short life, the mine did not escape tragedy. Once, a disheartened Finnish immigrant reportedly stood at the edge of the 980-foot shaft and announced "I'm going to yump" before leaping to his death. The tipple and the other mine buildings were dismantled and moved to the Brophy mine in Bearcreek in 1918. (JPL.)

Boyd Methodist Episcopal Church is seen here just before it was dismantled. Ironically, the church building began its life as a Carbonado saloon owned by Claude Banta. In 1920, the building was purchased, and it was so difficult to move that Rev. H.B. Woods reportedly offered to step to one side if the men moving the building felt tempted to swear. (JPL.)

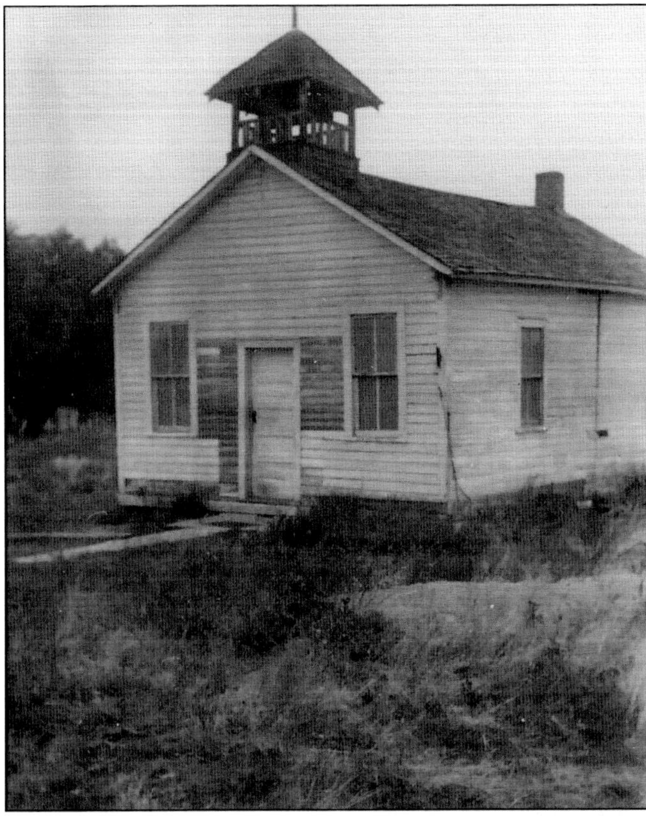

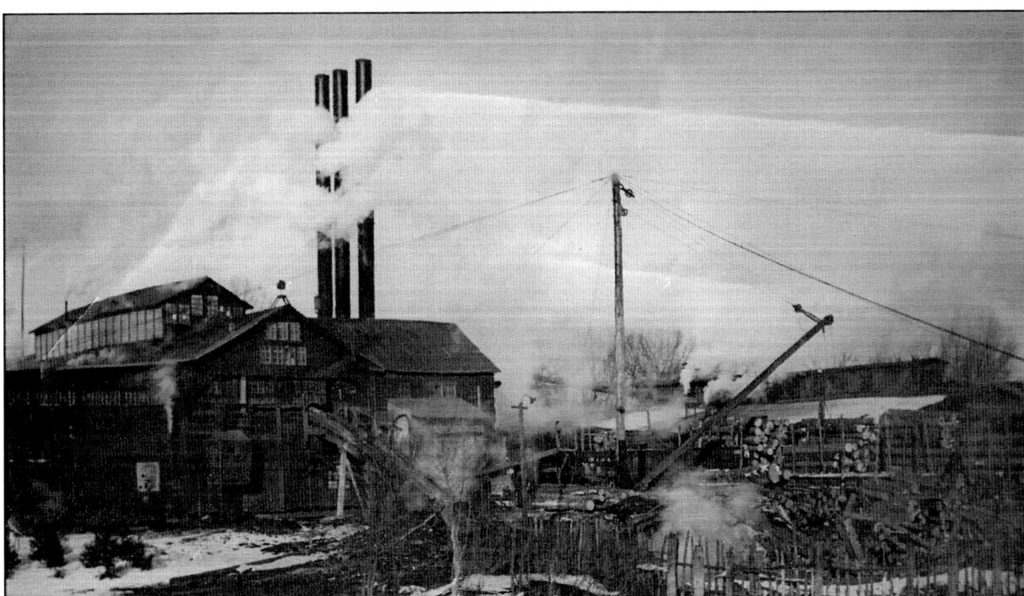

Mines required massive support in the form of craftsmen and resources. Some mines employed almost as many carpenters and masons as miners. Timber, for mine supports and numerous other applications, was in such high demand that timber-processing facilities were often located right next to the mine, as in Carbonado, which also had its own brick factory. (CCHS.)

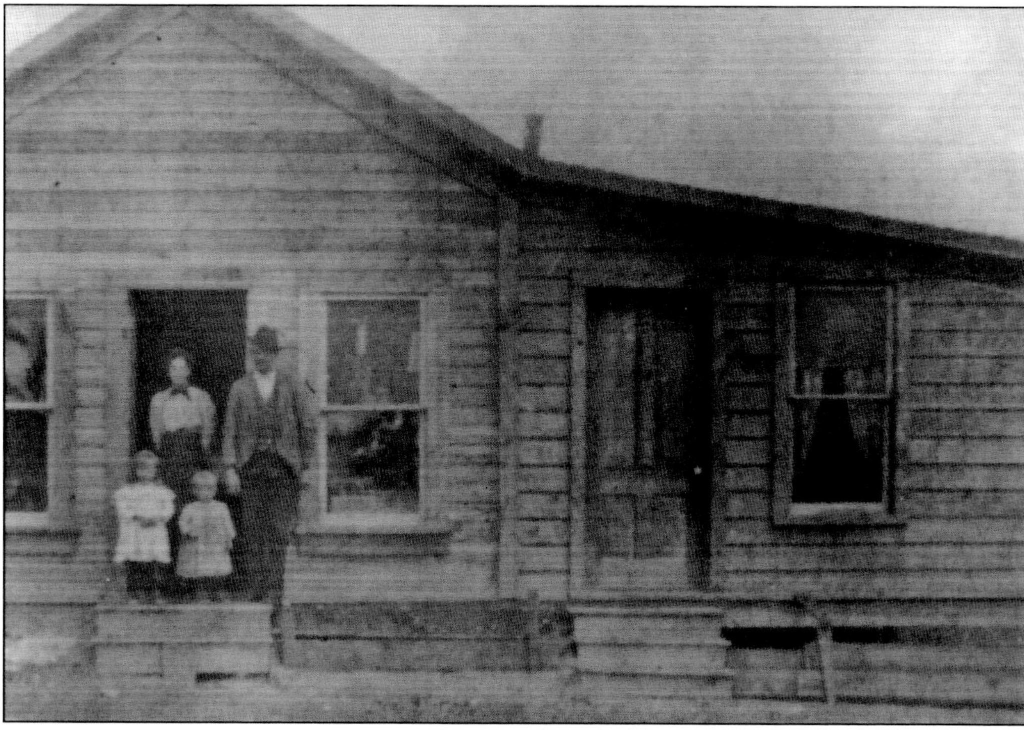

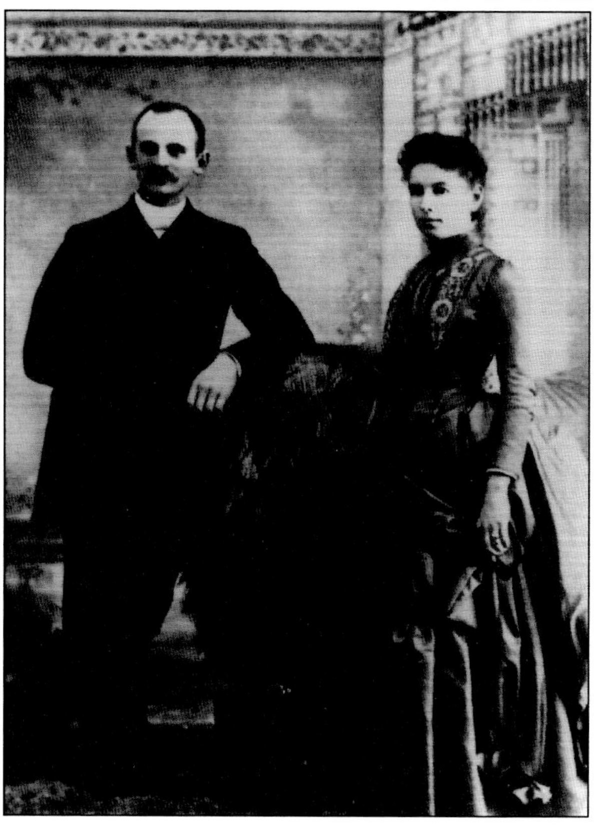

Above, Alfred and Mabel Croonquist stand on the front porch of their general store in Carbonado with their two oldest children, Mabel and Stanley. The store's biggest customer was the Anaconda Copper Company, which set up food credit accounts for its miners at the store. Alfred Croonquist built the structure, which included living quarters behind the door on the right. (CCHS.)

Alfred and Mabel Croonquist are seen here in their 1888 wedding photograph. The Croonquists were among the first merchants in Carbonado in 1899. Alfred, a Swedish immigrant, was a merchant in Livingston when he met 18-year-old Mabel, a teacher. After the store in Carbonado closed in 1901, Croonquist opened a mercantile store in Red Lodge. (CCHS.)

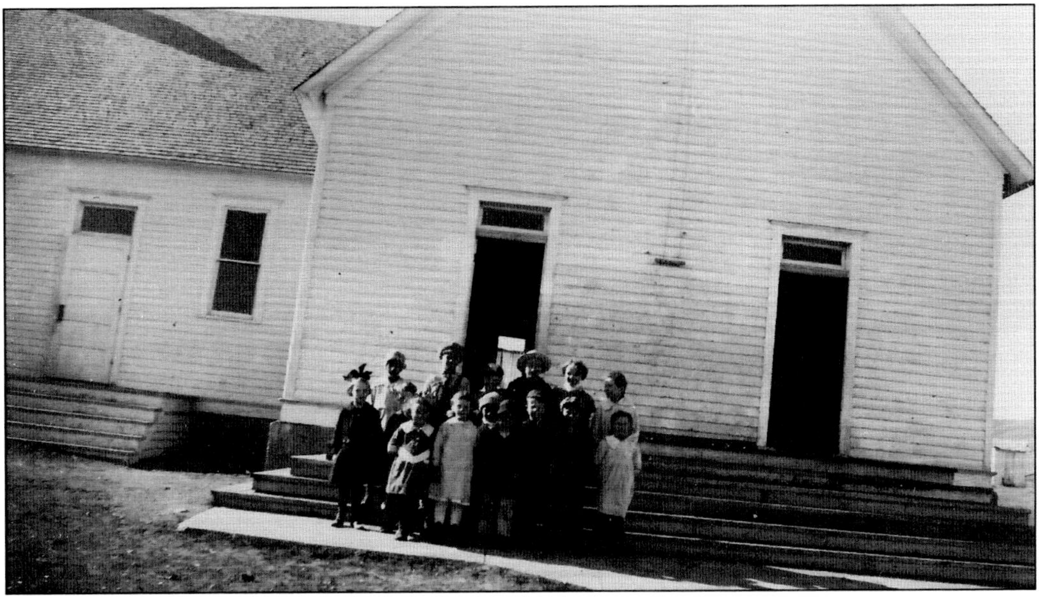

The Carbonado school opened in 1897 but was replaced by a second, larger school in 1901, seen above in a 1919 photograph. The two-room school was built with volunteer labor on land donated by the Anaconda Copper Company. Classes as large as 40 students attended grades one through eight. The students standing on the porch in the 1919 photograph below are, in no particular order, Lawrence Hughes, Delmer Walker, Ruby Ward, Ellis Taylor, Mayre Ward, Edna Kirkhart, Grace Adamson, Celeste Ward, Dean Hughes, and Donald Anderson. Their teacher was Queenie A. Saby. Other early teachers included Charlotte Dilworth and Miss Thomas. Shortly after this photograph was taken, the school was moved to Boyd, where it is still used as a community center today. (Both, Woody.)

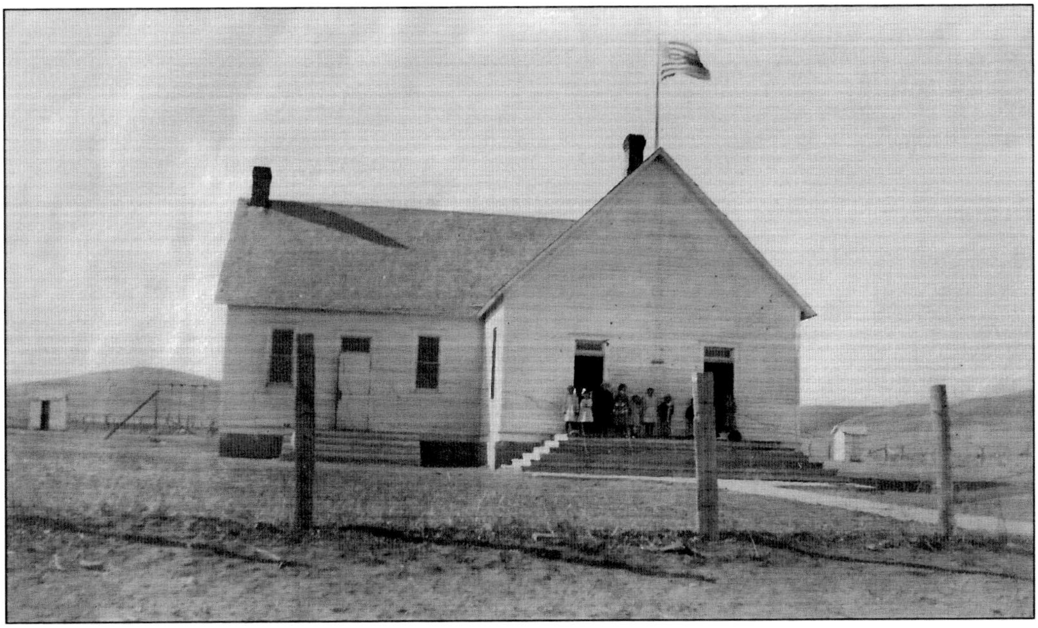

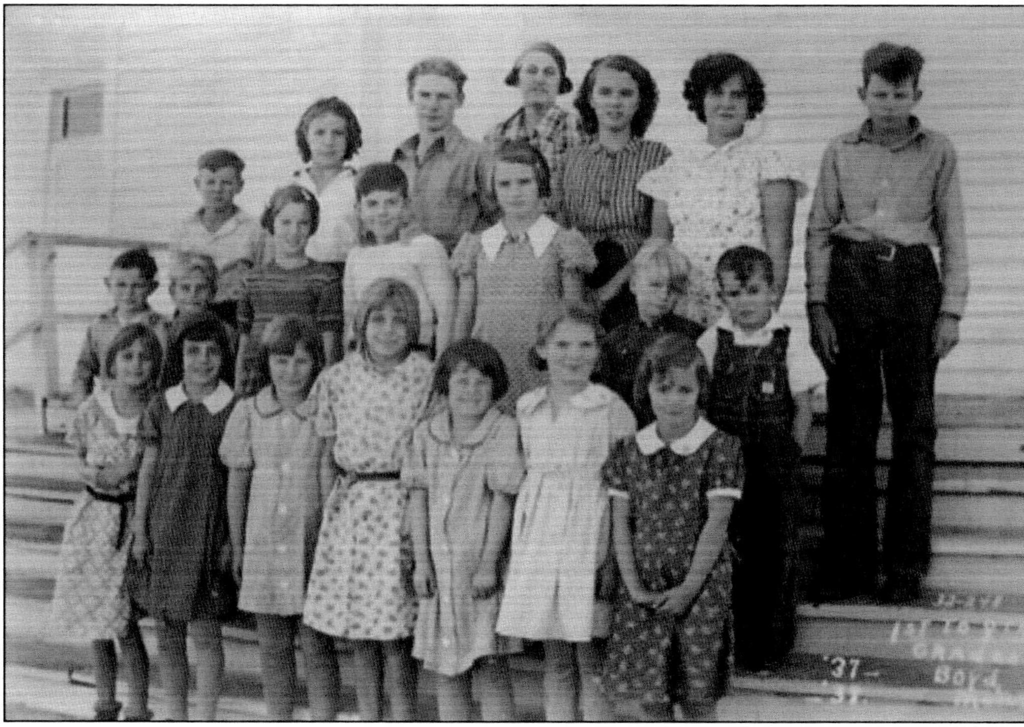

Students from grades one through eight are seen above in 1937 at the Boyd school. At its peak, the town had over 50 residents. The school still stands today, although it was recently converted to a community center. (CCHS.)

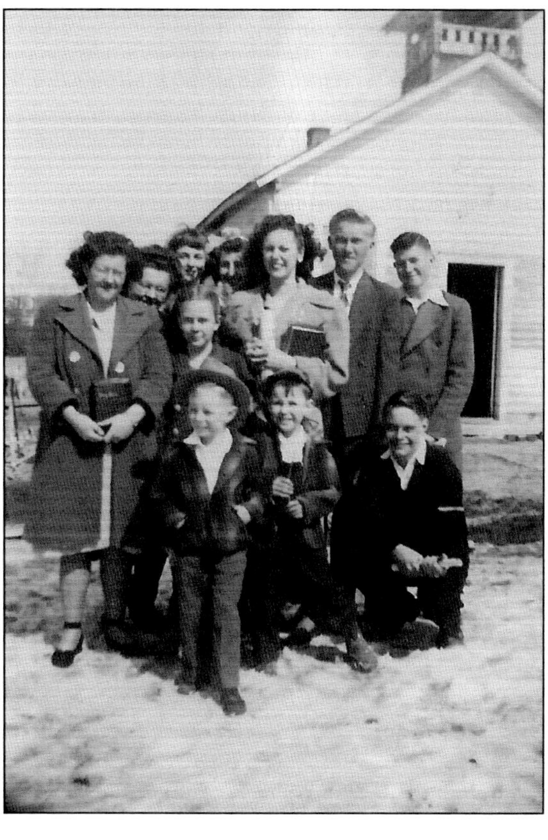

This Sunday school class stands outside the Boyd church in 1950. From left to right are (first row) Kurt Comack, Bill Comack, and ? Hull; (second row) Thelma Kirkhart (Woody), unidentified, Violet Comack, Marvin Crook, and Jay Legget; (third row) Velma Kirkhart, Joyce Shoop, and Claire Shoop. One of the two grain elevators that once served Boyd is in the far left background. (Woody.)

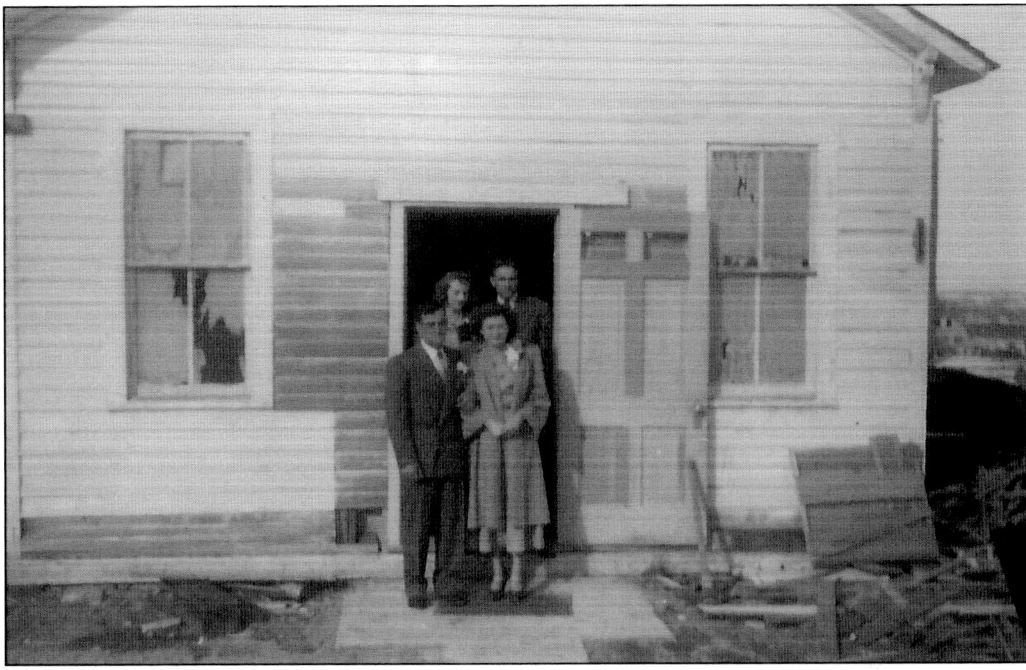

The 1950 wedding of Warren and Betty Taylor (first row) was one of the last official ceremonies performed at the Boyd church. Judging from the debris piled in the front yard, deconstruction of the church began prior to the happy union. (Woody.)

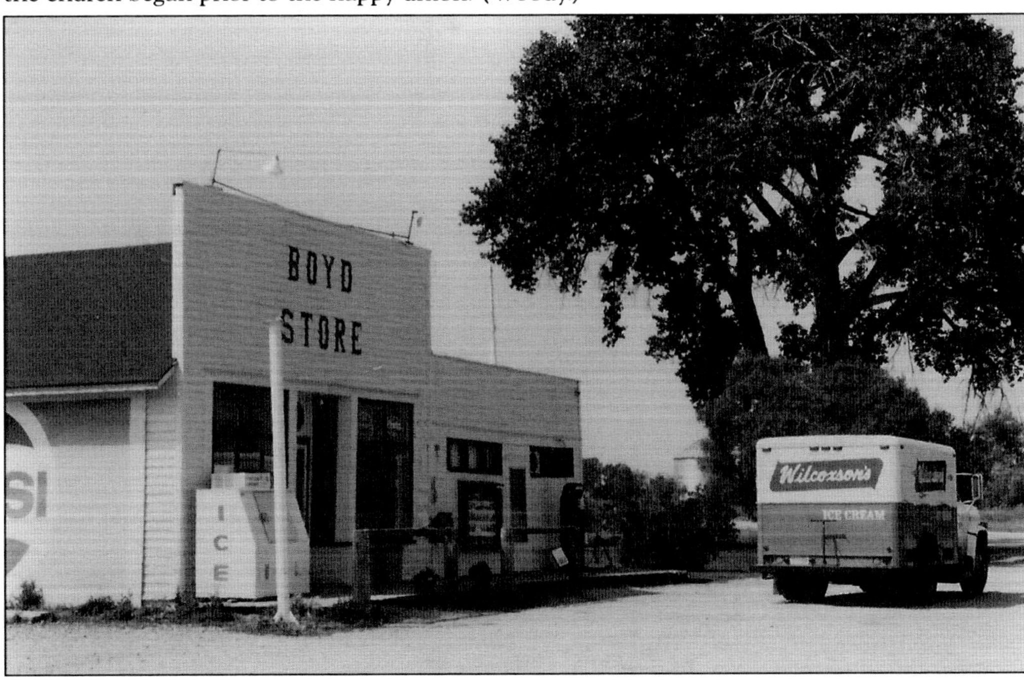

The Boyd Store was built in 1908 by R.N. Doughty on land donated by town namesake John Boyd. The store was a classic general store with a wooden boardwalk and a post office inside. Seen here around 1980, the store survived despite many changes in ownership. It was last open in 2008. (CCHS.)

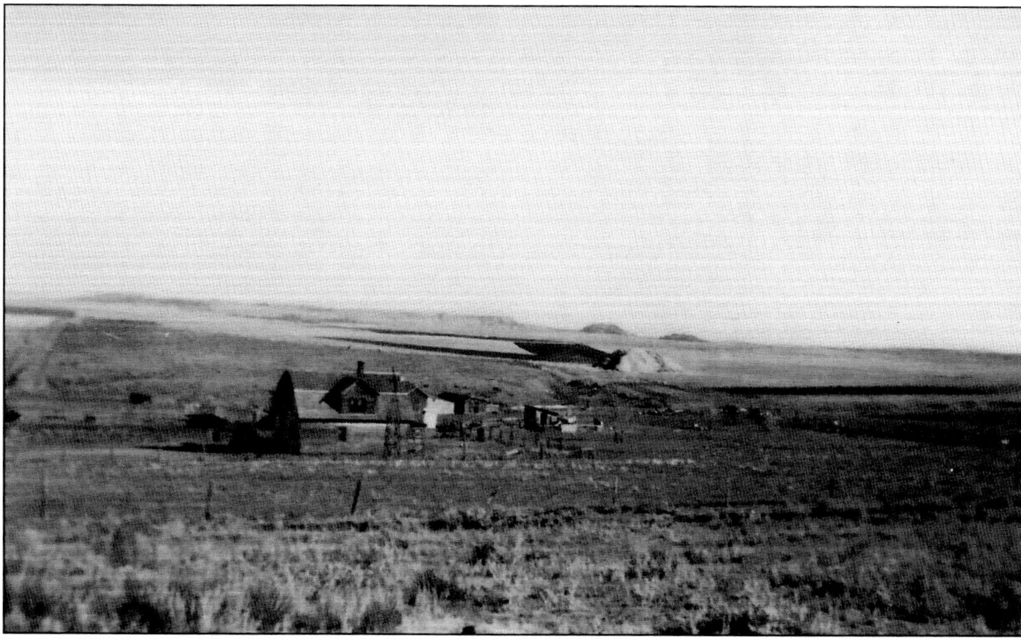

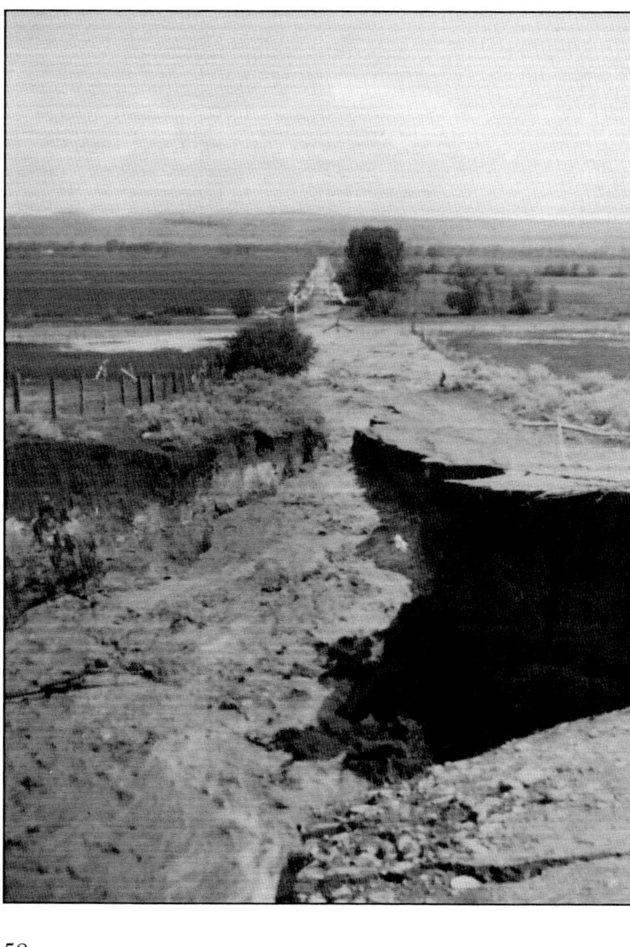

The Pryor Mountains are in the background of the photograph above, which looks east at the Cow Creek homestead of Adam and Margaret Mae (White) Wakenshaw. Adam was an adventuresome miner, coming to Montana by way of the Yukon, where he had prospected for gold. He worked in the Carbonado mines and farmed on the homestead. (Wakenshaw.)

After a dry winter, the spring rains of 1936 were at first greeted as a blessing against drought and grasshoppers, which thrive in dry weather. Locals in Boyd changed their minds, however, when heavy rains between May 31 and June 2 led to massive runoff and flash flooding. As is often the case, the downpour did little to assuage the drought, which struck that summer anyway. (JPL.)

Five

Cooney Reservoir, Willow Creek, Red Lodge Creek, and Volney Creek

In an attempt to lessen the threat of periodic floods and drought, and to bring irrigation to tens of thousands of acres of farmland, residents of the Rock Creek Valley pushed for the creation of Cooney Reservoir, located eight miles west of Boyd. In 1936, a dam was completed near the confluence of Red Lodge and Willow Creeks, about six miles upstream from where Red Lodge Creek flows into Rock Creek. It was originally going to be called Red Lodge Creek Dam, but when Montana governor Frank H. Cooney passed away while in office in 1935, it was decided to name the new water impoundment after Cooney, who had done much to endorse water conservation programs throughout the state.

Cooney Reservoir not only brought irrigation to many farmers, helped avert floods, and eased drought conditions, it also became one of the most popular state parks in the Montana system, attracting boaters and fishermen alike. West of Cooney Reservoir, Red Lodge Creek, Willow Creek, and Volney Creek wind through a great open space of golden brown foothills peppered with some of the oldest ranches and homesteads in Carbon County.

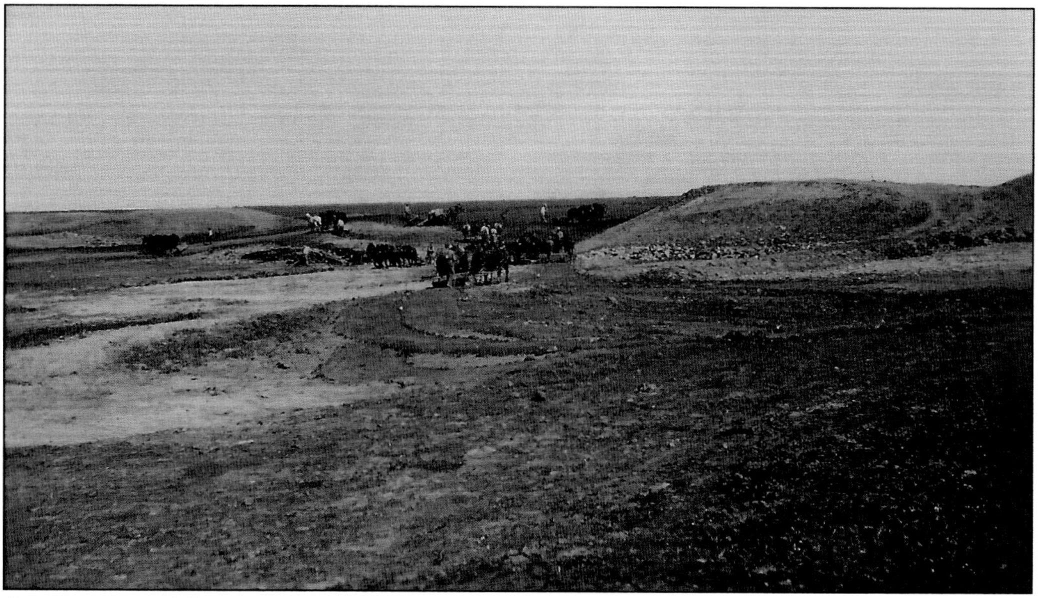

Construction of Cooney Reservoir commenced in 1935 with the clearing of land. Here, horse-drawn graders and dozers build up the earthen dam structure. This photograph was taken by John Henry Collins VI of nearby Fox, who worked as a foreman for the Utah Construction Company, the dam's contractor, which also built Hoover Dam. (Collins.)

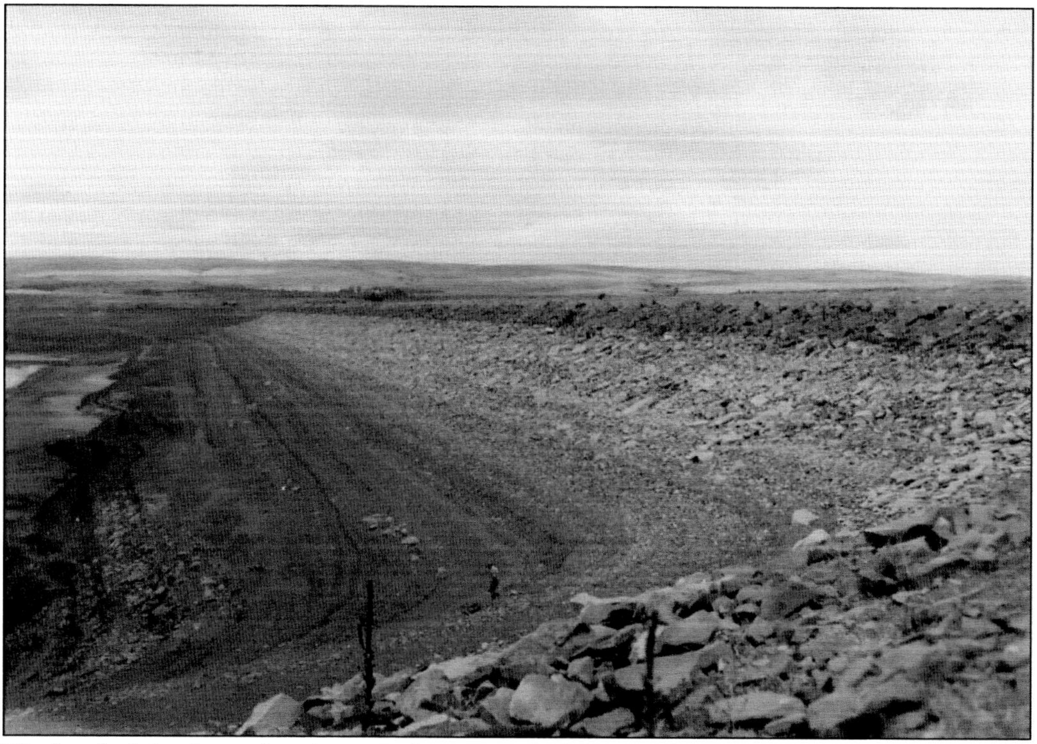

The head of the dam takes shape at the east end of Cooney Reservoir as a lone worker makes his way down its face. The earth-fill dam is 97 feet high and 2,260 feet across its crest. It has a capacity of 28,230 acre-feet of water. (DNRC.)

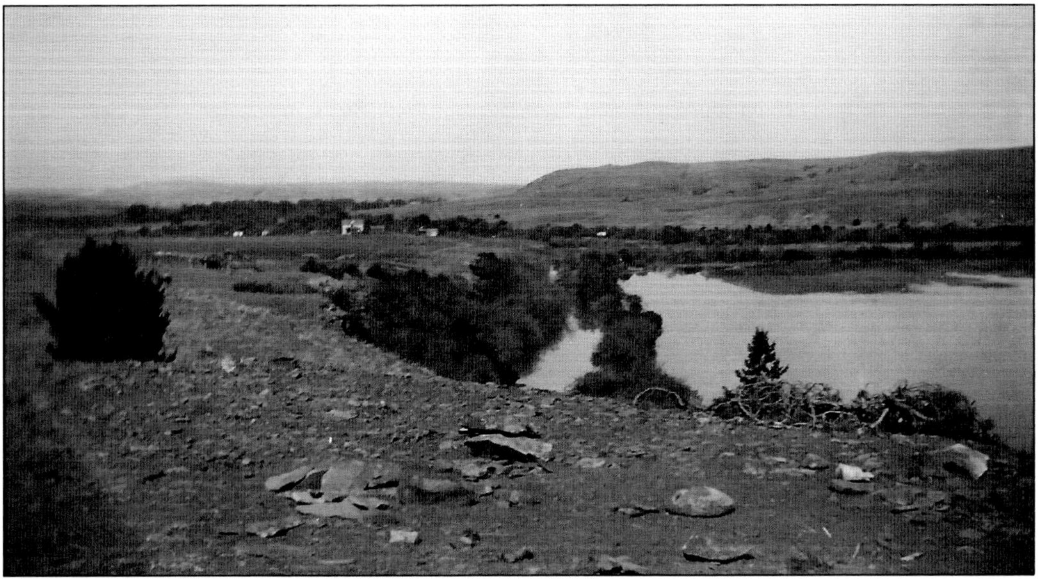

Water fills up near the Willow Creek inlet of Cooney Reservoir in this John Henry Collins VI photograph. The reservoir provides irrigation water to approximately 20,000 acres of farmland downstream. The shoreline stopped well short of the Otto Marshall place, seen in the distance. (Collins.)

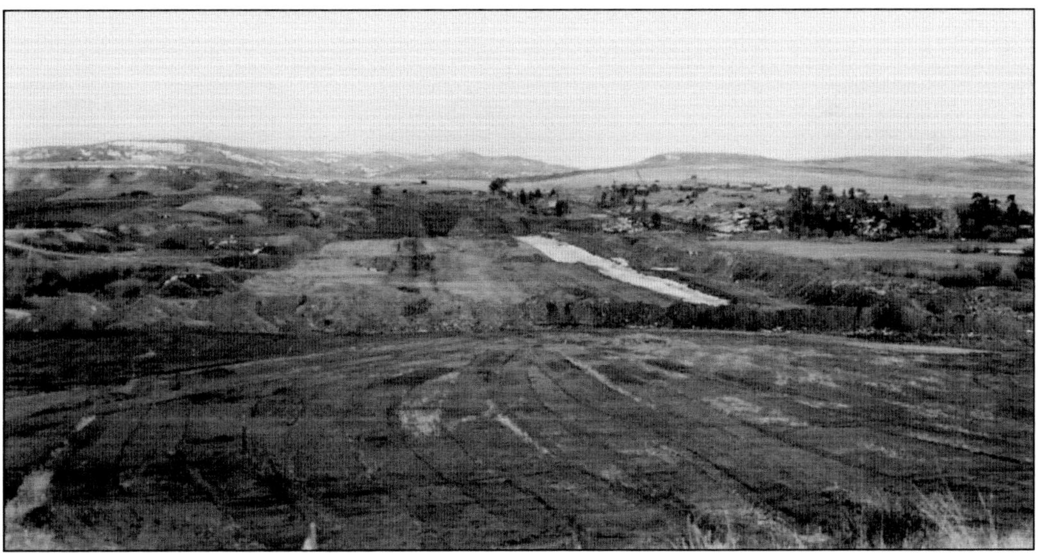

This photograph shows the small valley at the confluence of Rock and Willow Creeks that was flooded to create Cooney Reservoir. At one time, Roland Robertson's family owned a ranch there. The family sold the ranch in 1935, following the death of Robertson's father. Work on the dam began soon after that. Robertson remembered the ranch as being in a beautiful, productive valley. (DNRC.)

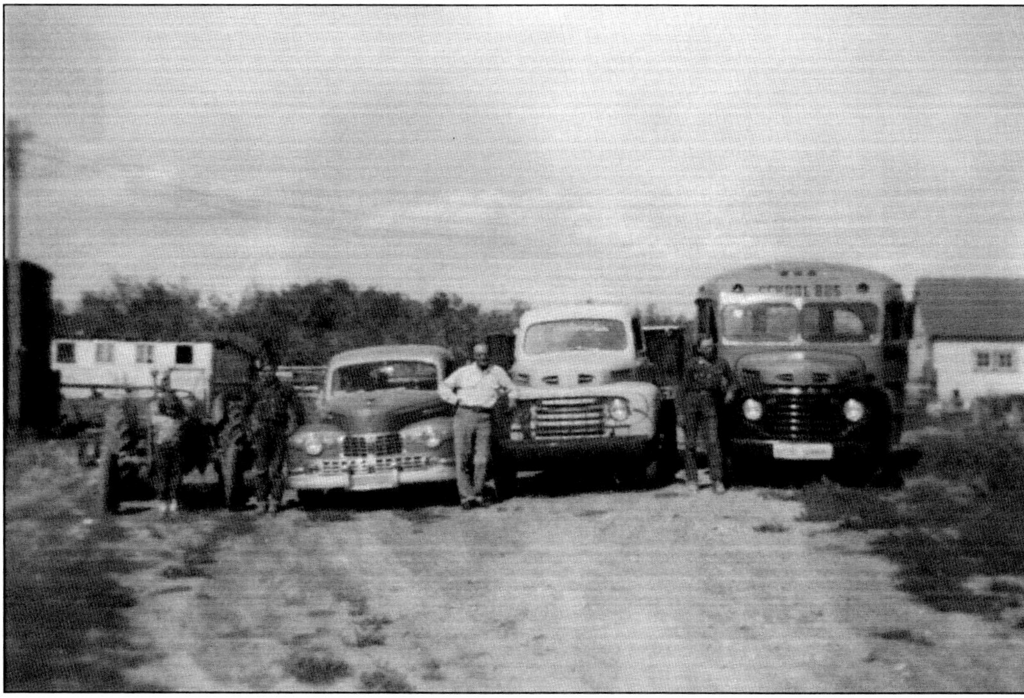

While most local residents viewed Cooney Reservoir as only an irrigation resource, it was also a state park. Otto Marshall thought it might attract people for recreation and saw a commercial opportunity. In 1946, he and his three children began selling concessions out of the back of a 1946 Lincoln. His sons, Gene and Wally, drove around the shore selling bait, candy, soda pop, and hand-rolled cigarettes to fishermen, campers, and boaters enjoying postwar leisure time. Above, from left to right, Barbara, Gene, Otto, and Wally Marshall pose in front of the family vehicles. Below, spring mud at Cooney Reservoir forced Otto Marshall to buy a tractor to periodically free his other vehicles from the muck. (Both, Herbert.)

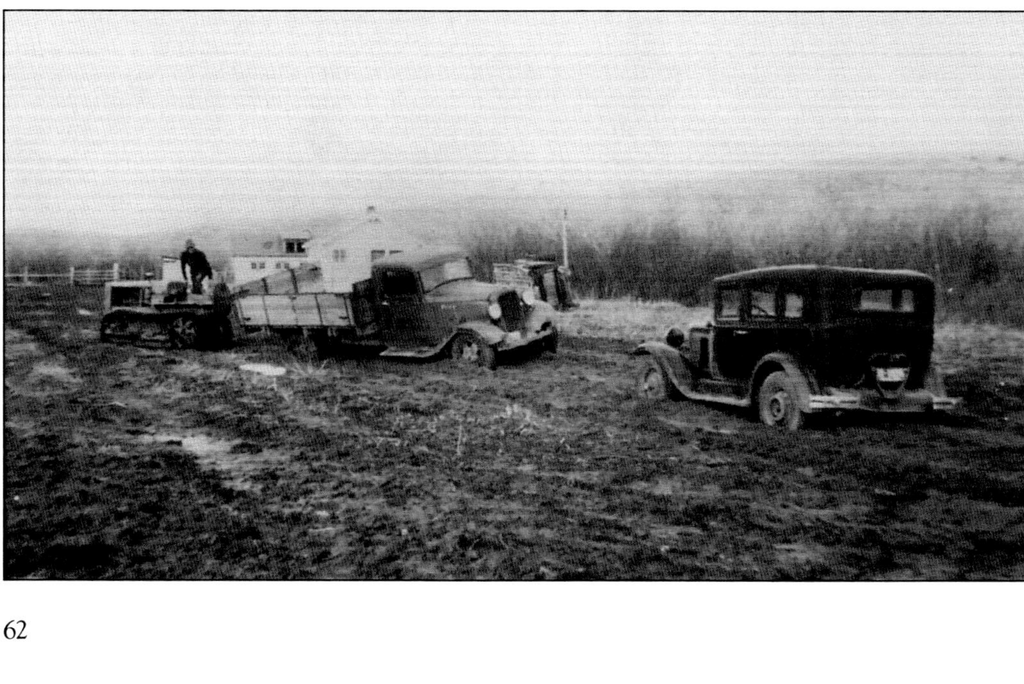

After two successful seasons selling concessions out of his 1946 Lincoln, Otto Marshall built a small canvas- and plywood-covered stand just south of the dam in an area now named Marshall's Cove in his honor. Barbara Marshall (Herbert) is seen here behind the counter in 1948, when the stand expanded its menu to sell hot dogs and hamburgers. (Herbert.)

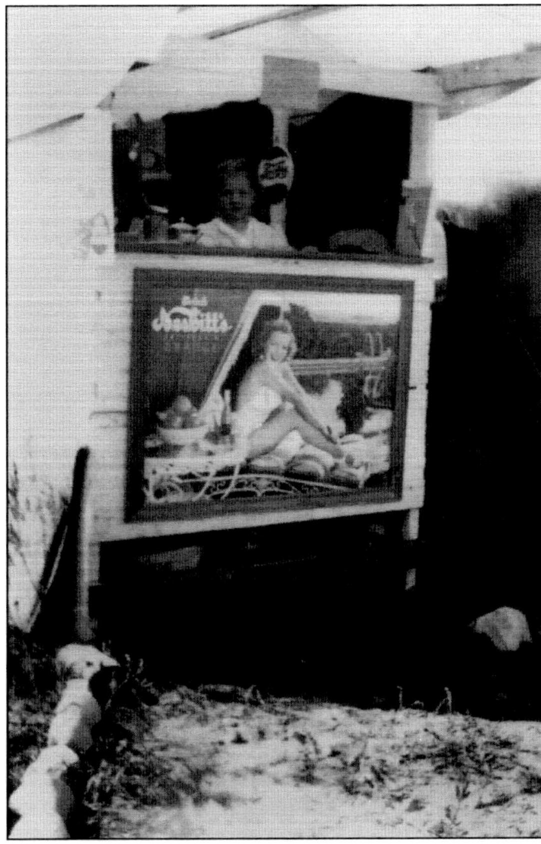

Barbara Marshall (Herbert) is seen below on the far left with her classmates on the first day of school in 1945. Her father, Otto, drove the bus for the Roberts school district and kept the bus at home. On winter days, before engine-block heaters, he stored the bus in an underground garage he had dug into a nearby hillside and insulated with hay bales. (Herbert.)

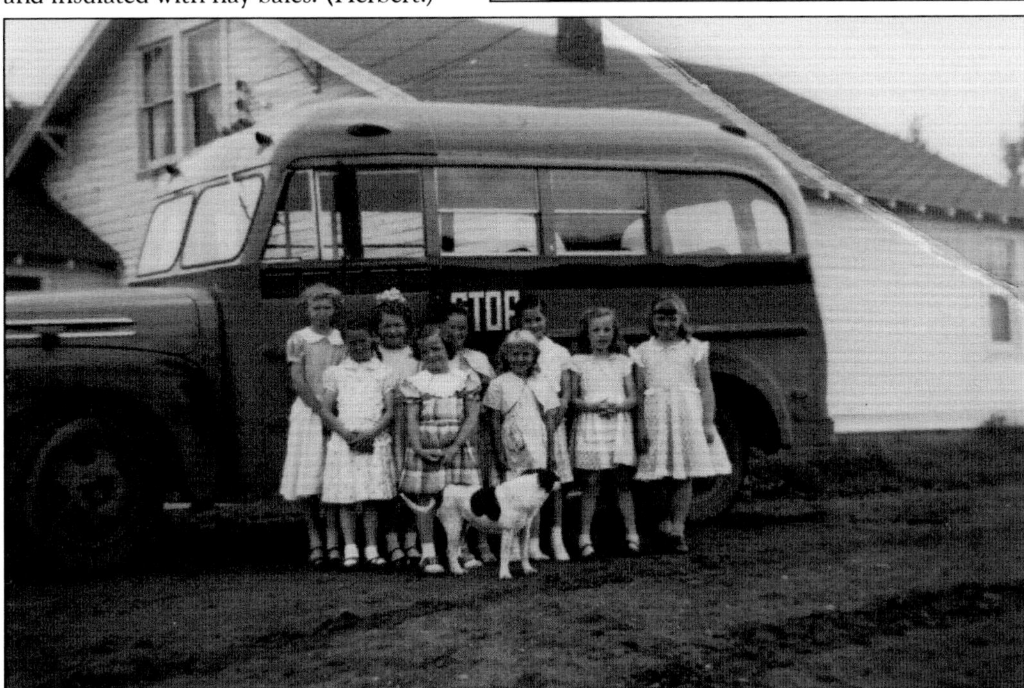

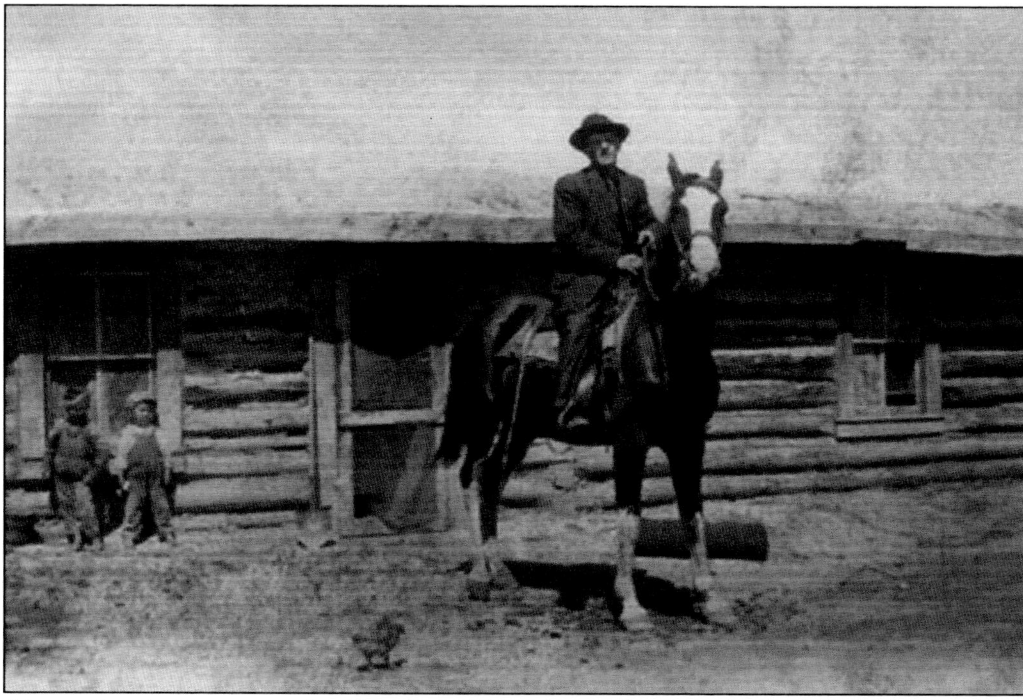

Above, Gunder Hoines stands tall in the saddle in front of his Volney Creek homestead with two of his children nearby. Hoines and his brother Sven were among the earliest settlers on Volney Creek, having squatted on it in the 1880s when it was part still part of the Crow Reservation. The brothers moved away briefly but returned in 1906 to homestead on the land they had previously squatted on. Sven moved to Canada a few years later, but Gunder stayed and raised sheep. He is seen below holding a plow while five of his children play on it. (Both, Hoines.)

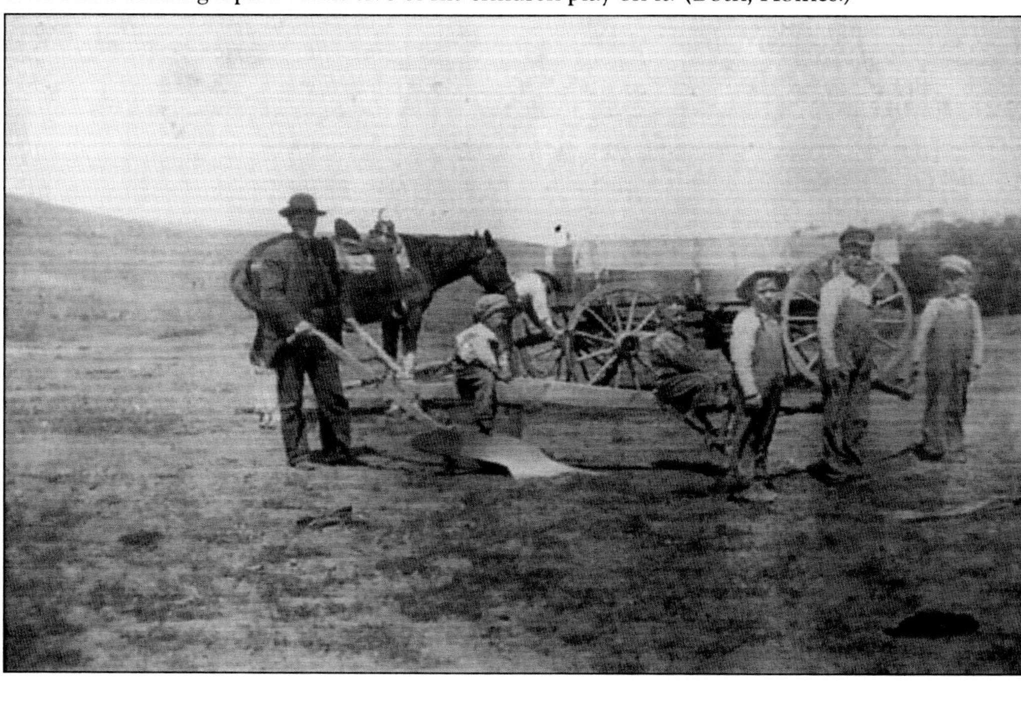

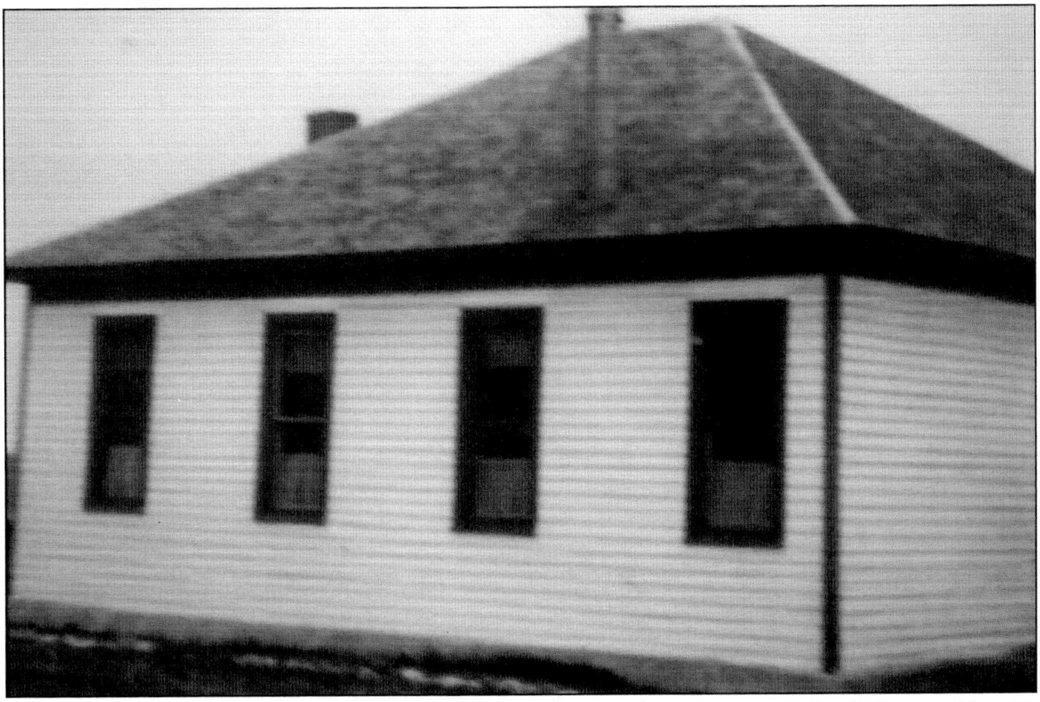

The Volney school (above) was the second school in Carbon County School District No. 10. The school served grades one through eight and operated from 1909 until 1947, when it was consolidated into the Luther School District. During its time, the school was located on James Burnett's land. Below, students pose on a teeter-totter in front of the school. Mae and Edwin Luoma are fourth and fifth from the left, respectively. (Both, CCHS.)

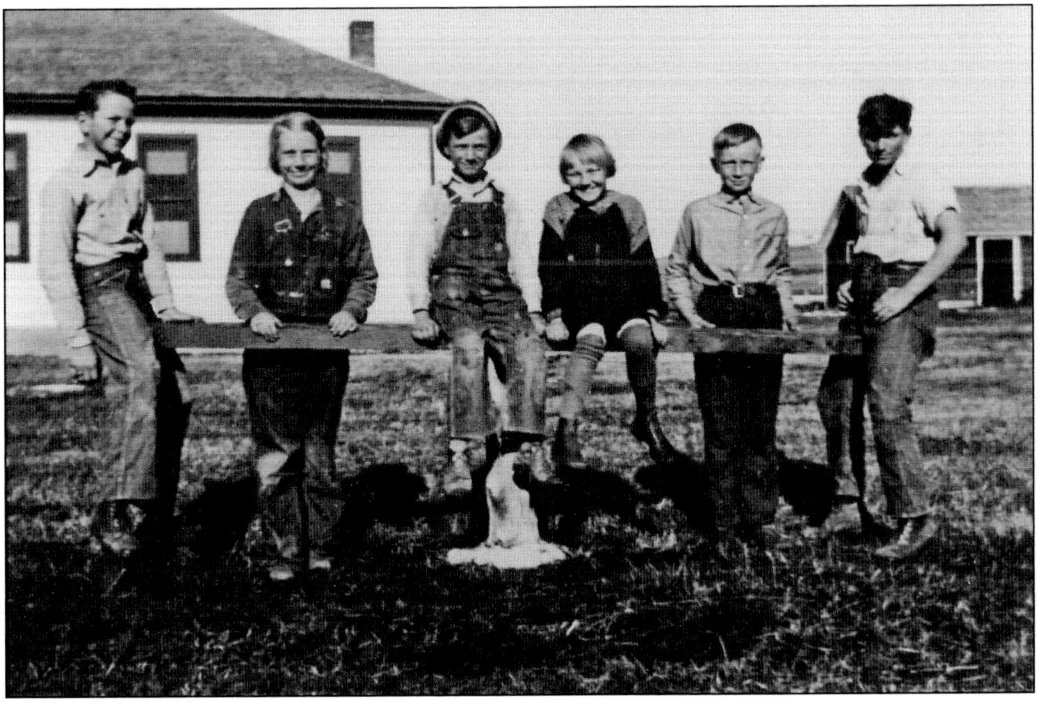

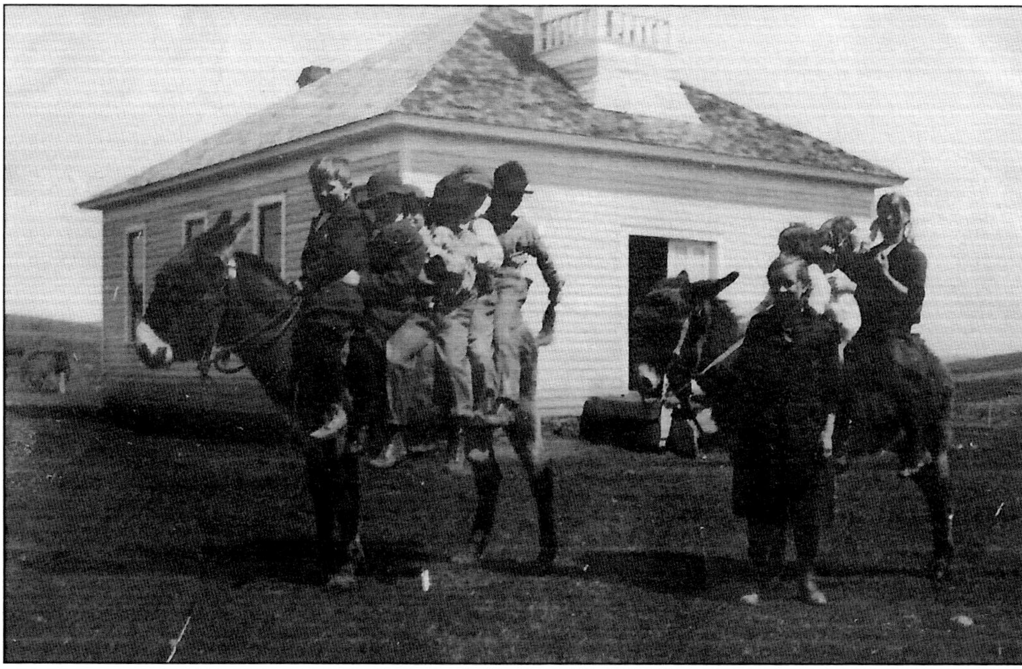

School buses were not yet used when this photograph of Volney Creek school students was taken around 1910. Seen here piling onto two donkeys, some students rode more than five miles each way to school every day in all but the worst weather. (Thayer.)

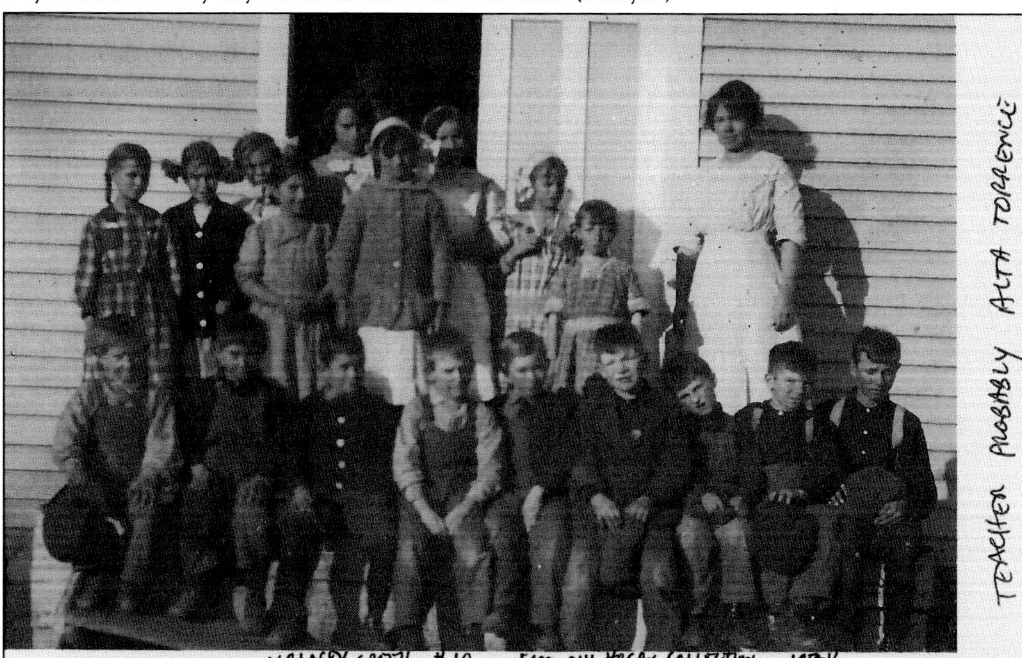

This photograph of Volney Creek students was taken by Carbon County school superintendent Nora Hogan "Nog" Ogden between 1913 and 1916, during the tenure of teacher Alta Torrence. None of the students are identified, but the Tjeltveit, Hyem, Boggio, Fiveland, and Indreland families were some of the first to settle in the area. (Hogan.)

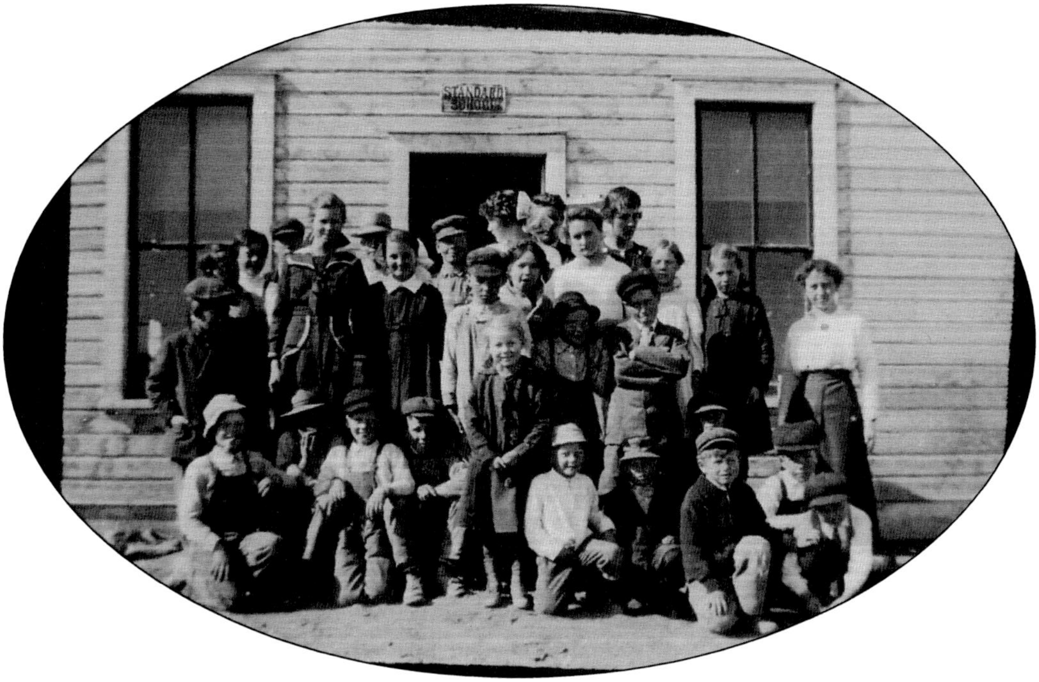

The Weast school was on the lower end of Volney Creek, near where it drains into Red Lodge Creek. The "Standard School" sign hanging over the door in this 1913 photograph was awarded to rural schools by the Montana superintendent of school instruction for meeting certain standards of excellence, including the education and certification of teachers, lighting, facilities, and parent participation. (Hoines.)

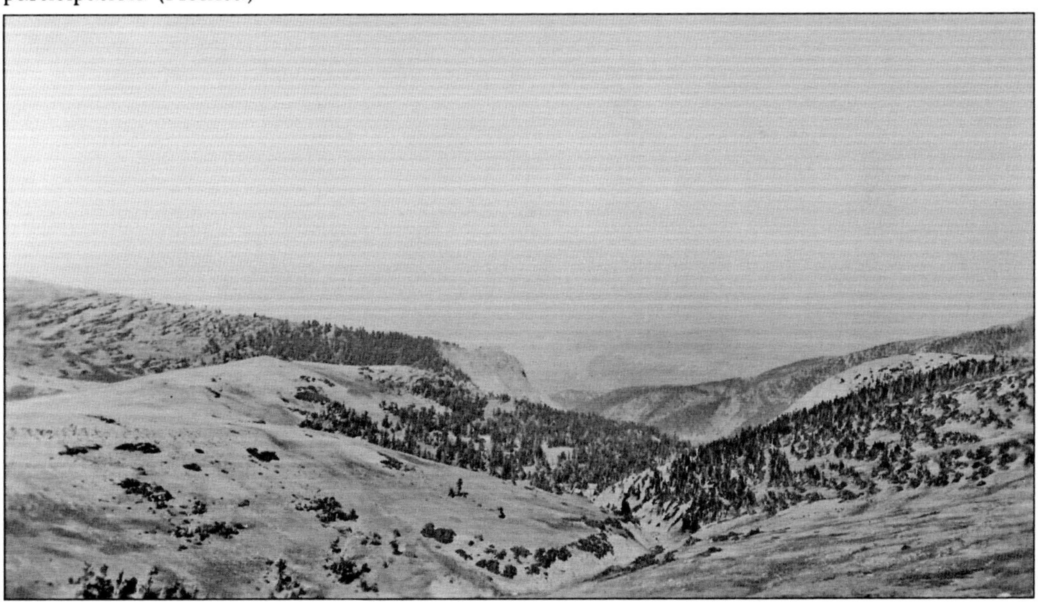

Red Lodge Creek starts high up on the Rock Creek Plateau, about 9,000 feet above sea level. The plateau is situated between the 10,179-foot Butcher Mountain to the north, the 9,905-foot Bare Mountain to the east, the 9,707-foot Crow Mountain to the west, and the 11,056-foot Grass Mountain to the south. By 1893, more than 25,000 sheep were ranged in this area. (CCHS.)

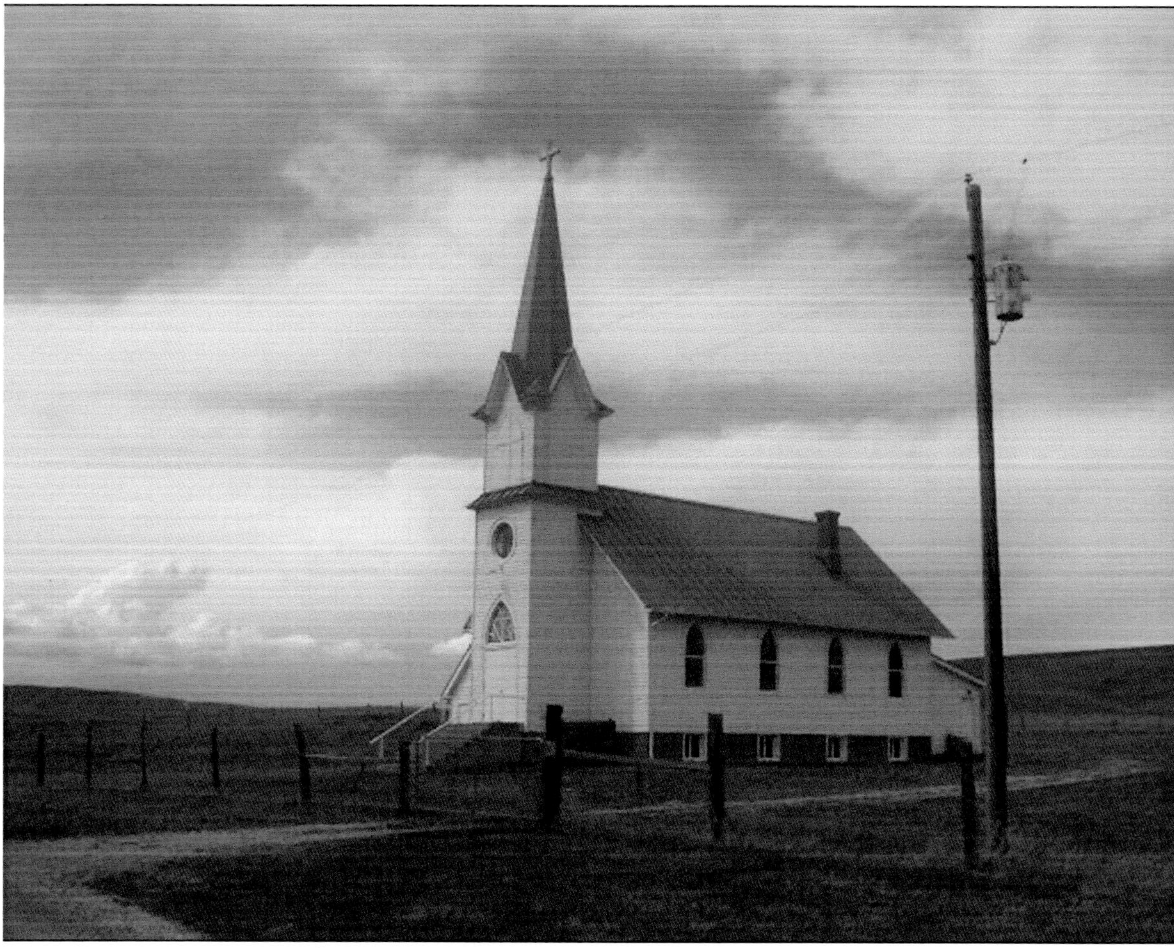

In 1904, a group of Norwegian immigrants in the Red Lodge and Volney Creek valleys, tired of making the long trek by horse and buggy into Absarokee for church, founded St. Olaf Lutheran Church. For the next 20 years, services were held in area homes. In 1919, Absarokee carpenter John Lee was hired to construct a church building 30 feet wide by 40 feet long. In 1921, with the help of many volunteers from the congregation, it opened. The original heating system was a simple cast-iron stove. It was often said that the building finally warmed up just as everyone was leaving. The building is still maintained by the community for weddings, funerals, and selected services. The church stands as a memorial to the Norwegian settlers whose dedication created this elegant, simple structure. Note the "two-holer" outhouse on the far right in this contemporary photograph. (CCHS.)

Six

Luther, Roscoe, Linley, and Alpine

In western Carbon County, the tawny foothills meet the steep, evergreen-blanketed slopes of the Absaroka Mountains. Rich grazing land attracted many early settlers, who started the communities of Luther, Roscoe, Linley, and Tony. The town of Roscoe, 16 miles northwest of the county seat in Red Lodge, was formerly called Morris. It was named after the first white settler, Robert O. Morris, who established a small community there between 1875 and 1883. Roscoe's first post office was established in 1901 under the name Morris. The name changed in 1905. The area around Roscoe saw the first oil wells drilled in Montana. A considerable amount of cattle and sheep ranching still thrives in the area. Today, it is also known for the Grizzly Bar and Restaurant.

Luther and Linley were once known as Carbon County's "twin cities," but they never grew into that ambitious nickname. Luther was named for the man who bought the townsite from George Kuhl. Linley got its start on the Walter Linley Ranch about a quarter mile from Luther. A school was opened on the Cecil Linley homestead in 1896. Linley gradually faded as Luther established itself in later years with a store, a school, a saloon, a post office, a gas station, a lumberyard, a blacksmith shop, and a hall. Today, the school, fire hall, and a church survive in Luther.

Alpine, nestled in a deep canyon on the shores of East Rosebud Lake on the westernmost edge of Carbon County, is a small community of vacation cabins and homes that dates back to the 1890s. Settlement in the canyon began when a former Army officer and Indian agent, Maj. Henry Armstrong, petitioned the federal government to allow him to purchase 105 acres there in 1894. Until 1916, the lake was named after him.

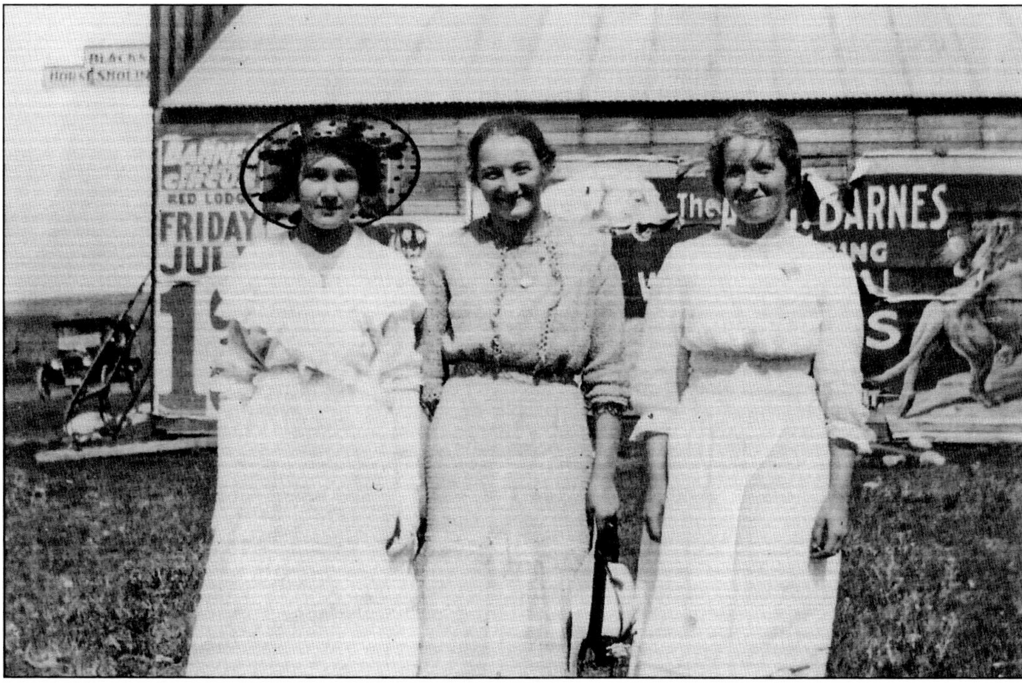

From left to right, Annie Yates, Ruth Yates, and Dorothy Cunningham stand in front of Lyal Brown's blacksmith shop in Luther on July 4, 1917. According to billboards on the side of the shop, the Barnes Circus was set to visit Red Lodge in the weeks following Independence Day. (Thayer.)

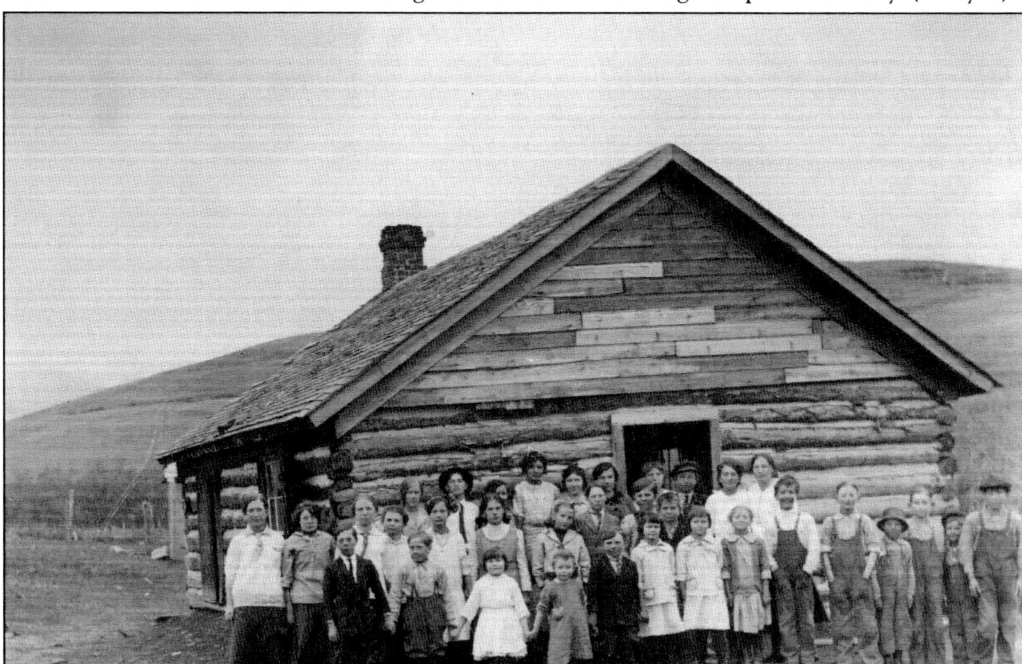

Built in 1896, the Luther school sat on the homestead of Cecil Linley until it was moved one mile east of Linley in 1908 to a second location known as the Breck/Isom site, where it sat until 1917. Students are seen here outside the school in 1914. (CCHS.)

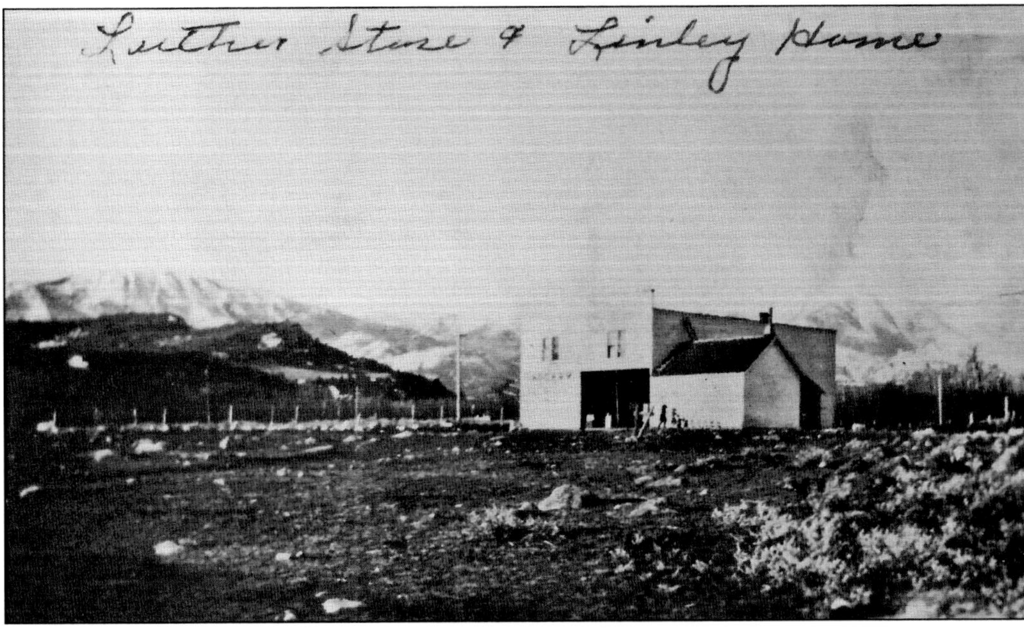

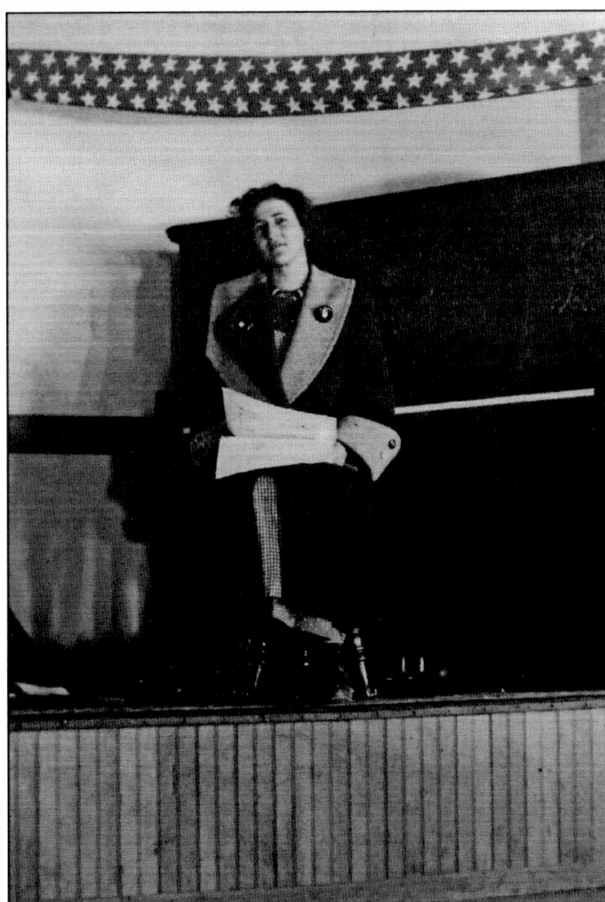

Walter Linley's store (above) was a community center in early Luther. It housed a grocery store, a gas station, and an upstairs dance hall. The Linley family home is to the right of the store. The store also housed the post office from 1902 to 1907. Grace Luther, who lived on the Luther ranch, a quarter mile from Linley, got the postal contract in 1908, after which Linley soon fell by the wayside. At right, Leila Linley sits at the piano on the small stage inside the dance hall. (Both, CCHS.)

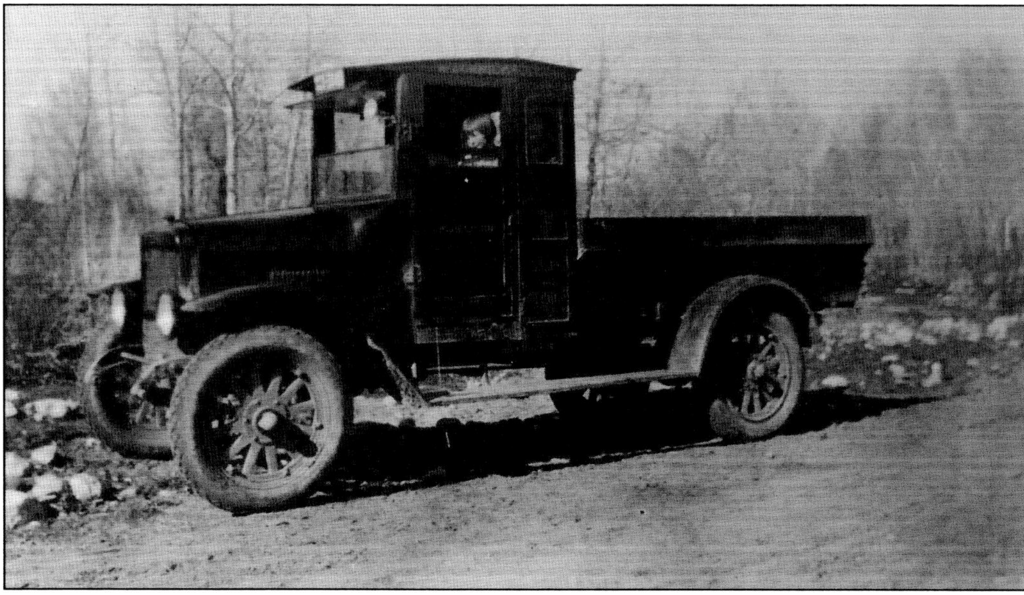

John M. Anderson sits in the driver's seat of a 1925 McCormick-Deering International Harvester truck, known as a Red Baby, that belonged to the Luther grocery store. The Red Baby was used for deliveries but was touted as a means of transporting implement dealers out into the field to better understand their clients' needs. (Linley-Pogue.)

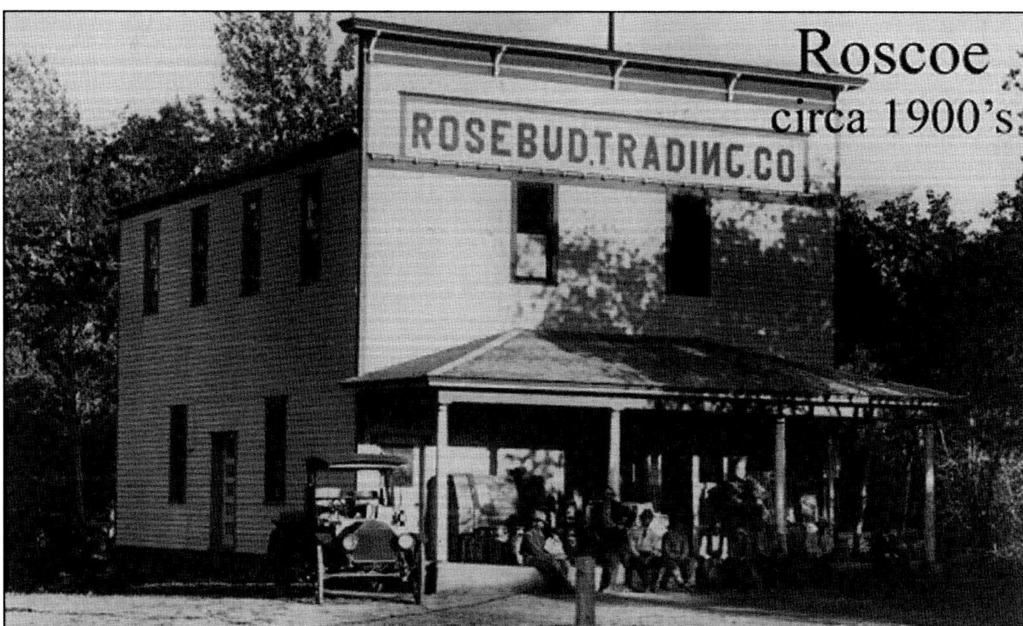

Roscoe townspeople are seen here on the porch of the Rosebud Trading Company around 1900. Originally named Morris for its first settler, Robert O. Morris, the town's name was changed to Roscoe in 1905 because the postal service kept confusing it with the town of Norris in Madison County. (CCHS.)

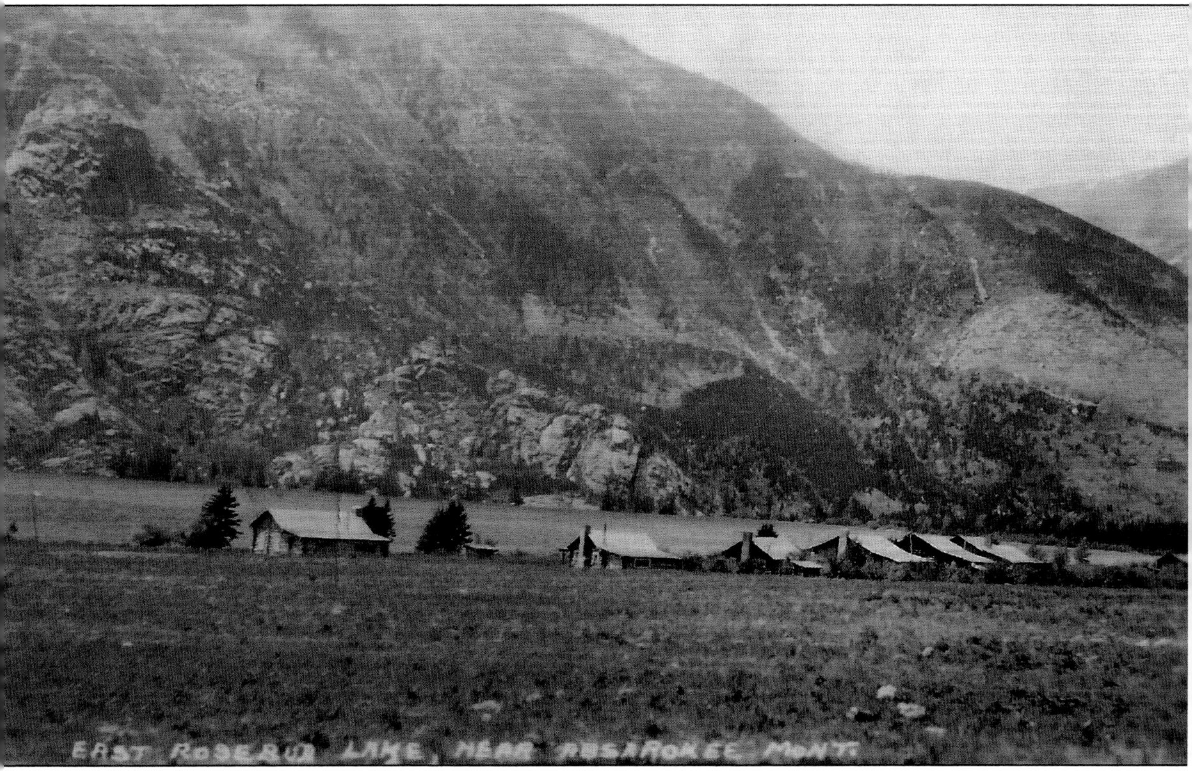

Nestled on the shores of East Rosebud Lake, Alpine is a small community of vacation cabins and homes dating back to the 1890s. In 1908, the first road for car travel to the lake was built. In 1911, the East Rosebud Lake Association was formed for the purpose of buying and selling land around the lake and for maintaining a summer resort and dude ranch. The lodge was built in 1914. In the early years, it was managed by John Branger and his family. The lodge housed a post office that opened on November 3, 1914, and closed on March 31, 1943. It was reestablished in 1945 before closing again in 1953. (Thayer.)

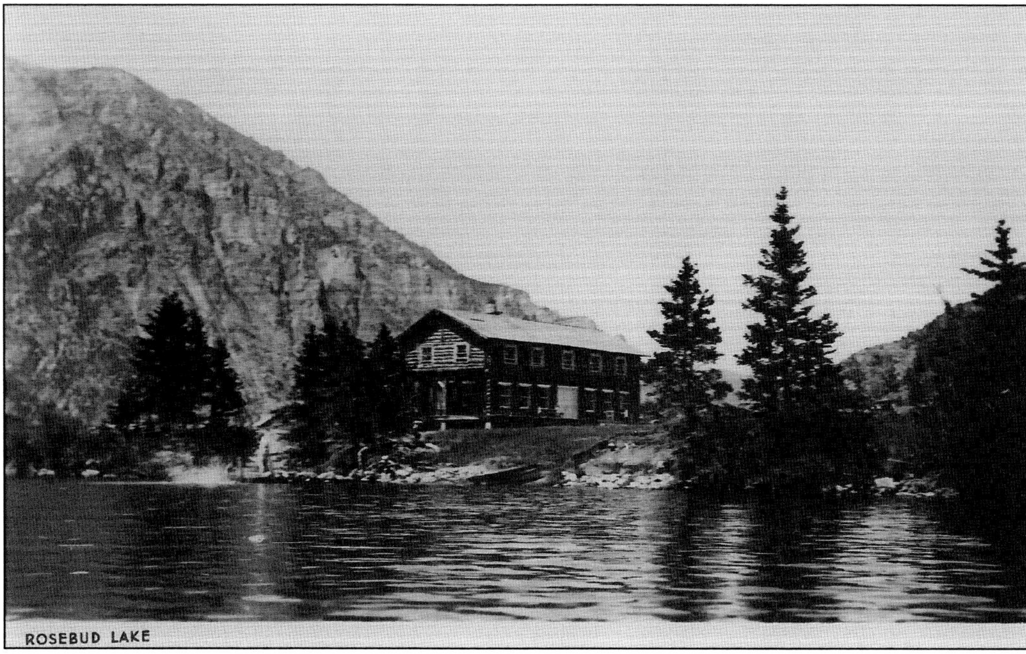

More than 25 cabins were built on the shores of East Rosebud Lake between 1912 and 1920. In 1996, nearly half the homes in the area were destroyed by the Shepherd Mountain fire. Today, the lodge still survives and includes a small convenience store. The area has long been regarded as one of the most scenic locations in Montana. (Thayer.)

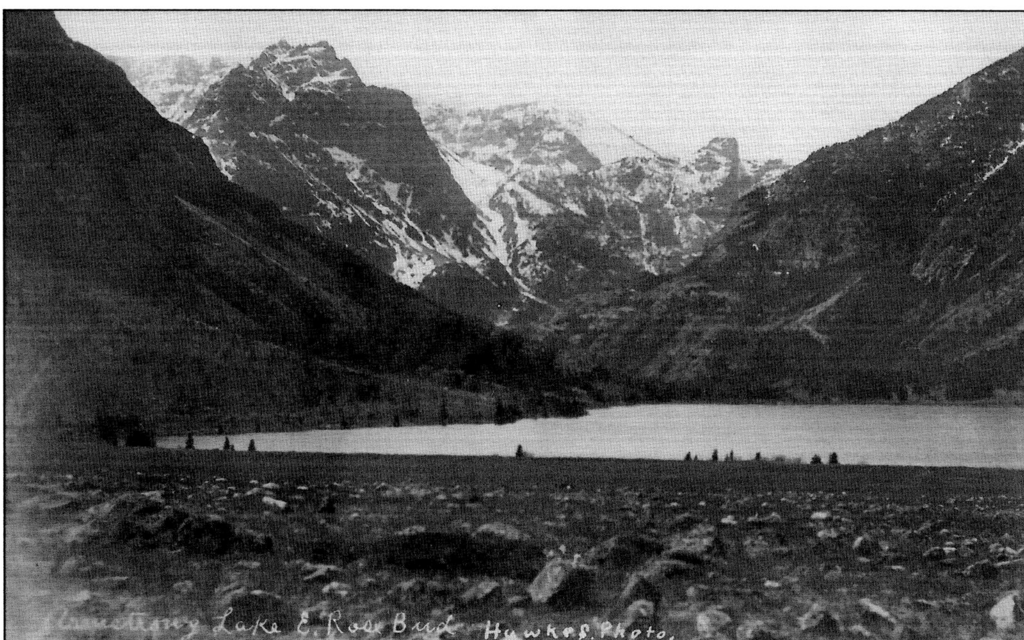

Dwellings have yet to be built in this early view of East Rosebud Lake, then known as Armstrong Lake. On this postcard, addressed to a Miss Francis Carr, the sender asks, "Do you think that you would enjoy a little fishing here? Those mountains are pretty rough but make a fine view." (Thayer.)

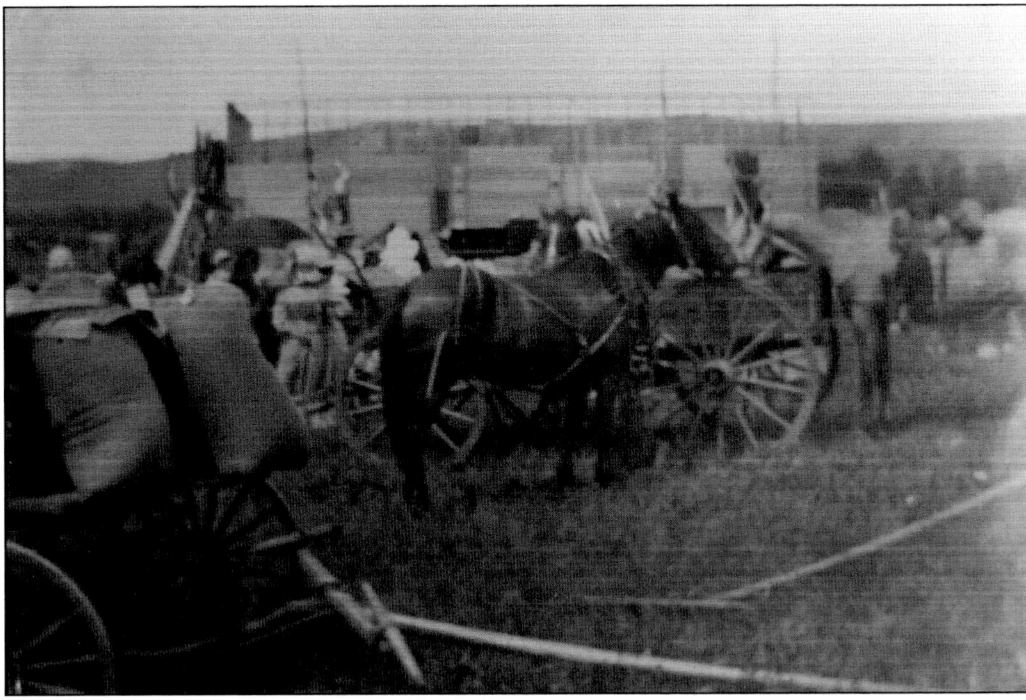

The communities of Volney Creek, Luther, Linley, and Tony turned out for the construction of the Tony church, seen in these rare photographs from around 1900. The church was close to the Tony school, northeast of Luther. Early area settler Thomas Yates did much of the construction. Above, horse teams and wagons full of supplies wait in the foreground while the church's walls are being framed. Below, women dressed up in their Sunday hats prepare a picnic for the men. The church was so close to the Tony school that it was often used for special programs associated with the school. (Both, Thayer.)

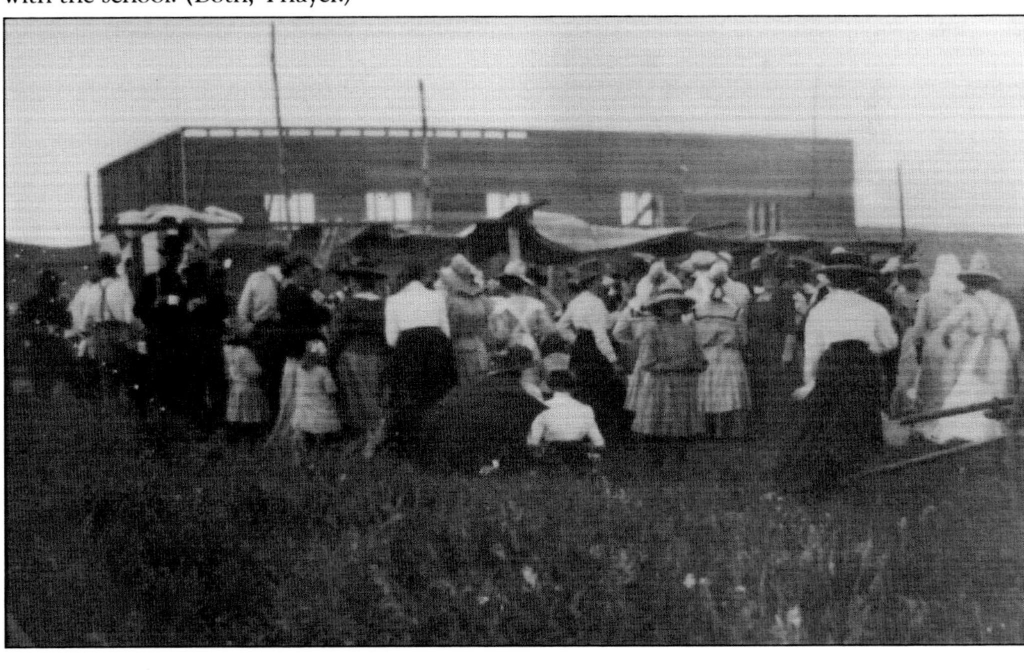

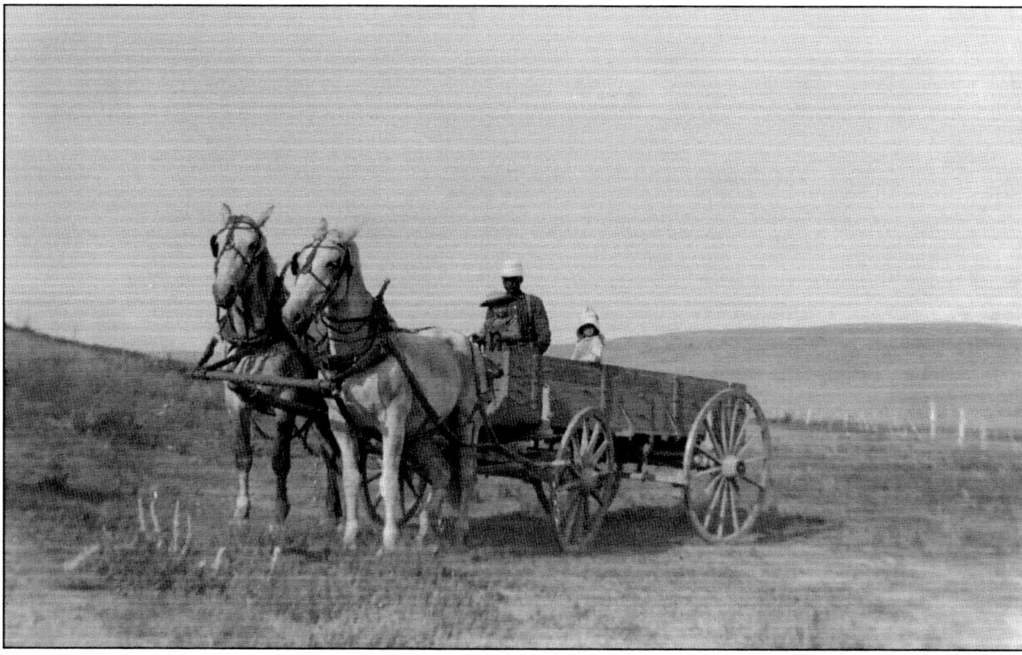

Jacob Durst and his two oldest children, Ronald and Margerie, ride in the family wagon near the family's homestead in Tony, about a half-mile from the Tony school. Jacob was born in Iowa and moved west shortly after marrying his wife, Nellie, a schoolteacher from Ohio who later taught at the Tony school. (CCHS.)

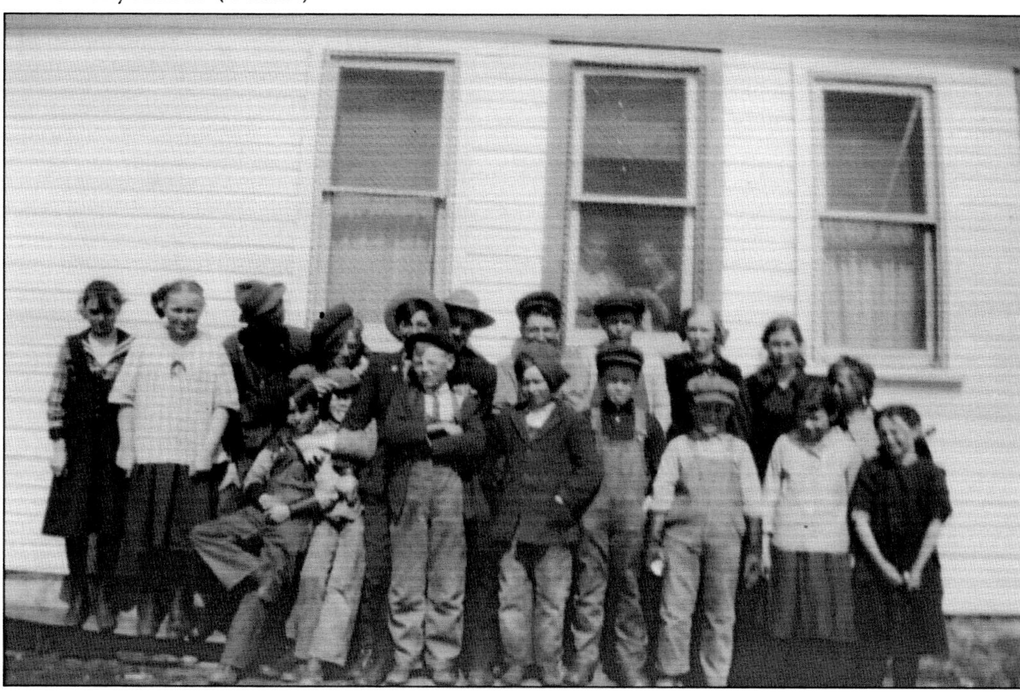

Vernice McBroom (right) and a fellow teacher peer out the window in this 1930s photograph of students at the Tony school. The school was built on February 28, 1903, on an 80-acre parcel of state land near the Hutton and Stewart homesteads. It closed in 1949. (CCHS.)

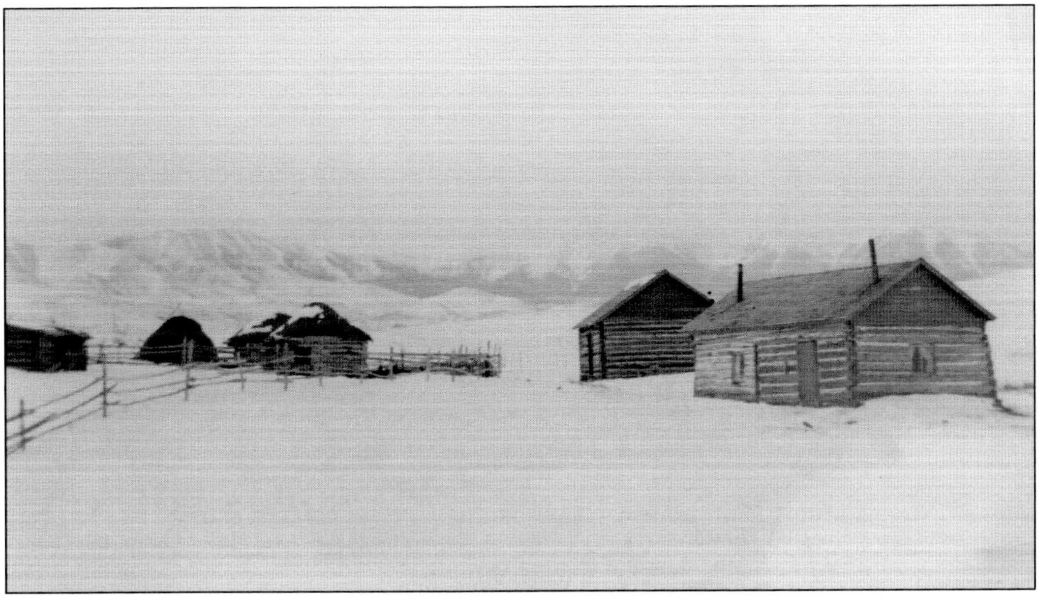

Above, in 1895, the stout cabin (right), corral, and outbuildings of the Durst homestead are besieged by snow and look dwarfed by the mountains. By the time the photograph below was taken, around 1910, Jacob Durst had built a more substantial home, the back porch of which he and his family are posing on. The Durst homestead was just half a mile from the Tony school. From left to right are Jacob, Ronald, Margerie, Rhoda, and Nellie Durst. (Both, CCHS.)

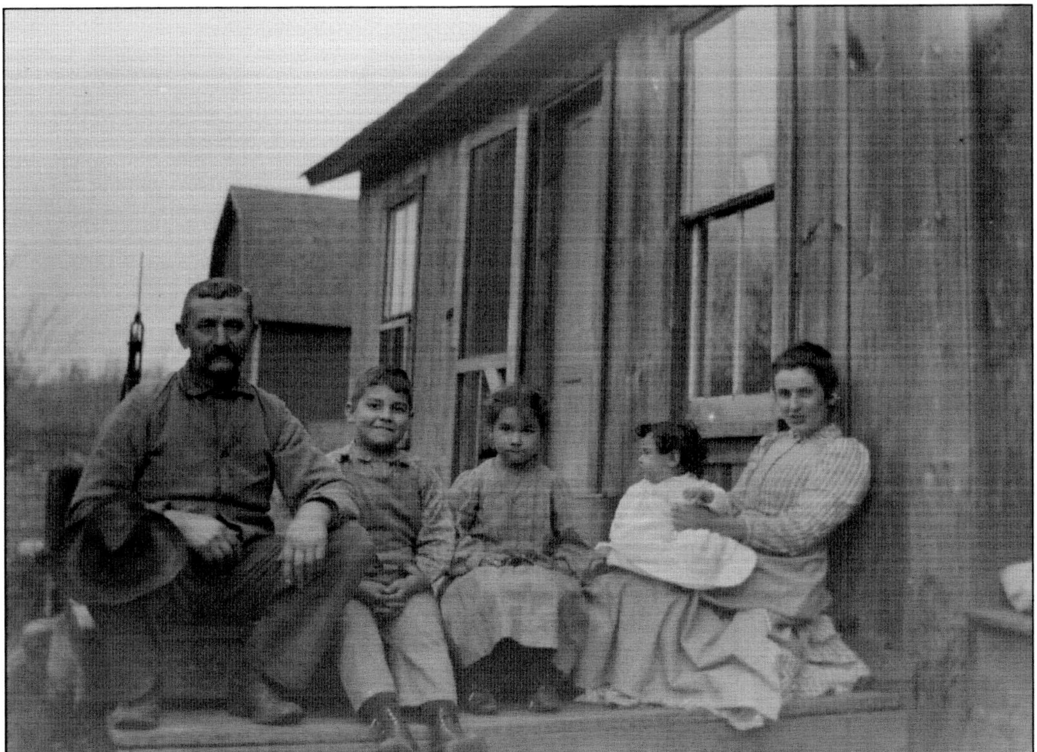

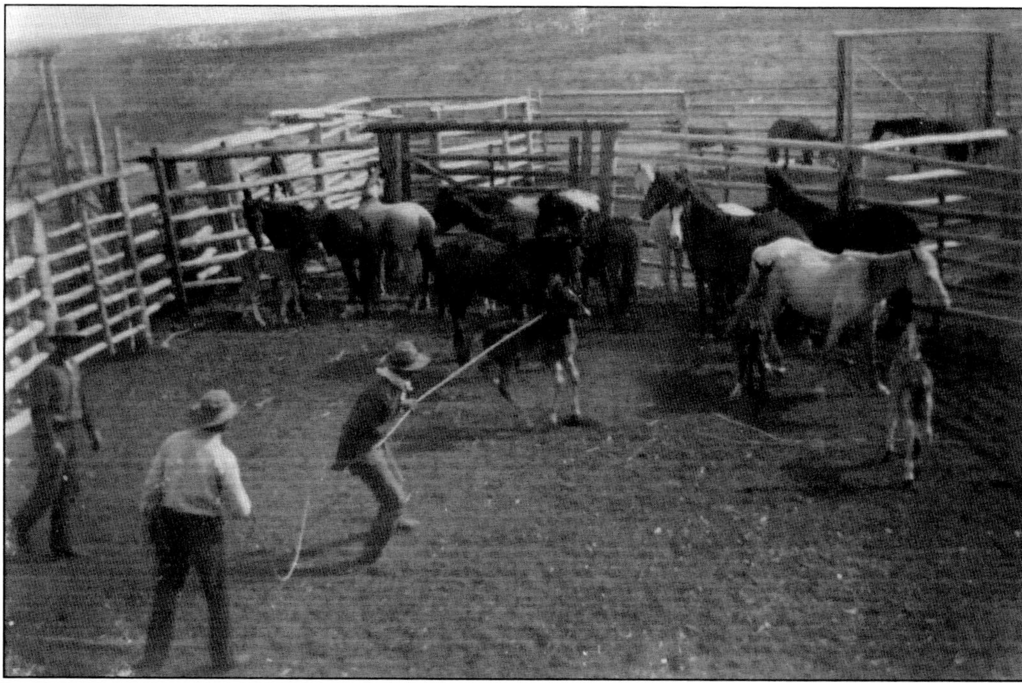

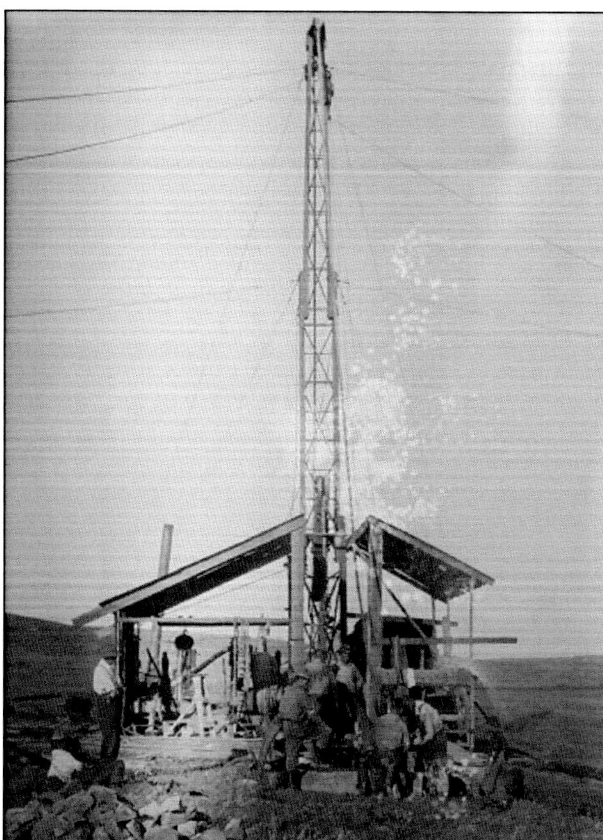

Above, ranch hands rope a colt on the Dilworth cattle ranch near Luther. One of the earliest settlers to the region, Charles Dilworth was the first postmaster in what became Carbon County in 1884. With over 5,000 head of cattle, Dilworth was often referred to as the "cattle king of Carbon County." (CCHS.)

Helena millionaire Thomas Cruze is believed to be the first person to drill for oil in Montana, in 1889 on Butcher Creek about six miles from Roscoe. The justification to drill there came from the Butcher Creek Seeps, where asphalt residue had puddled on the surface. The nine wells he drilled came up dry and were abandoned. (CCHS.)

Seven

Roberts

Roberts began as a stagecoach stop named Coulee Creek about a quarter mile east of the town's current location. In 1889, a railroad station called Merritt was established, but the name was changed because it was too close to Merrill, another stop on the Northern Pacific's vast rail network. On April 1, 1896, the Roberts post office was established. The town's name comes from Frank Roberts, a well-loved express messenger who carried parcels and mail on the train between Red Lodge and Billings. He was so well-loved that in 1904, after stealing $5,000 from a bank shipment he had been officially entrusted with so he could pay outstanding saloon tabs and other debts, friends in communities all along Rock Creek Valley chipped in to help him repay what he had stolen and lobbied on his behalf to have the charges dismissed. Shortly afterward, he moved to Kansas City, Missouri.

The community, however, continued to grow. Cattle, sheep, turkeys, and chickens were among the livestock that thrived in the pastures around Roberts. Grains, hay, beans, and peas accounted for much of the crops. By 1909, Roberts had three grain elevators, a general merchandise store, a clothing store, a livery and feed stable, a lumberyard, a dairy, a schoolhouse, a church, and several saloons. The rich grazing lands surrounding town made it the largest shipping point for poultry and wool in the county.

Many settlers saw Roberts as an escape from the coal mines in Red Lodge. Some miners, especially Finnish and Italian immigrants, worked all day in the mines then traveled 13 miles to their homesteads in Roberts to tend crops and livestock in the hope of creating a better, safer life in the open air. The railroad pulled up the tracks in 1981, but the ranches and farms around Roberts remain a vital part of the county's agricultural economy. The town still has several hundred residents and features a high school, a saloon, a gas station, a post office, a café, and several churches.

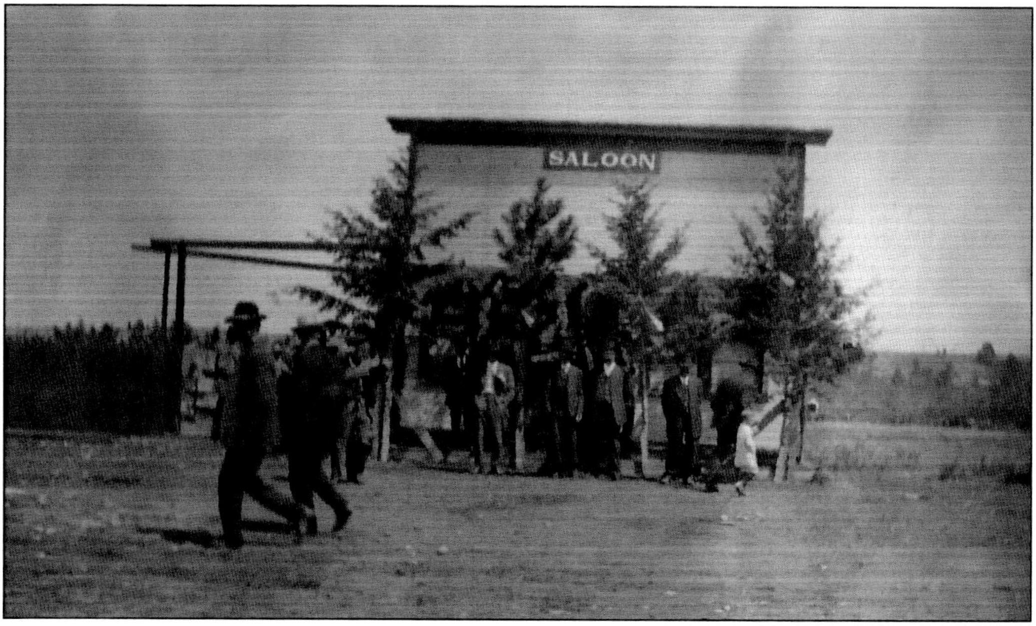

John Carrigan opened the first business in Roberts, Carrigan's Saloon, in 1893. Here, patrons stand outside the hastily constructed building. Note the hastily planted saplings being propped up in the background. It stood across First Street from where the New Deal Bar would be erected in 1933. (Hogan.)

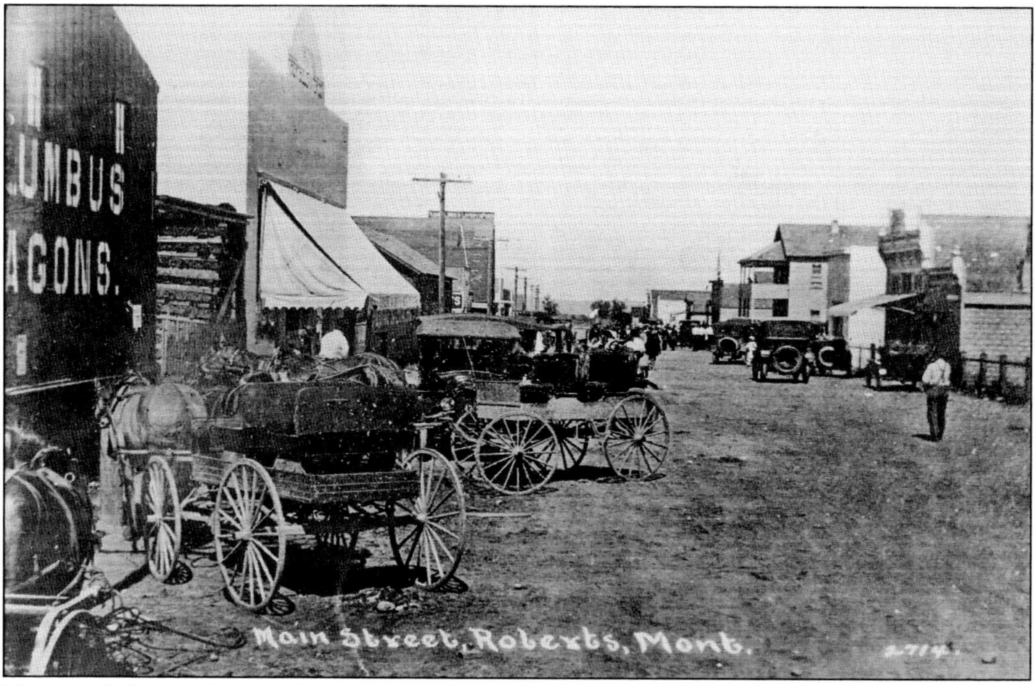

This north-facing photograph from around 1920 shows wagons and automobiles mingling on First Street in Roberts. People's light garments and the awnings over the Roberts Elevator Company (left) and Bertrand's clothier store (right) suggest a hot summer's day. Beyond Bertrand's is the two-story Roberts Hotel. (CCHS.)

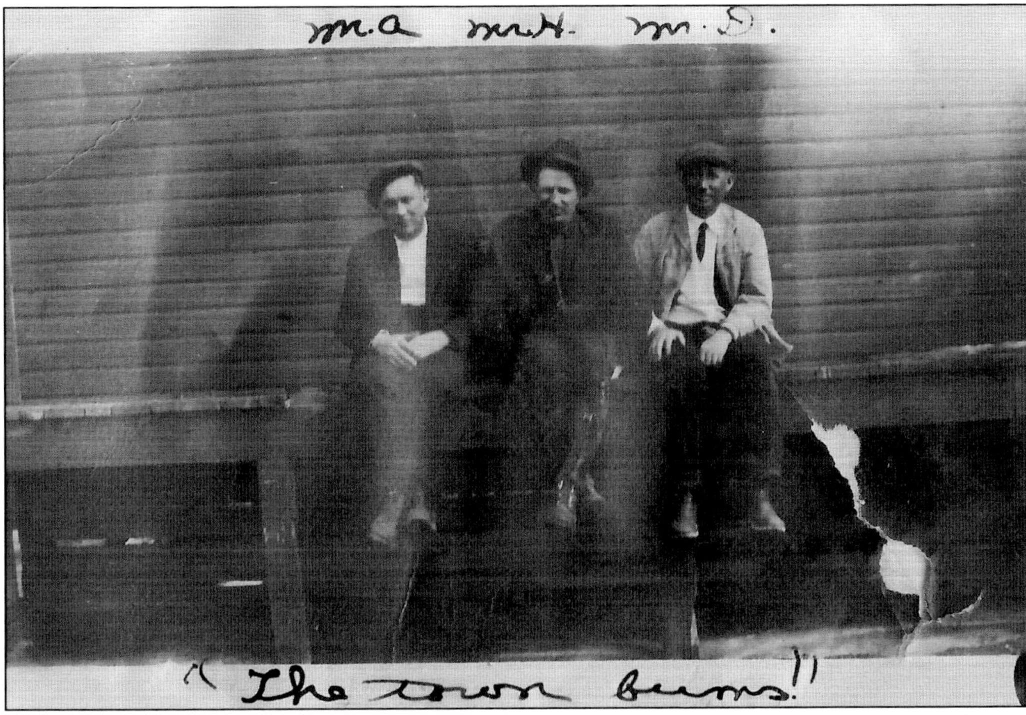

While this 1926 photograph is titled "The Town Bums," that description could not be further from the truth. From left to right, they are John Abramson, Emil Heikkila, and unidentified. Abramson was the vice president of the Roberts Elevator Company, and Heikkila was the general manager. The company sold groceries, farm equipment, coal, hardware, and guns but did not have a grain elevator. The interior photograph of the store below shows its normal display of wears, as well as a young employee standing beside a table full of Easter items. Today, the Roberts Elevator Company building is used by the Roberts Volunteer Fire Department. (Both, CCHS.)

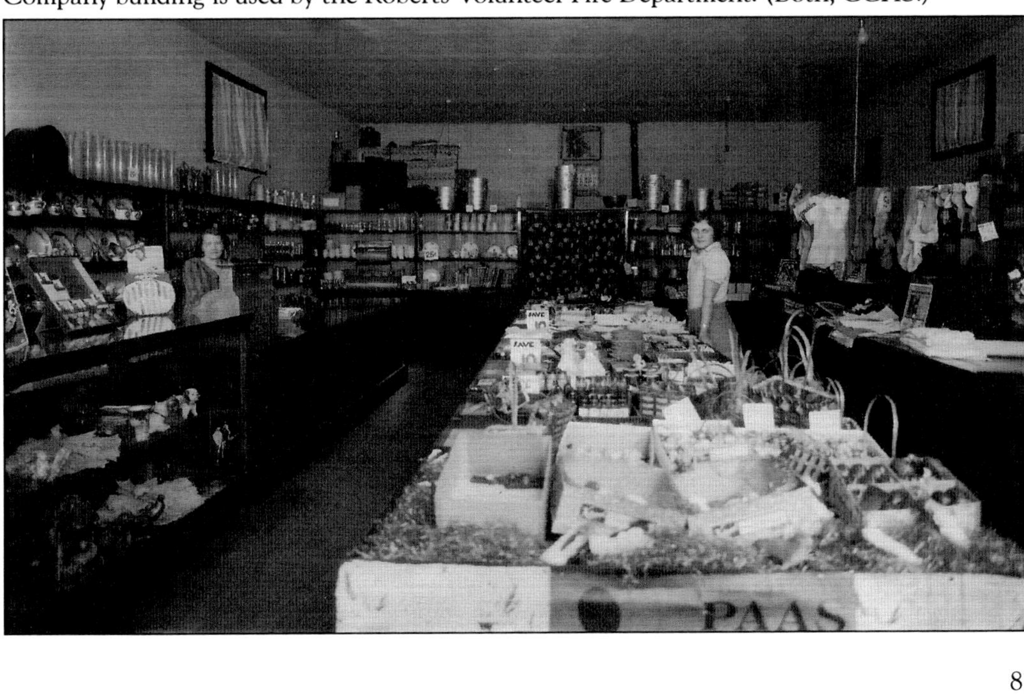

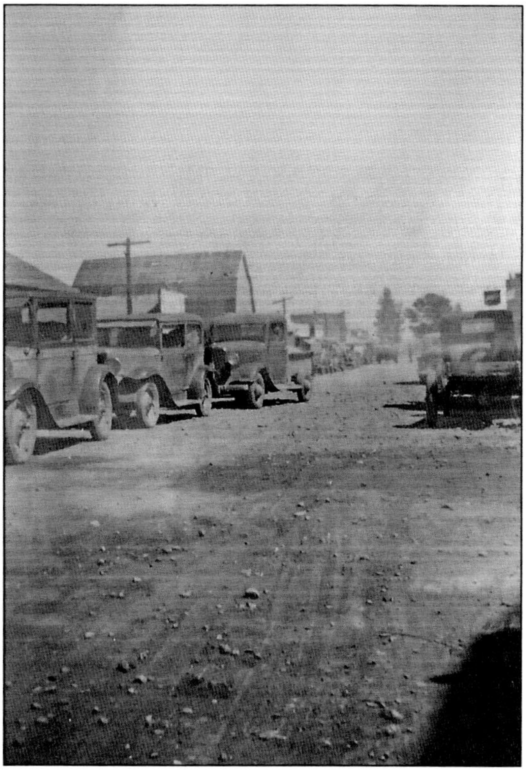

Cars and trucks from area ranches line First Street to ship their wool to market. In July 1926, Roberts area sheepherders shipped six boxcars of wool totaling nearly 250,000 pounds and worth $100,000. It was the most wool ever shipped at one time from any one place in Carbon County. (Bertolino.)

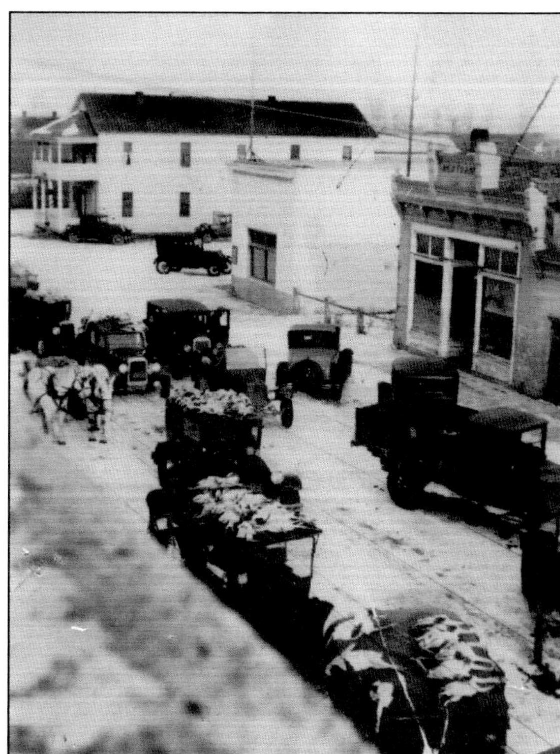

Roberts was a main shipping point for poultry, as this 1920-era photograph illustrates, with freshly killed chickens and turkeys draped from cars and trucks on Main Street. The buildings are, from left to right, the Roberts Hotel, Roberts State Bank, and Bertrand's clothier store, which later became a boardinghouse. (CCHS.)

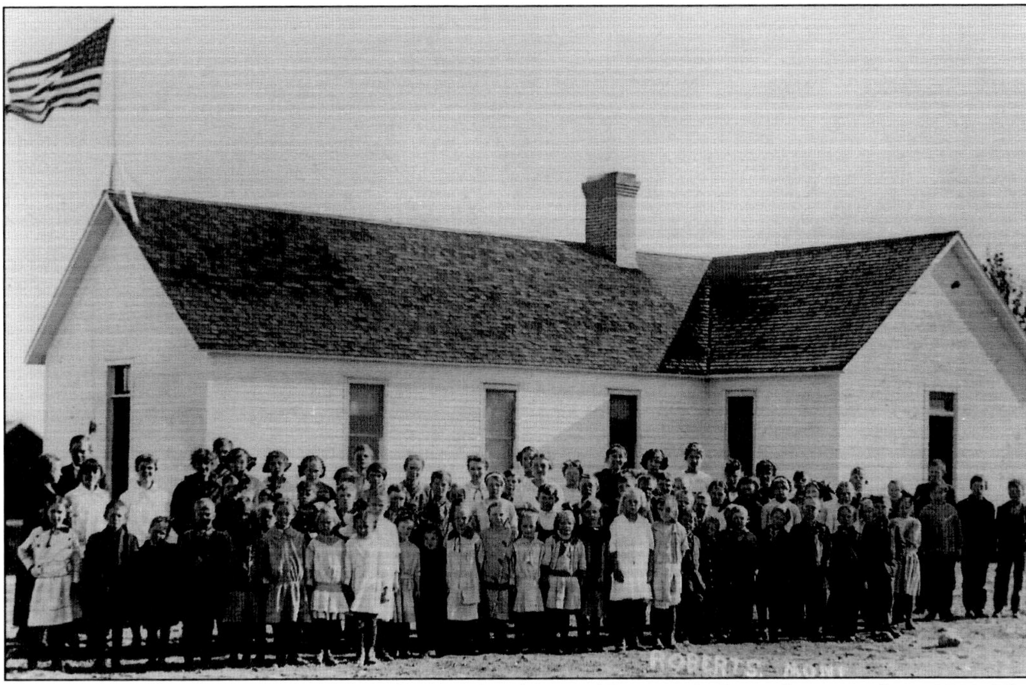

Above, students from the second Roberts school assemble outside for a photograph in 1914. The first Roberts school, built in 1897, was a one-room log cabin with a dirt floor. Blanche Wayman, Martha Holland, and Estelle Province were among the first teachers. In 1917, a new brick, two-story Roberts school (below) was built, with the high school on the first floor and the elementary school on the second floor. It was closed shortly after its opening due to the Spanish Influenza outbreak. The school served as a makeshift hospital for the epidemic's victims. The first graduating class, in 1923, consisted of Edith Hunt, Winifred Hunter, Ruth DeVries, Hannah Schanck, and Kenneth Weidman. The school motto defined the pioneer spirit of all who settled in Rock Creek Valley: "We climb, though the way be rugged." (Both, CCHS.)

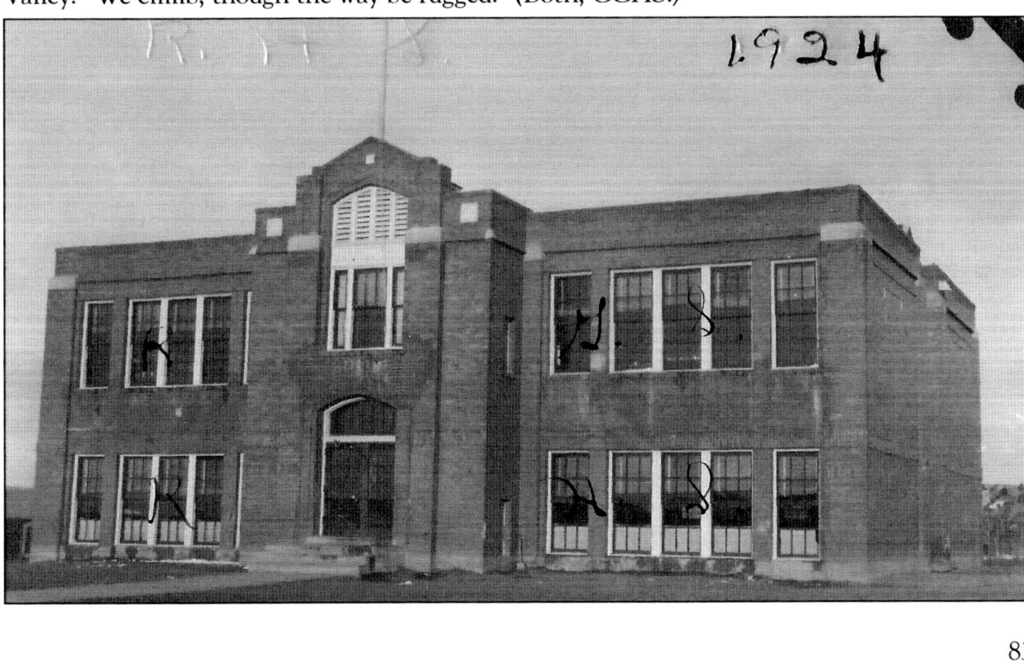

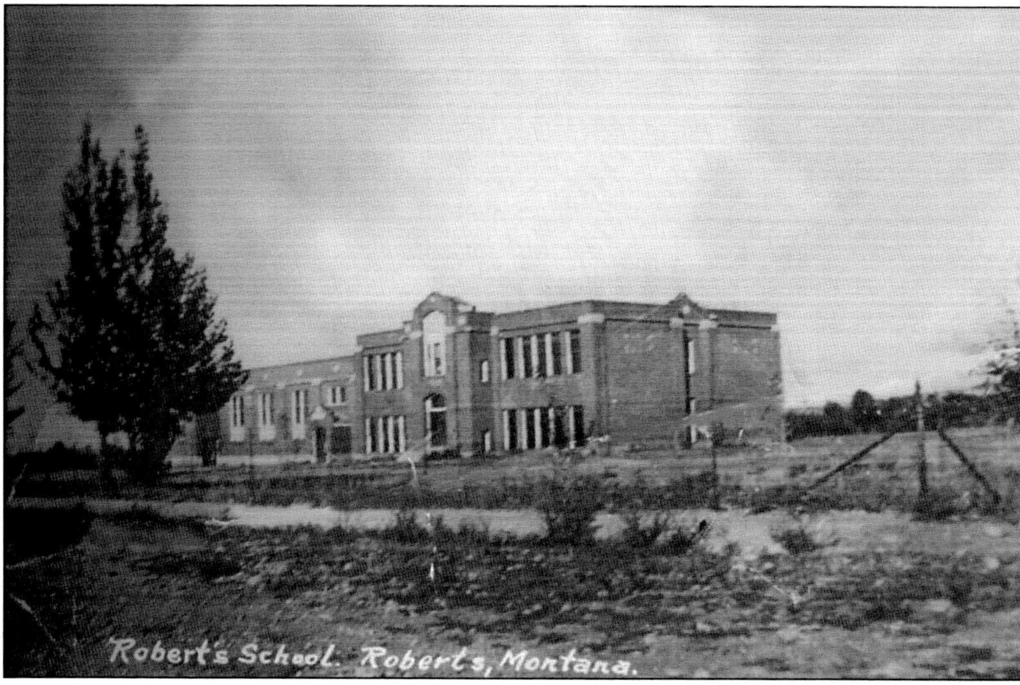

In 1929, a gymnasium (above) was added to the high school for its basketball team, the Rattlers. Prior to its construction, players practiced in the school's assembly room or in Silaka Hall, a converted barn. After completion, the gymnasium was considered the best facility of its kind in Carbon County, and it hosted most county athletic tournaments and exhibitions for years afterward. Below, the Roberts High School basketball team stands in front of Hogan's Cozy Corner on First Street after returning from the 1925 state basketball tournament. From left to right are James Deeney, unidentified, Roy Hunt, Sam Hunt, and four unidentified team members. (Above, Roberts School District; below, Bertolino.)

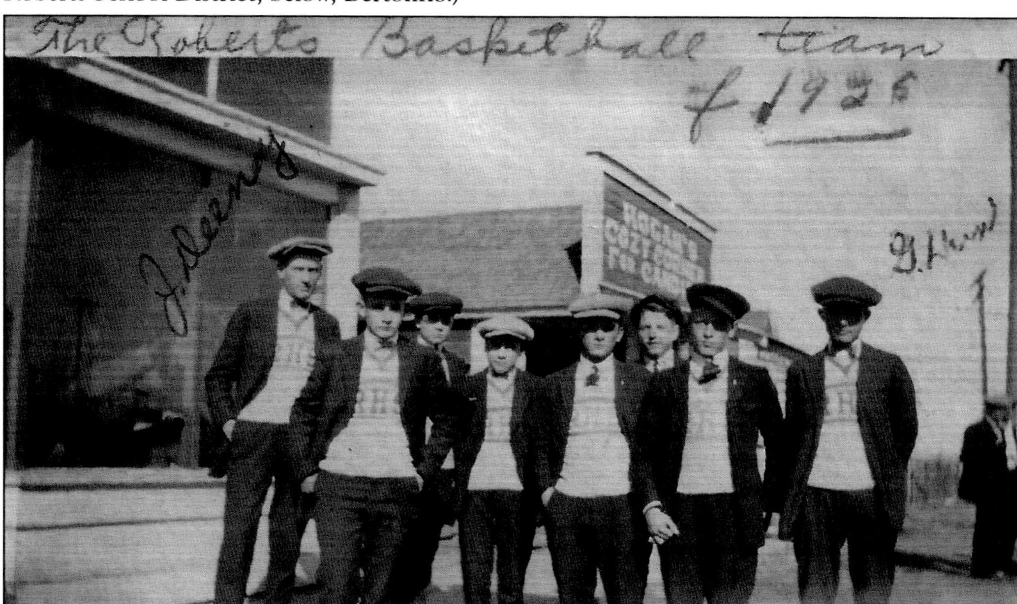

Seven jovial young Roberts residents playfully pretend to hop a boxcar out of town in the 1920s. Captions on the photograph read (clockwise from left), "Let's go. We're off. How far? When? Which way? Why? How come? Where to?" (CCHS.)

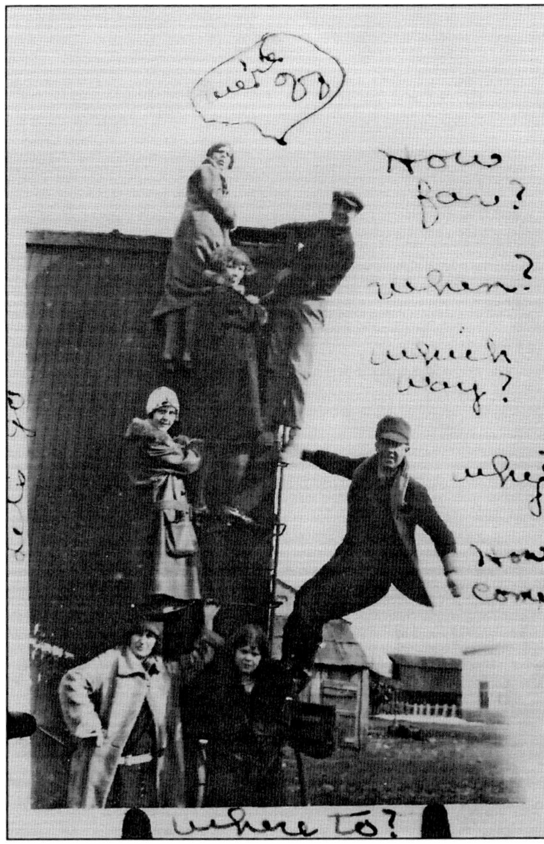

Below, prominent Roberts businessmen of the 1930s stand on a snowbank in front of the Occidental Elevator Company. Built in 1915 to hold up to 40,000 bushels of grain, the elevator was on the Northern Pacific right-of-way across from the section house. It burned down in July 1998. (Allen.)

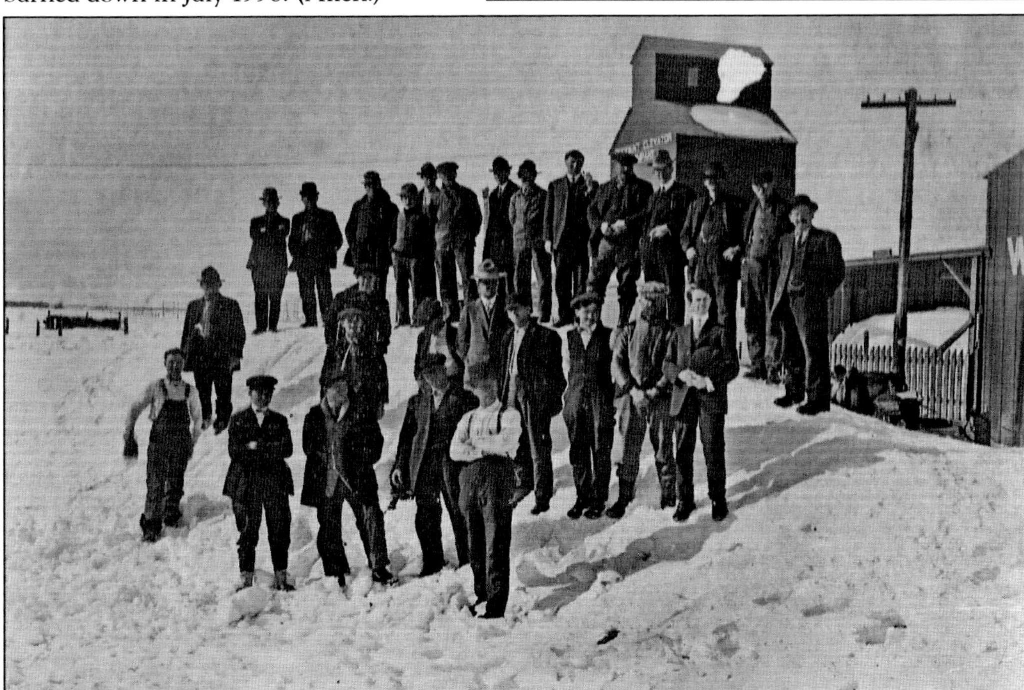

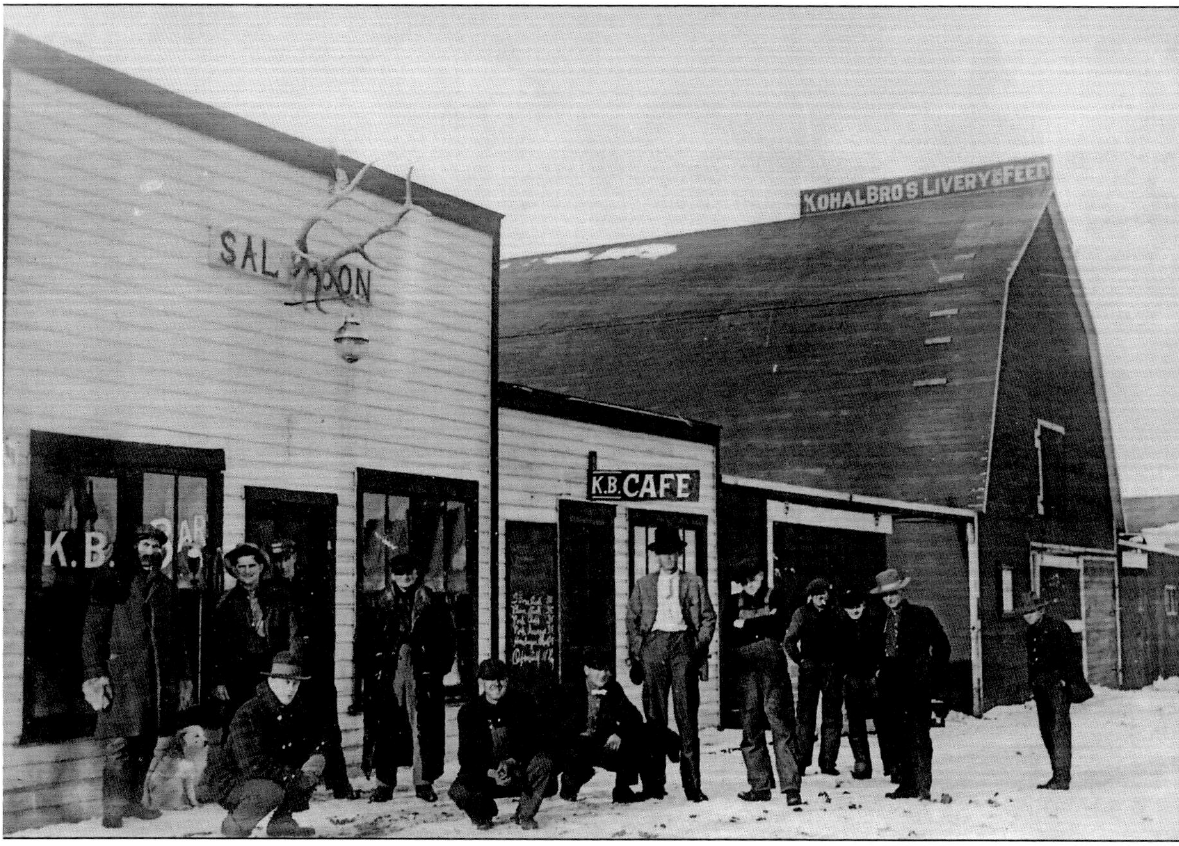

Locals stand in front of the Kohal Brothers (KB) block in 1916 in a photograph by prolific Carbon County photographer Kay (Psenda) Egenes. The Kohal brothers operated a saloon, a café, and a livery stable on the block. Egenes, born in 1906, amassed a huge photographic archive of Carbon County life up to her passing in 2005 at age 98. Her and her husband, Bernt, operated a newsstand and photographic studio in Red Lodge until 1978, when her photographer son Tom took over the studio, which remains a landmark today. A consummate artist, Kay Egenes took up oil painting in 1979 at the age of 73. (Flash.)

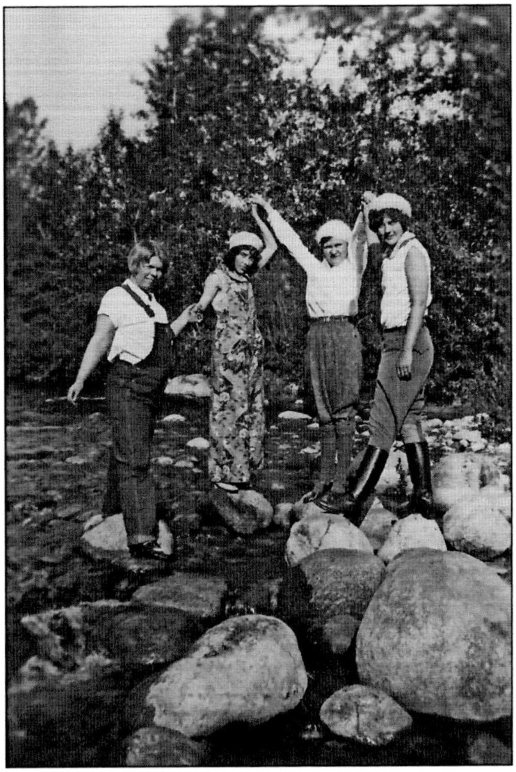

At right, young women dance among the rocks in Rock Creek on a hot summer day in the mid-1920s. They are dressed in the styles of the period, from the very casual but practical overalls to an outfit with the latest palazzo pants, which had wide flowing legs from the waist to the ankle and were stylish but still appropriate for an outdoor adventure. The two women on the right, in jodhpurs with riding boots, may have ridden their horses to the picnic. Below, the women enjoy a picnic lunch on the edge of Rock Creek. The water level is low in the summer, so the women stay dry but cool in the creek bed. (Both, CCHS.)

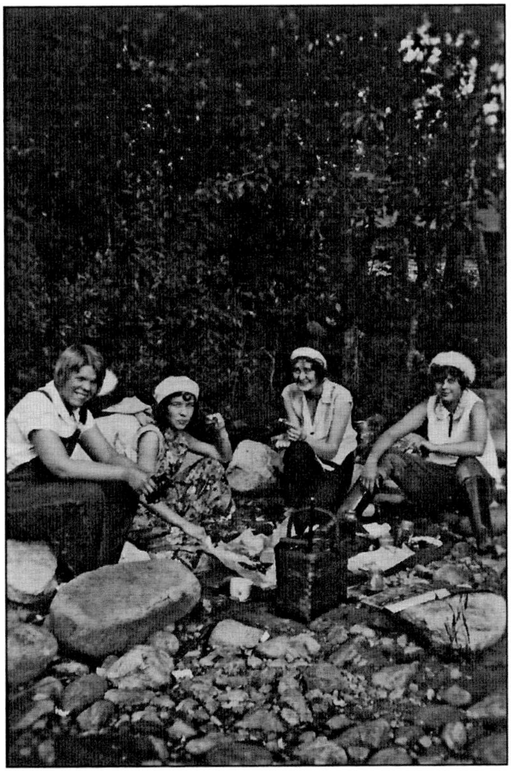

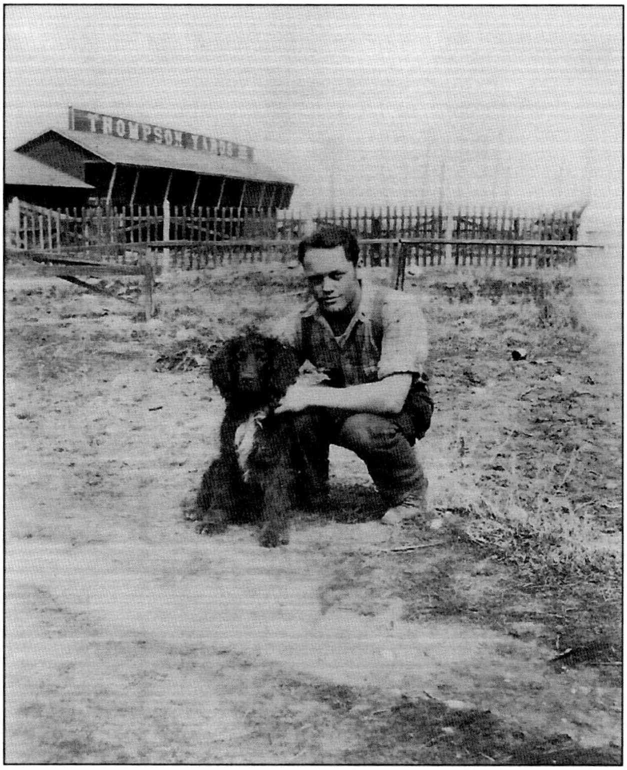

An unidentified man squats next to his dog in front of the Thompson lumberyard in the 1920s. Located southeast of the high school, the lumberyard was operated by Addison R. Moon and sold a variety of lumber and building supplies. (CCHS.)

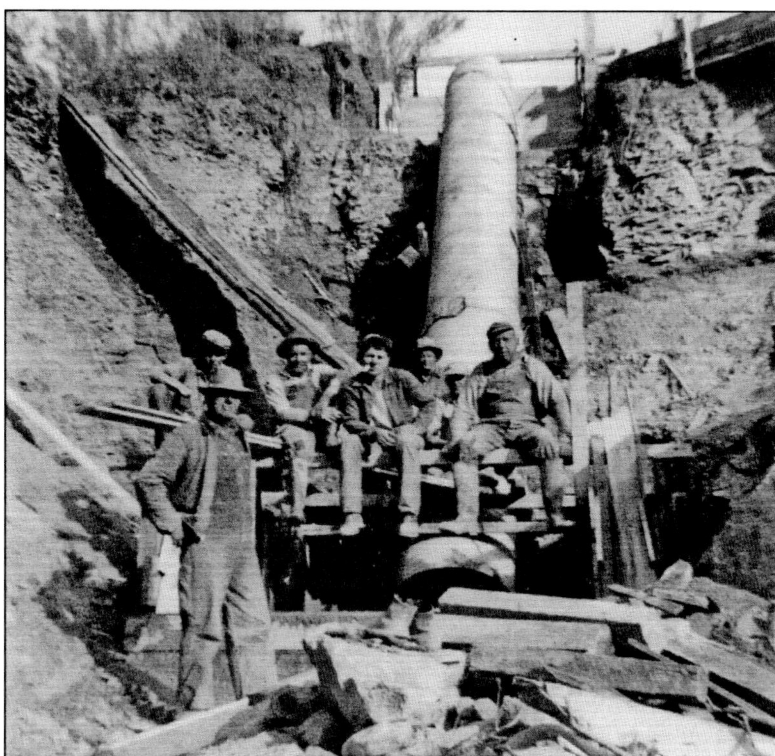

John Kotka (standing) and (from left to right) Clifford Long, Wayno Wallila, Donnie Wilson, Leonard Bell, Kris Kotka, and Joe Bertolino reconstruct the overflow flume on Finn Ditch in May 1957. The irrigation ditch was built in 1895 to provide water from Rock Creek to farms in the Roberts area. The 150 miner's inches it provided in 1895 grew to 1,626 by 1902. (Ayre.)

Identified only as "Momma and Bob," this mother and child wait at the Roberts depot in the 1920s. The Northern Pacific Railway started passenger service on the Rocky Fork Branch from Laurel to Red Lodge when the line opened in 1889. At first, passengers and mail rode in the caboose. Northern Pacific did not add regular passenger car service until 1903. (CCHS.)

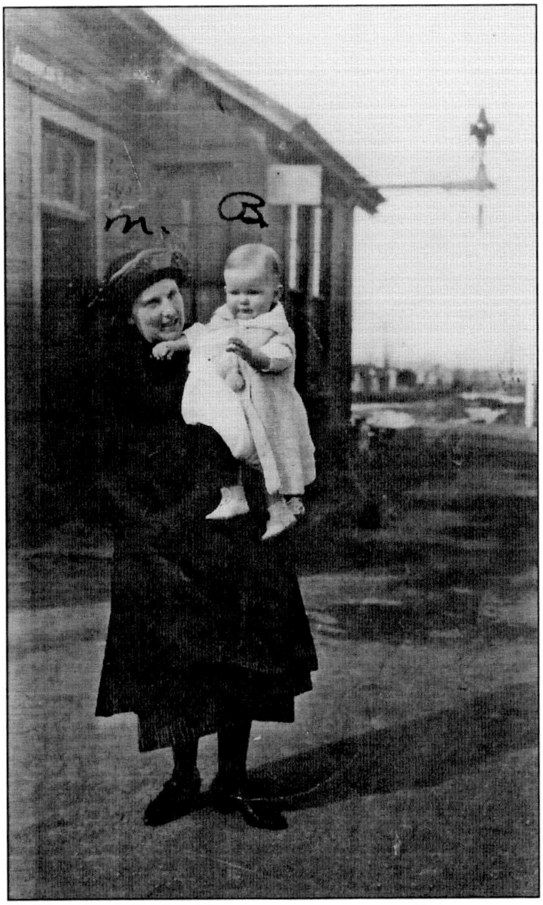

The young woman below stands on First Street in 1928, with the Roberts Hotel in the background. The hotel burned to the ground in 1930, but a bucket brigade kept the blaze from consuming adjacent buildings. The blaze led to the foundation of the Roberts Volunteer Fire Department. (CCHS.)

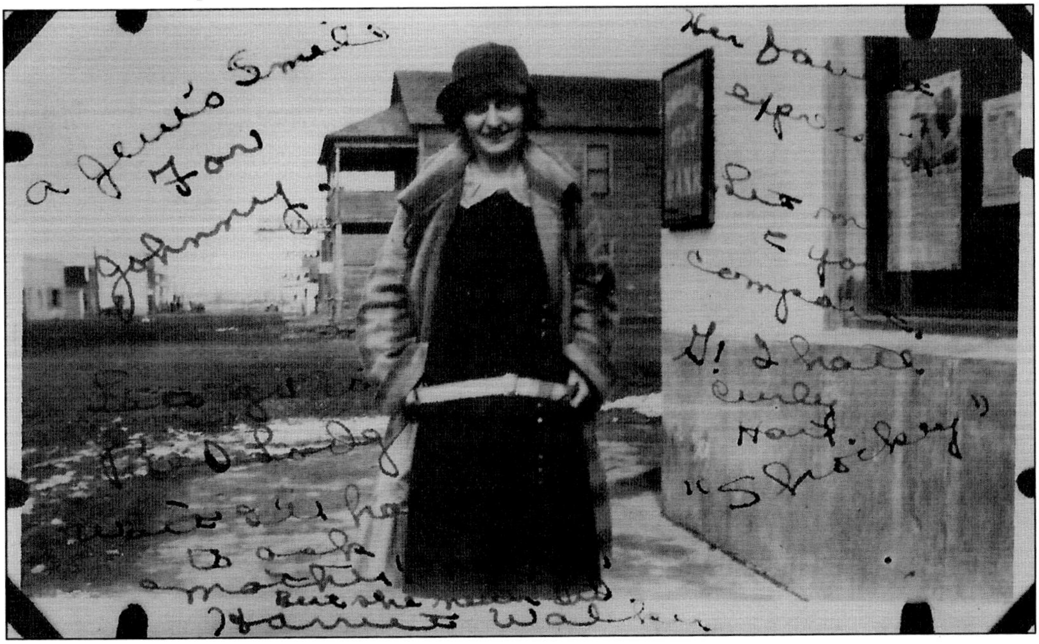

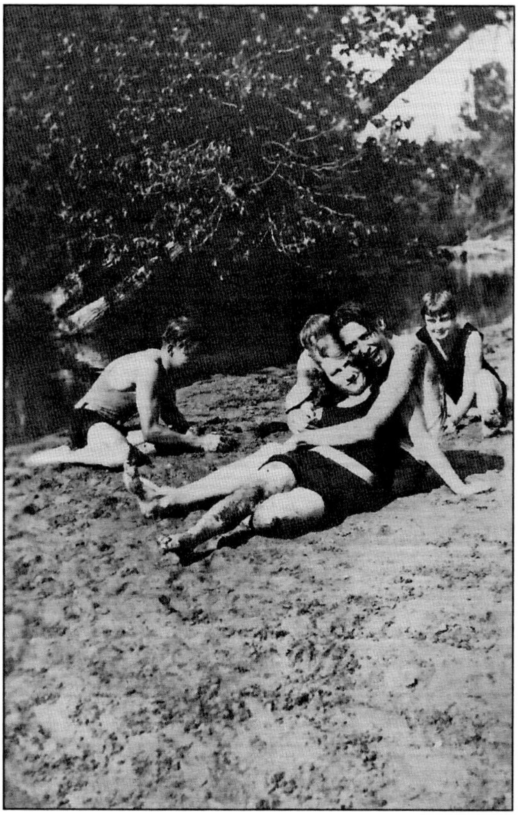

In addition to providing water for irrigating and plenty of trout for the frying pan, Rock Creek's countless swimming holes also kept residents, including these playful teenagers in the 1920s, cool on the hottest of summer days. Wool, knit bathing suits, the material of choice, helped people tolerate the cold water. (CCHS.)

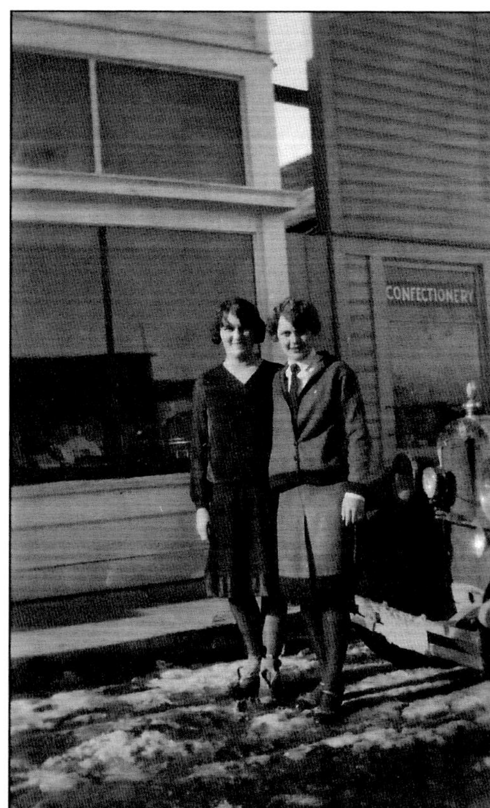

Though Roberts was a relatively remote agricultural hub far from major metropolitan areas in the 1920s, its residents embraced the cosmopolitan fashions of the age, as seen with these women, who had bobbed hair and were dressed in the couture of the day: one in a flapper dress and the other in a short skirt and a masculine shirt and tie, conveying a message of liberation. (CCHS.)

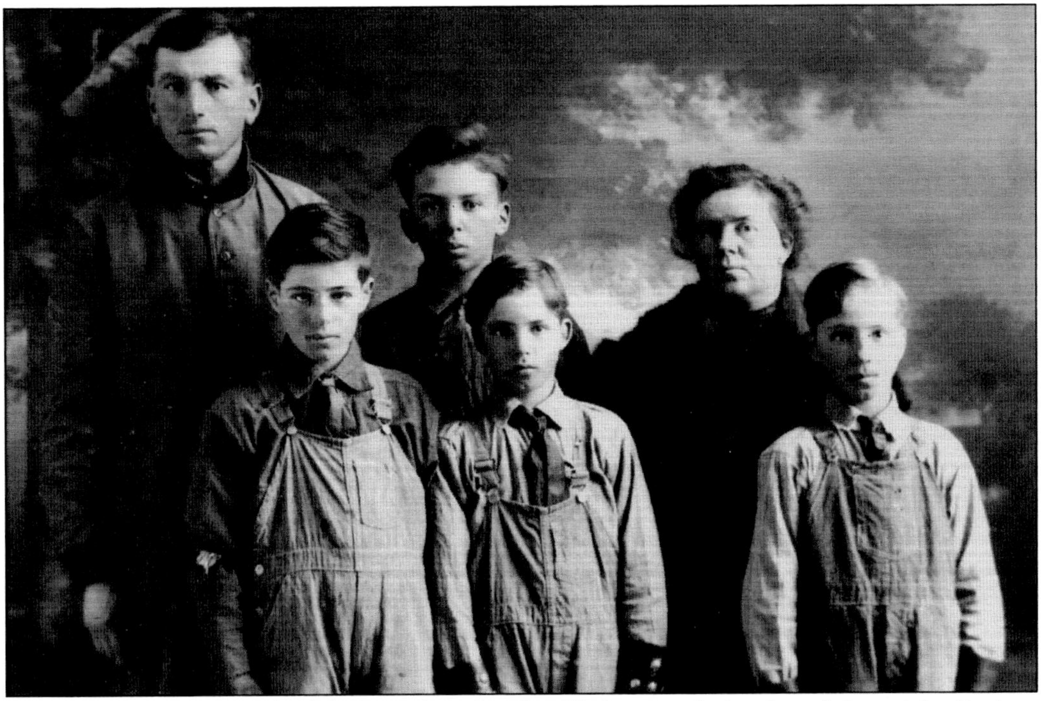

This 1920-era photograph of the Bertolino family of Roberts includes, from left to right, Batista, Pete, Joe, Dominic, Maria, and Batista Bertolino Jr. Batista "Batt" Bertolino Sr. came to work in the mines in Red Lodge. Wanting her sons to work in a less dangerous profession, Maria convinced Batt Sr. to purchase a ranch outside of Roberts on Willow Creek in 1916. (CCHS.)

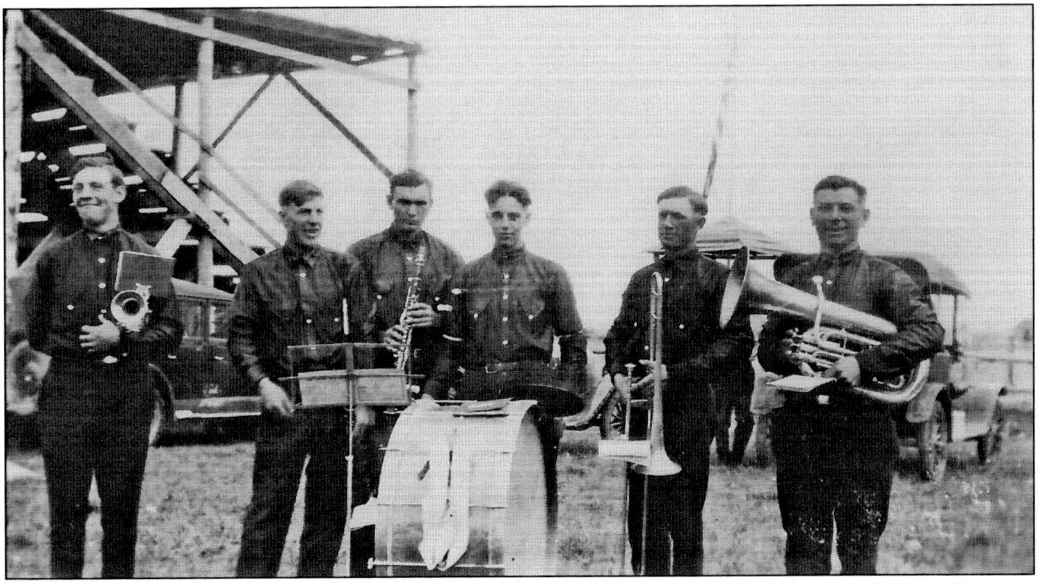

The Roberts Band included, from left to right, Joe Bertolino, Harry Hunter, Jimmy Hunter, Martin Patterson, Pete Bertolino, and an unidentified member. Pete Bertolino worked in Chicago as a musician but was killed when he was struck by lightning while back home helping with the harvest in 1926. He was 21. (Bertolino.)

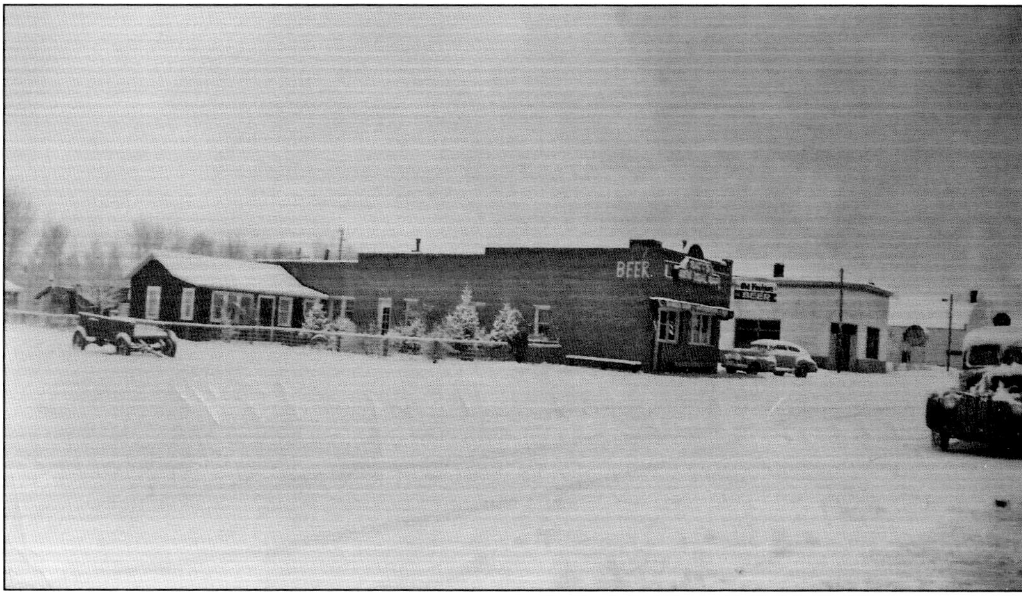

The above view of the east side of First Street shows the New Deal Bar in the late 1940s. The Bertolino family residence is on the bar's north side. To the south (right) of the bar is a farm implement store housed in the former Roberts State Bank building, which sits kitty-corner across First Street from the current post office. Beyond it is the arching roof of the Beartooth Garage. Operated by Solomon Homi, the garage had a ramp in back of the building leading to a basement where cars could be stored or serviced. Louise Bertolino took the photograph below of the Roberts High School Band playing in front of P.E. Howland's meat market in 1933. Band director Edwin Kansala is on the right, with the letter "R" on his coat. (Both, Bertolino.)

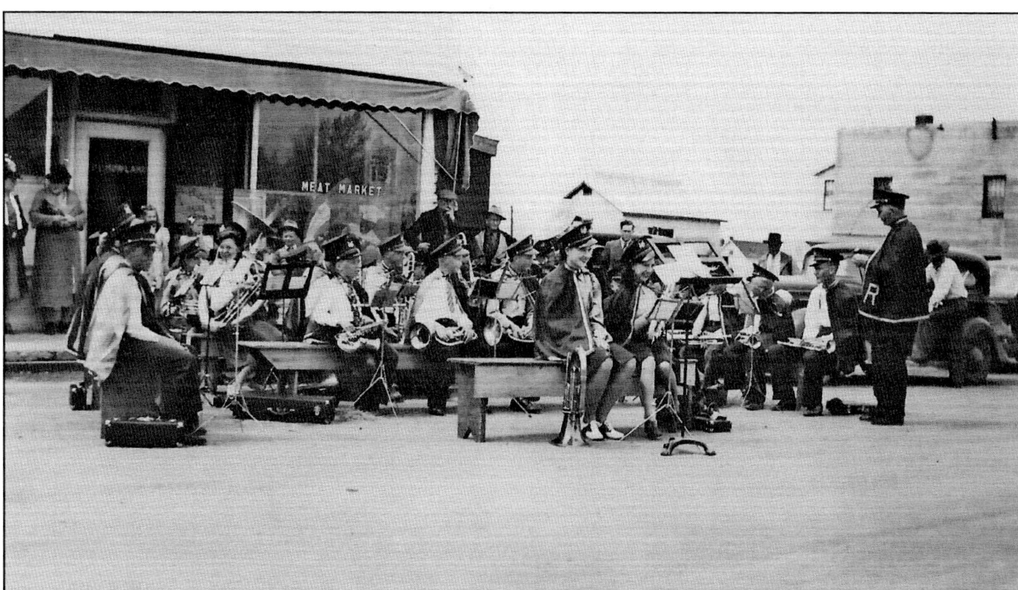

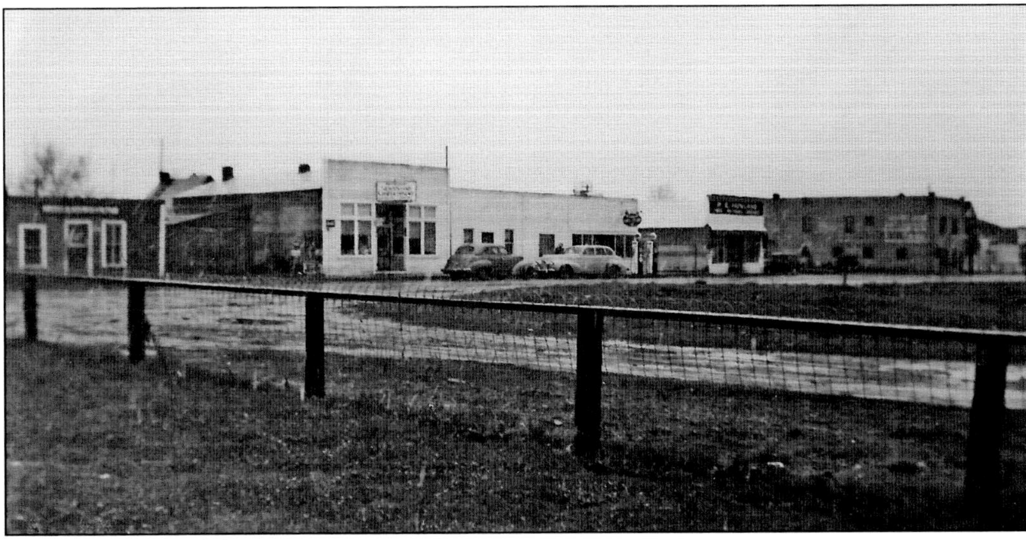

The view above of the west side of First Street shows, from left to right, McDonald's confectionery, Wilson's garage, P.E. Howland's meat market, and Winter's blacksmith shop. The single-story confectionery later moved into a two-story building across the street. Peter Howland operated Howland's store until he sold it to Ray and Pat Loyning in 1965. Batt and Louise Bertolino took the photograph at right of the Roberts Marching Band playing in front of the confectionery on Memorial Day 1939, when the confectionery was housed in a two-story building north of Wilson's garage. (Both, Bertolino.)

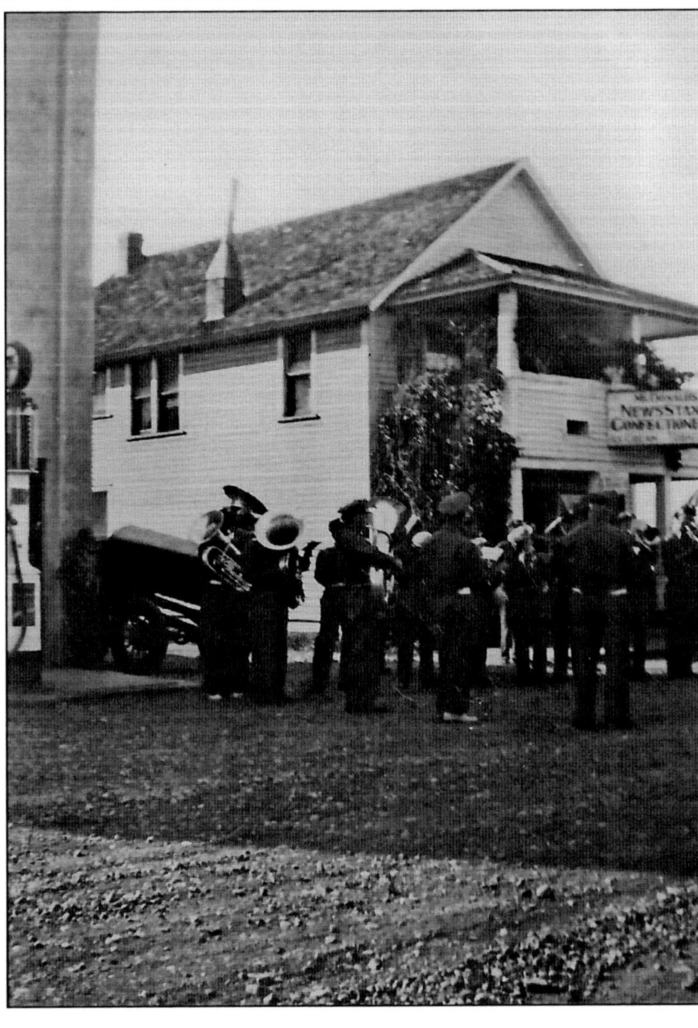

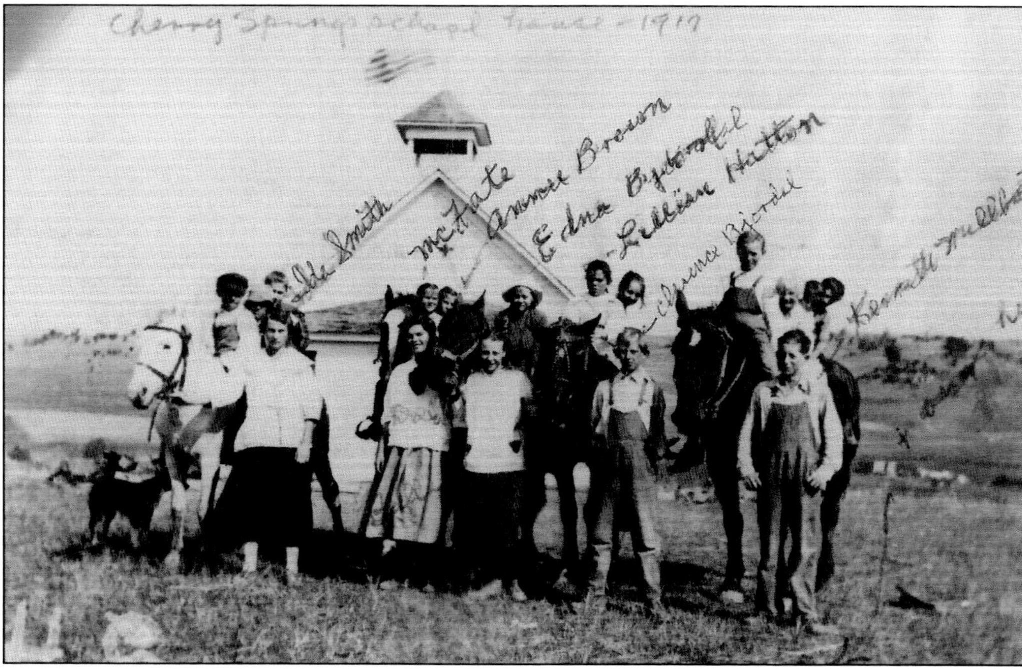

In the days before school buses, children often rode the family horse to school, as seen in this 1917 photograph of the Cherry Springs school. Located four miles east of Roberts, the Cherry Springs school operated from 1915 to 1939 and often served as a voting and gathering place for local farmers and ranchers. Below, Cherry Spring students pose for a photograph in 1919. They are, in no particular order, Edna Lochridge, Ida Smith, Lillian Hatten, Patrick McKennan, Anna McKennan, Kenneth Milbrath, Annie Brown, Thelma Brown, Daisy McFate, Jack McFate, John Saysell, Beatrice Saysell, Hazel Ballard, and Bella Ballard. (Both, CCHS.)

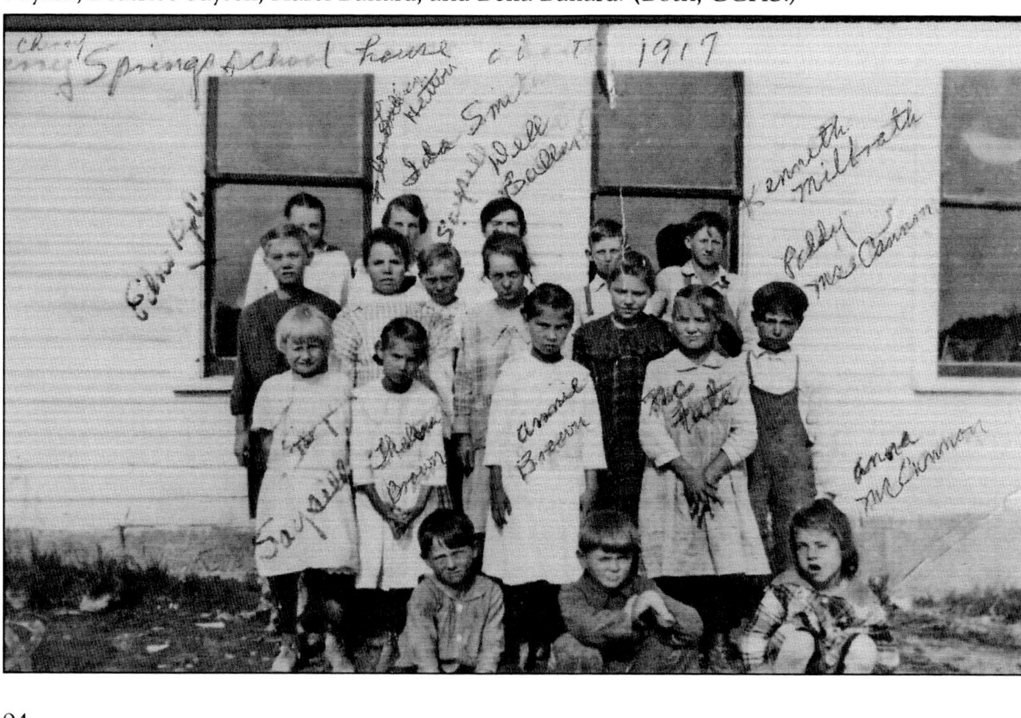

Eight

Fox and Kaleva Park

Located on Rock Creek halfway between Red Lodge and Roberts, Fox was the site of a railroad siding used as a shipping point by grain and hay farmers in this part of Carbon County. Named for Dr. J.M. Fox, the first manager of the Rocky Fork & Cooke City Railroad, Fox once had two grain elevators and was the largest grain shipping point in the county. Settled largely by Finnish immigrants, Fox once had a store, school, a post office, and a community hall to serve the surrounding homesteads. Such a large percentage of its early settlers were Finnish that a running joke in Fox was that the only place English was spoken was in the school, as the native tongue predominated both at home and in social settings.

Kaleva Park, two miles south of Fox, started as a gathering place for members of the Finnish secret society, the Knights of Kaleva, which began in 1898 in Belt, Montana, and shortly thereafter opened a chapter in Red Lodge. In 1902, Red Lodge hosted the first national convention of the Knights of Kaleva. In 1904, Red Lodge became home to the first women's Knights of Kaleva lodge. Today, the women's lodge has more members than any other women's lodge in the United States. In 1924, the Knights of Kaleva established Kaleva Park on 40 acres next to Rock Creek. There, Finns from Red Lodge, Fox, and Roberts could relax and enjoy time in the countryside. Over the years, the Knights of Kaleva opened Kaleva Park to the public. It is now available to all community groups for reunions, weddings, cookouts, and other functions.

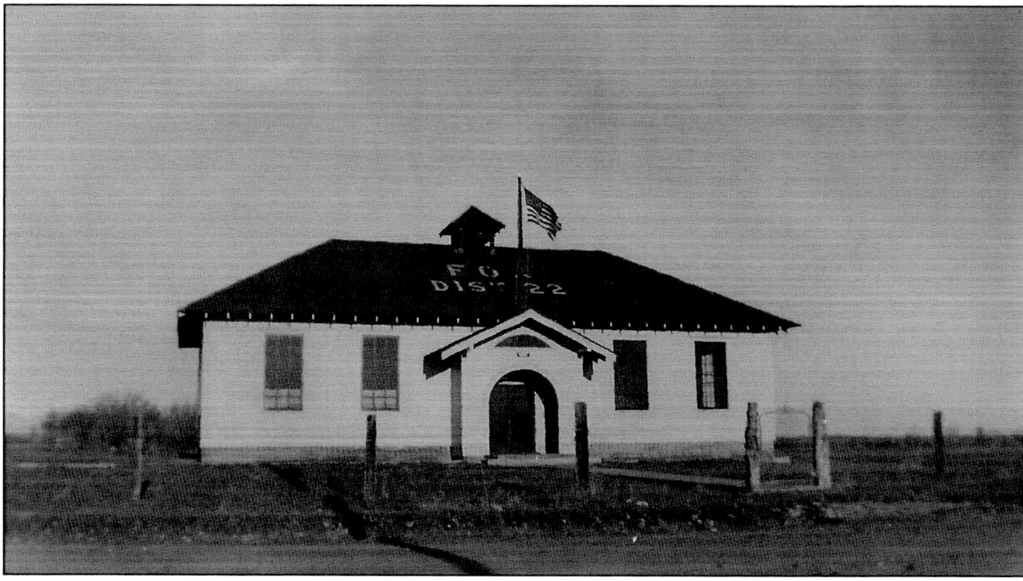

Social life in Fox revolved around two community gathering places, the Fox school and Fox Hall. Also known as the Valley school, the Fox school district was created on September 2, 1896. The very first school was located in a small log cabin on the Northy ranch. In 1909, it was replaced by a new building, seen above in 1940. Fox Hall (below) opened on February 28, 1914. Fox-area ranchers and farmers came up with the idea for a hall because it was too far to travel to Red Lodge or Roberts during long winter months. (Above, Redli; below, Lampi-Hassen.)

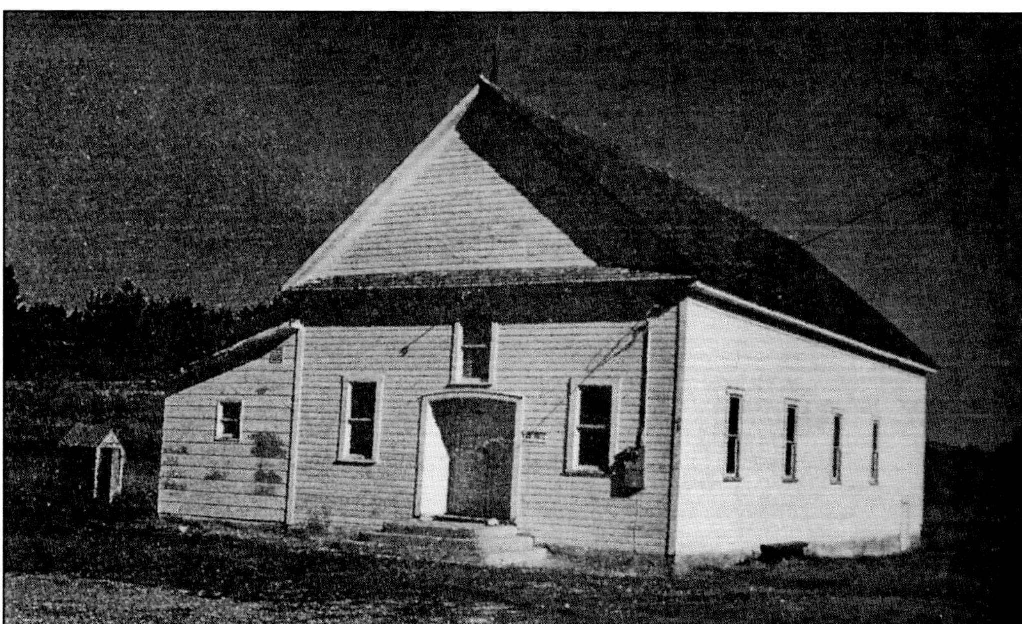

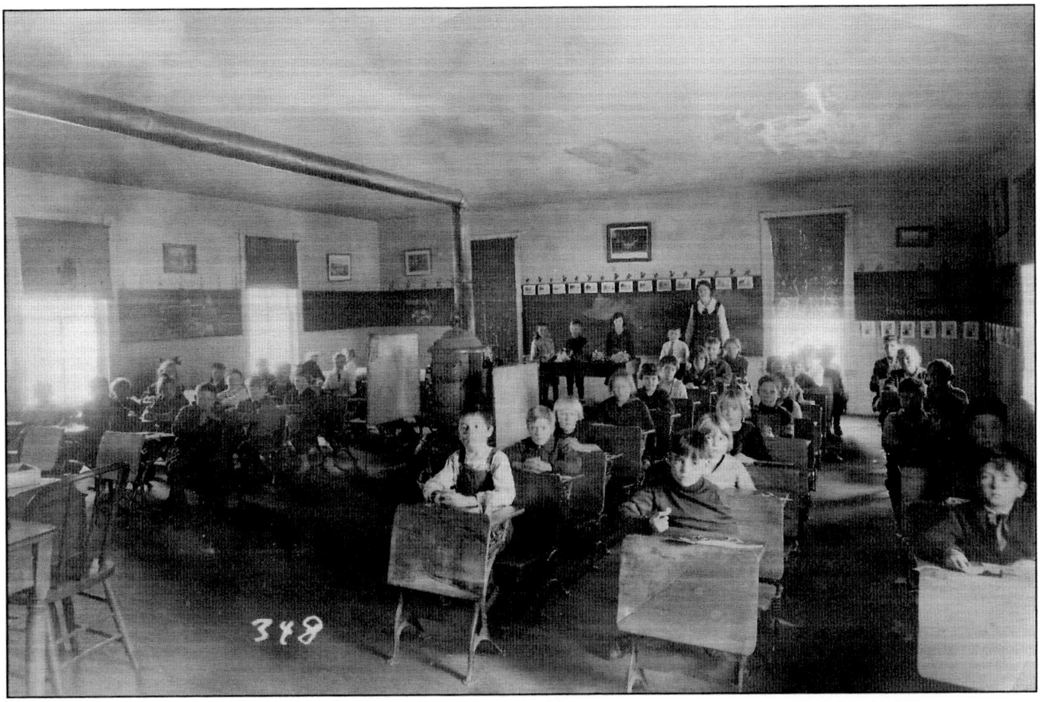

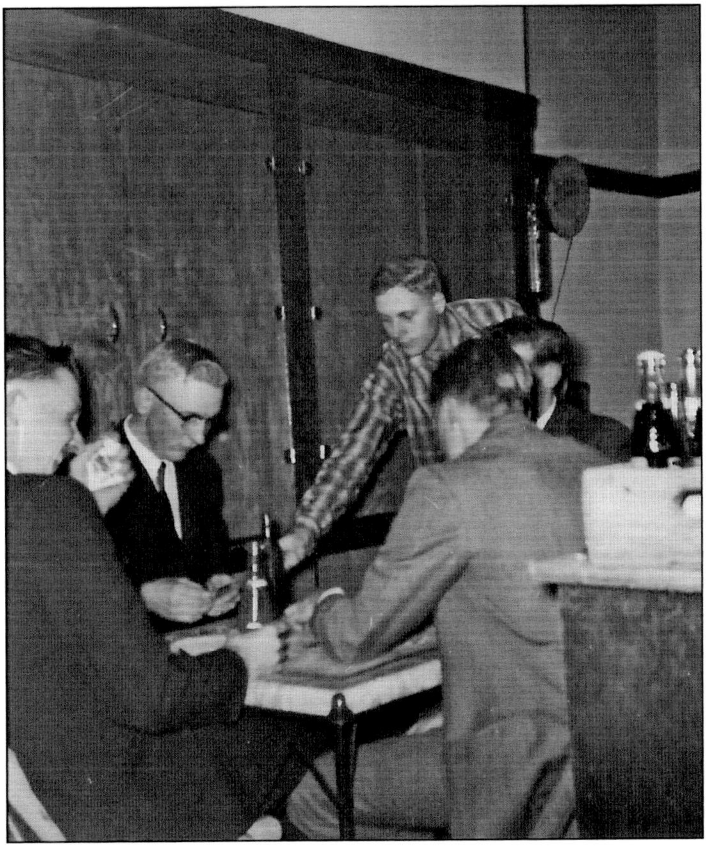

The rare photograph above of the interior of the Valley school, taken at Thanksgiving in the late 1910s, includes members of the Joki, Kamppinen, Korback, Koski, Kivikangas, Hyyppa, Hyvonen, and Johnson families. Teacher Janet Northy is seen in the back of the class. Hired for $70 a month in 1914, her salary was raised to $85 per month in 1918. The school's name was changed from Valley to Fox in 1922. The school disbanded in 1967. The school was also used for recreation, as seen by the men at right, who are enjoying soda pop and a friendly card game in the 1950s. They are, from left to right, John Collins, Robert Kero, Marvin Kivikangas, Harvey Joki, and Ron Kumula. (Above, CCHS; right, Redli.)

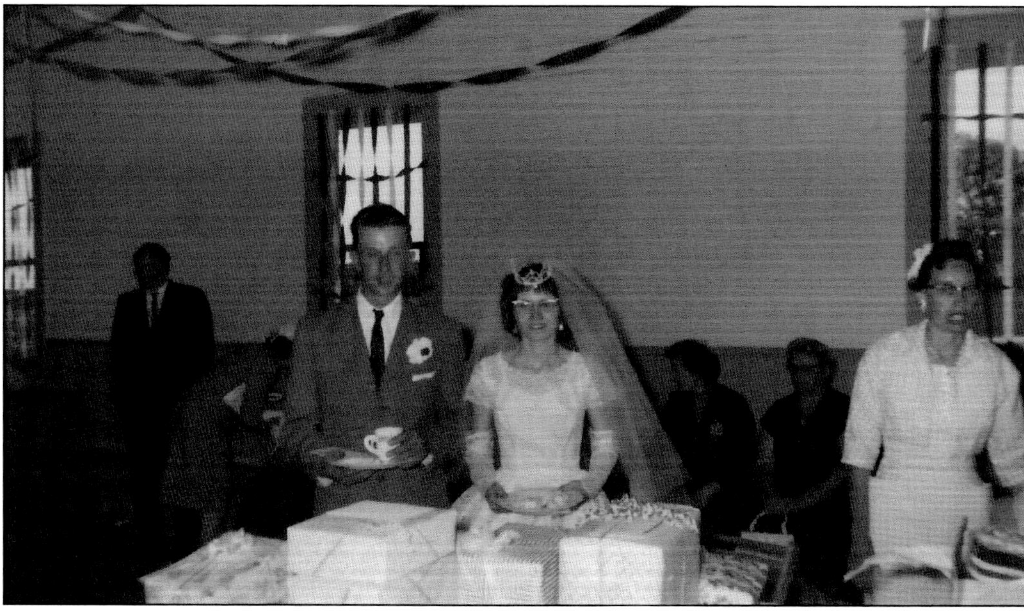

The wedding reception of John Henry Collins VI and Edna (Rowland) Collins took place at Fox Hall on June 10, 1962. Since opening in 1914, the hall hosted many area weddings, graduations, confirmations, dances, concerts, meetings, plays, and family reunions. Now part of a private residence, the hall was rented out for gatherings as recently as the 1990s. (Redli.)

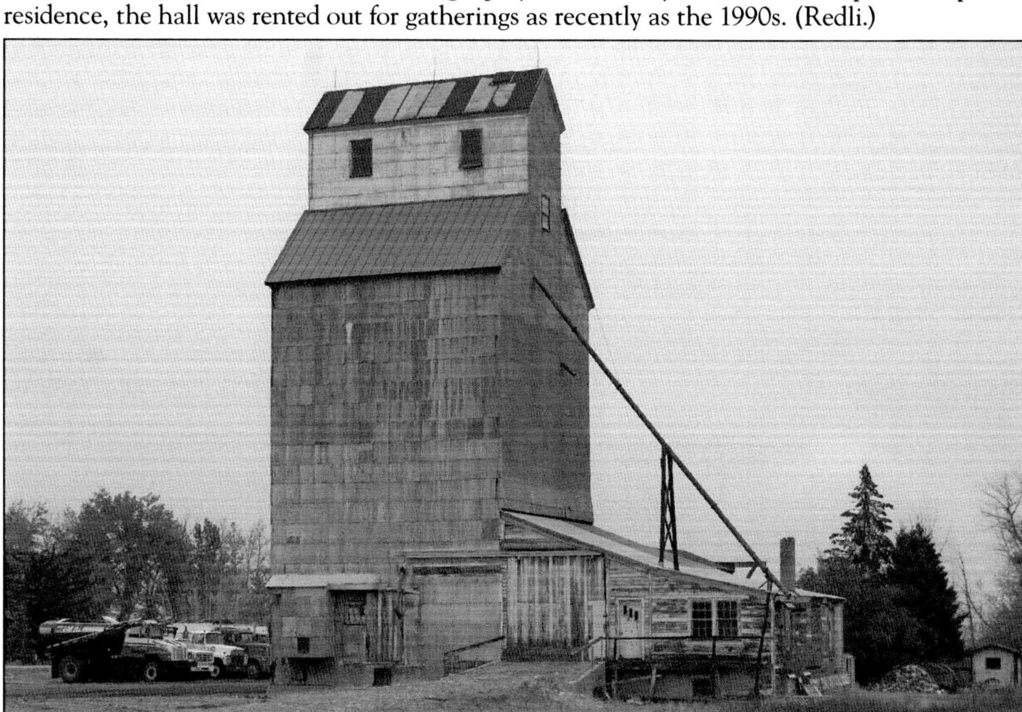

Standing next to Highway 212, the grain elevator is the most visible structure that survived in Fox. Built by Norwegian immigrant Goodman Gumsrud in the 1910s, the Atlantic Elevator Company at the Fox railroad siding was once the largest shipping point for grain in Carbon County. (Wallace.)

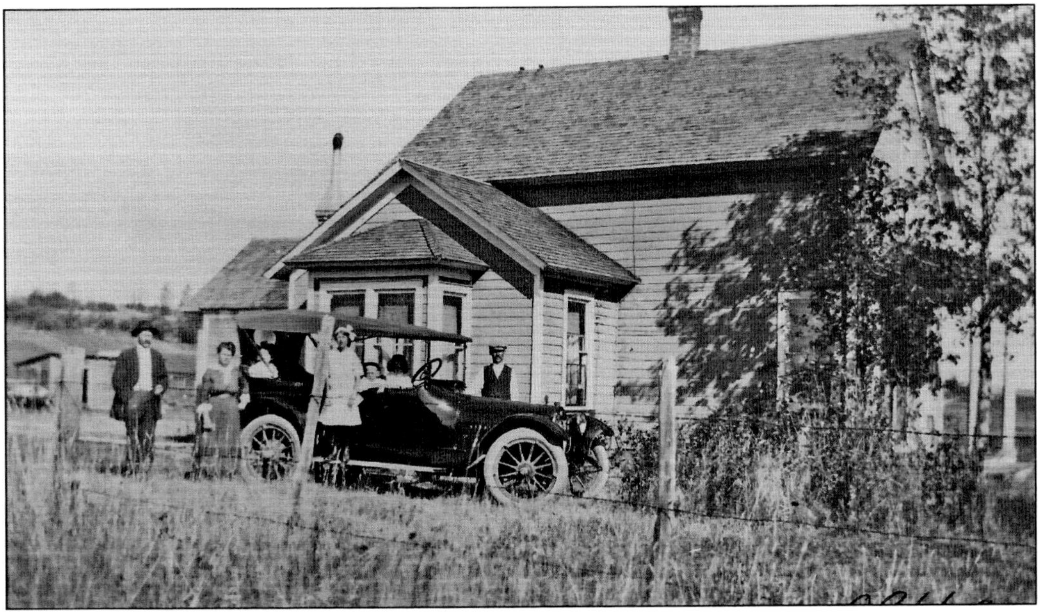

Above, members of the Puutio family are ready to take a Sunday drive in their 1916 Buick. They are, from left to right, Otto, Sophia, Sadie, Sylvia, Arthur, Arnie, and Alfred Puutio. Alfred and Sophia Puutio settled in the Fox area in 1906, living in a log cabin until moving to a second farm in 1911 and into the house seen in the background. On the second farm, Alfred and his cousin Otto, a miner in Red Lodge, built the large dairy barn below, which the Puutio children sit poised in front of on their horses with the family dog standing by. In 2004, it was included in Montana's Heritage Barns Program. (Both, CCHS.)

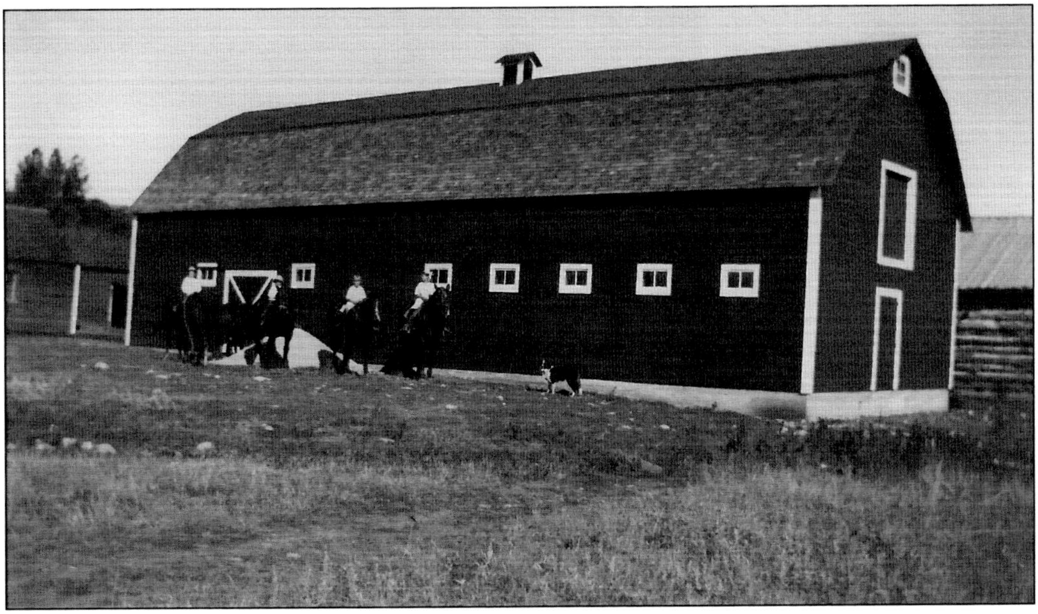

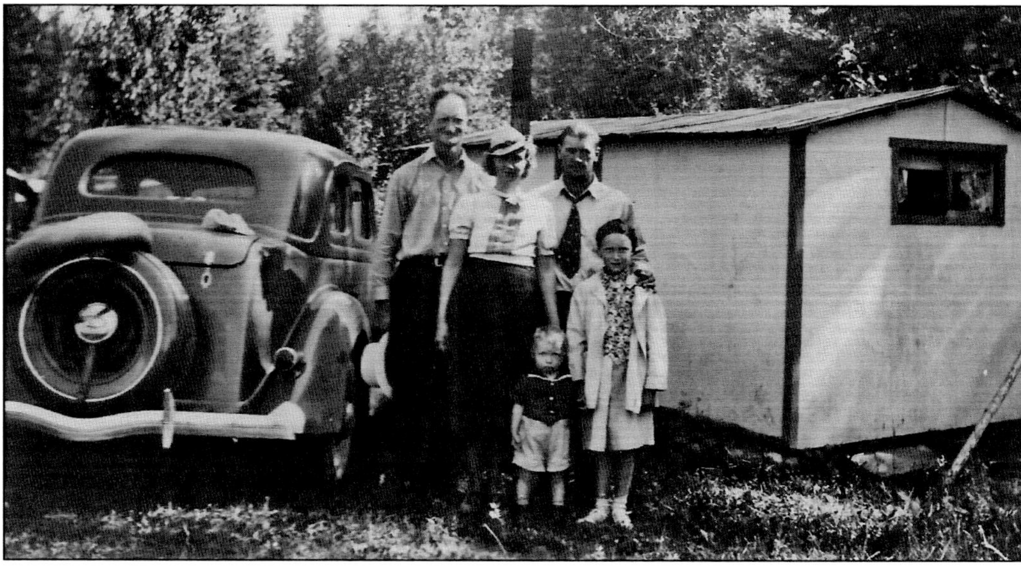

The Collins family is seen above in 1937 on their homestead in Fox. From left to right, they are John Henry Collins V, Alice (Lahti) Collins, Elmer Collins, John Henry Collins VI, and Alice "Babe" Collins. At the time of the photograph, the family was living in the bunkhouse to the right, waiting for their permanent home to be moved from the nearby mining community in Bearcreek about 10 miles away. The Collins house, after it had been moved from Bearcreek, is seen in the background of the 1950-era photograph below. In it, Ervi Johnson is haying and Alice "Babe" Collins (Johnson) stands to the far right. (Both, CCHS.)

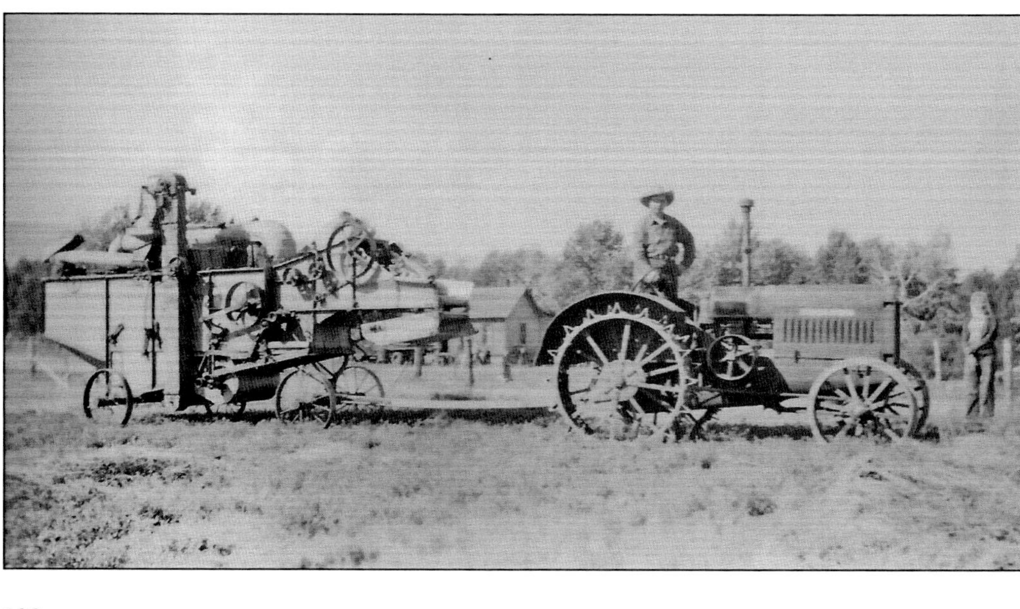

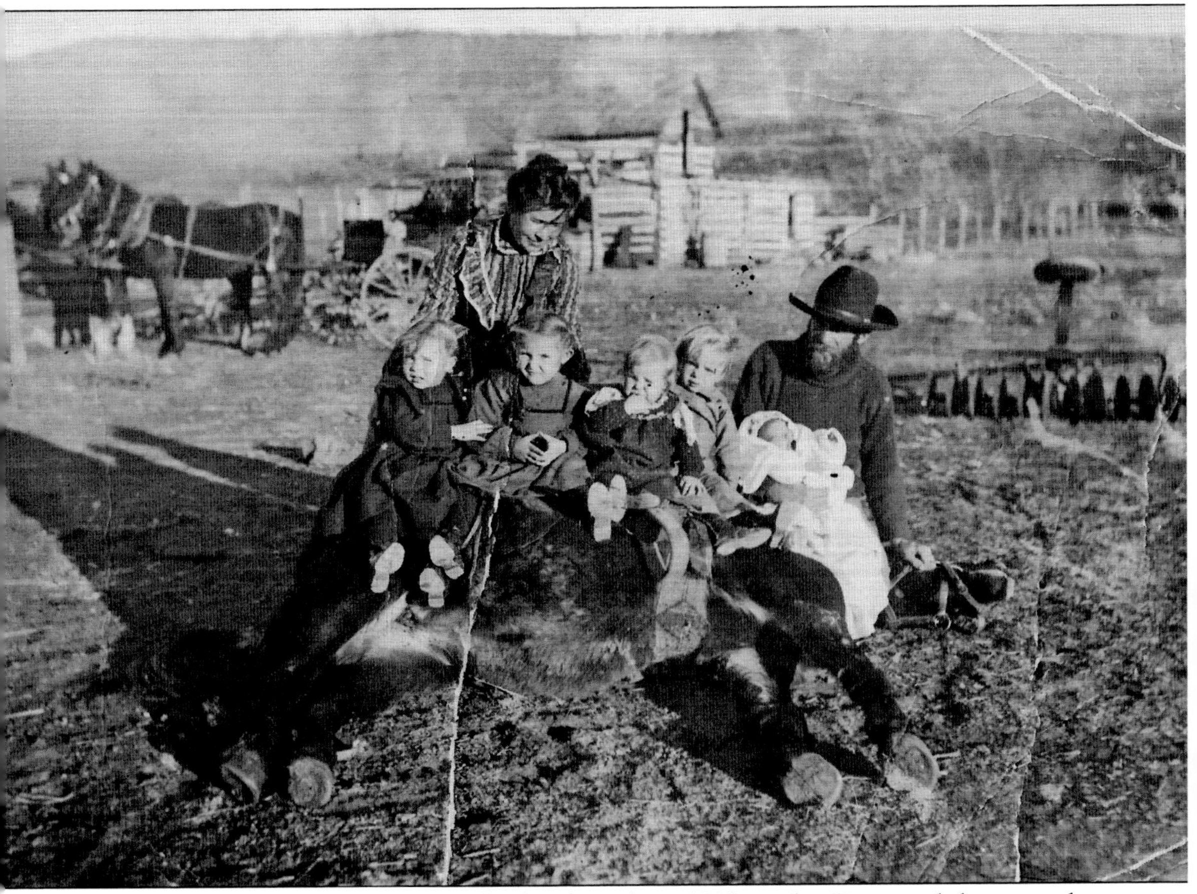

The Greenough family children sit on the family mule in 1905 on the Greenough homestead in Fox. They are, from left to right, (first row) Alice, Vena, Ida, Frank, and Thurkel "Turk" Greenough; (second row) Myrtle and "Packsaddle Ben" Greenough. From these humble beginnings, the Greenoughs went on to become one of the premier rodeo families of all time. Sisters Alice and Marge and brothers Frank and Turk were known as the Riding Greenoughs and enjoyed celebrity status, riding in rodeos all across the United States, Australia, and Europe. Turk was a three-time saddle bronc world champion who was briefly married to famous fan dancer Sally Rand. Alice was a four-time saddle bronc world champion who continued to work as a stunt rider on the television show *Little House on the Prairie* in her 70s. Their father, "Packsaddle Ben," was a successful mountain guide and one of the few people remembered fondly by Martha Jane Canary, better known as Calamity Jane. (CCHS.)

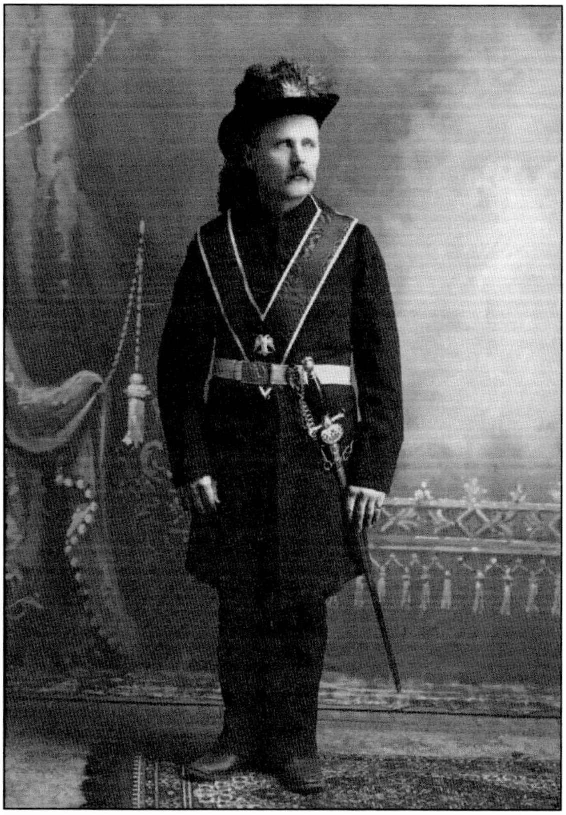

Red Lodge Finnish immigrant Jacob Kivikangas is seen here in his Knights of Kaleva uniform. Organized to preserve Finnish culture and traditions, the Knights of Kaleva was among the earliest secret societies in Carbon County. In 1910, families of Finnish descent made up a quarter of the population of Red Lodge and an even larger percentage in outlying areas like Fox and the settlements around Kaleva Park. (CCHS.)

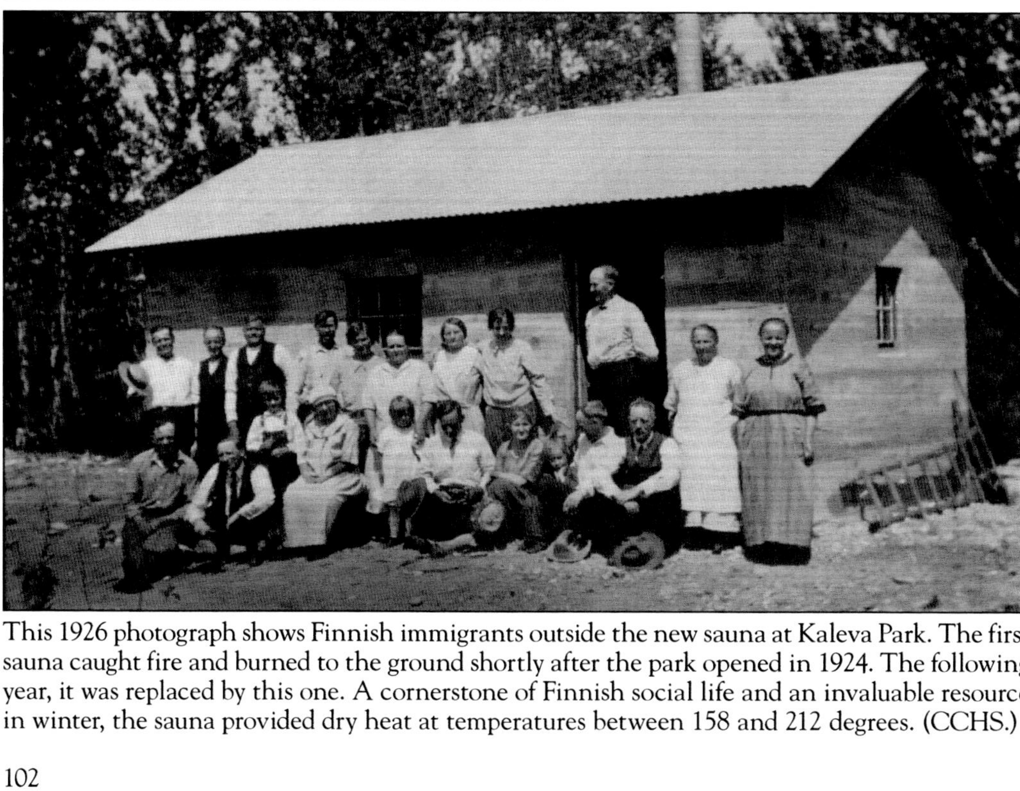

This 1926 photograph shows Finnish immigrants outside the new sauna at Kaleva Park. The first sauna caught fire and burned to the ground shortly after the park opened in 1924. The following year, it was replaced by this one. A cornerstone of Finnish social life and an invaluable resource in winter, the sauna provided dry heat at temperatures between 158 and 212 degrees. (CCHS.)

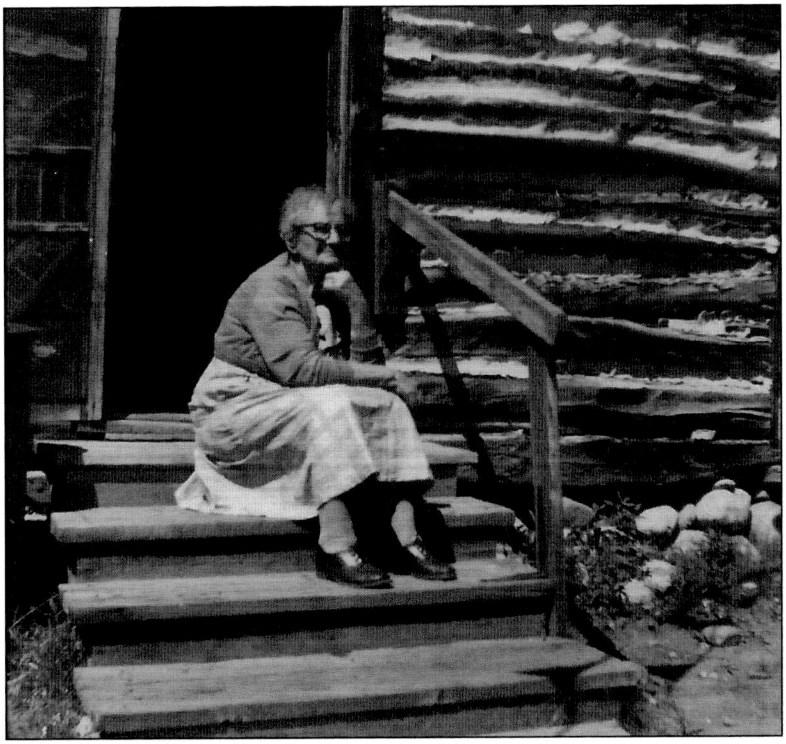

Lydia Karvonen takes a break from cooking to rest on the cookhouse steps at Kaleva Park in 1957. Picnics were usually held on long, linen-covered tables. Trout and smoked whitefish caught in Rock Creek were served. Farmers would bring unripened "farm cheese," fresh-churned butter, and cream for pastry desserts. (Johnston.)

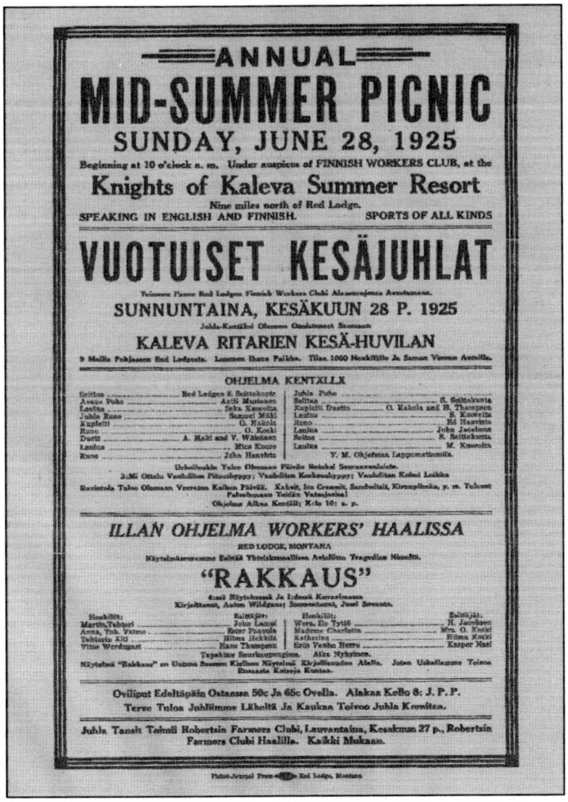

Every year around the summer solstice, the Knights of Kaleva hosted a midsummer picnic called *Vuotuiset Kesäjuhlat* at the Knights of Kaleva summer resort, or "Kaleva Ritarien Kesä-Huvilan" in Finnish. The midsummer festival included sporting events, music, plenty of food, and drama. The bottom part of this poster announced the play *Rakkaus*, which is the Finnish word for "love." (Herbert.)

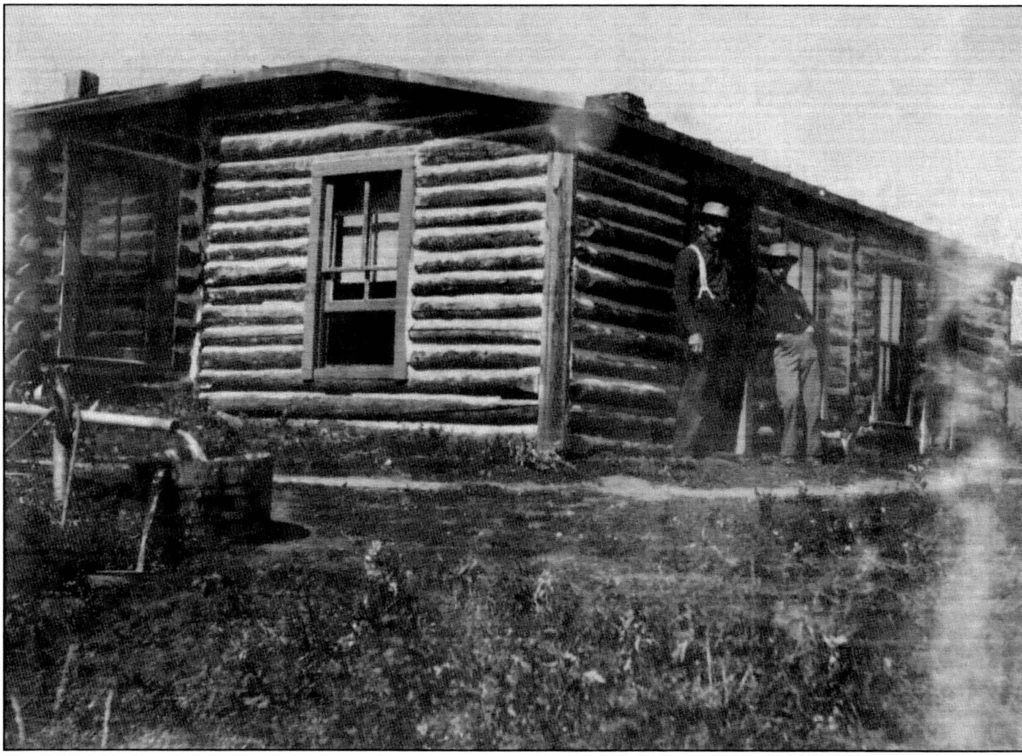

Above, John L. Maryott (left) is seen on the Maryott homestead with an unidentified man in the 1890s. Settled in 1886, it is one of the oldest homesteads in Montana. On his ranch, near Rock Creek and about three miles south of Fox, Maryott was one of the first settlers to tap the creek for irrigation. He also ran a dairy farm, which used a waterwheel to power its cream separator and butter churn. Maryott found prosperity early, as he was one of the only ranches around to supply men building the Rocky Fork Branch in 1889. Below, Maryott uses a handcrafted sleigh to keep his livestock fed during the harsh winters. (Both, CCHS.)

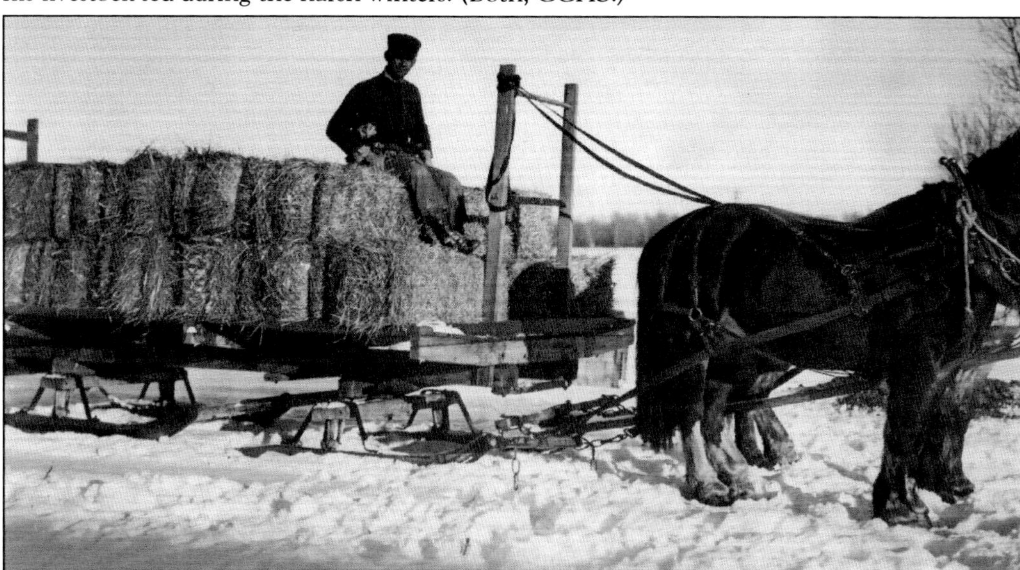

Nine

Red Lodge

Prospector James "Yankee Jim" George first discovered coal deposits along Rock Creek in 1866 near the future site of Red Lodge. Ownership of George's claim eventually passed into the hands of L.J. Platt. An energetic developer, Platt set up a small mining camp called Rocky Fork near the confluence of Rock Creek and its west branch just south of Red Lodge. The name Villiard, after Northern Pacific president Henry Villiard, was briefly considered before the name Red Lodge was chosen in reference to the many lodges the "red man" had in the area. The area had been part of the Crow Indian Reservation, but an agreement was reached in 1882 that allowed development in the Red Lodge area.

Red Lodge became the area's first permanent settlement in 1884, with the opening of a post office and stage stop. The rapid growth of the young town coincided with arrival of the Northern Pacific Railway in 1889. By 1891, the area became Montana's leading coal producer. Town lots were platted by the Rocky Fork Town & Electric Company, a subsidiary of the mining company, which in turn was owned by the railroad. By the mid-1890s, businesses had moved from the old townsite, and Red Lodge's new commercial center developed rapidly.

Although half of Red Lodge's population was foreign-born, the buildings erected between 1895 and 1936 generally reflect American trends rather than traditions of the various ethnic groups. Fraternal organizations, doctors' offices, ethnic clubs, bawdy houses, and hotels occupied the upper floors of downtown buildings.

When the last mine was closed in 1932, Red Lodge's economy briefly soured. But by 1936, the completion of the Beartooth Highway to Yellowstone National Park brought tourism to Red Lodge. Tourism is still Red Lodge's chief industry, with prime attractions like the Festival of Nations, the Home of Champions Rodeo, the Beartooth Motorcycle Rally, and the Winter Carnival.

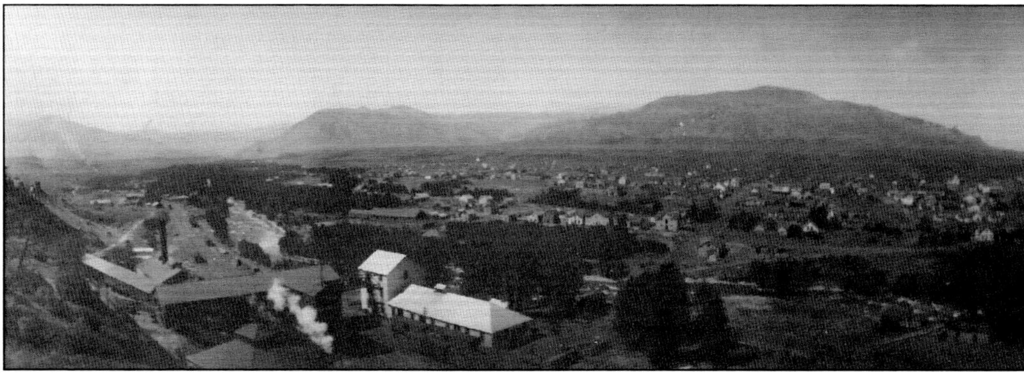

The East Side mine stands prominently in the foreground of this panoramic view of Red Lodge around 1900. The Rocky Fork Coal Company opened the mine in 1887. By 1891, it employed over 400 miners and extracted an average of 800 tons of coal per day. After having financial difficulties, the company was taken over in 1898 by the Northern Pacific Railway. (CCHS.)

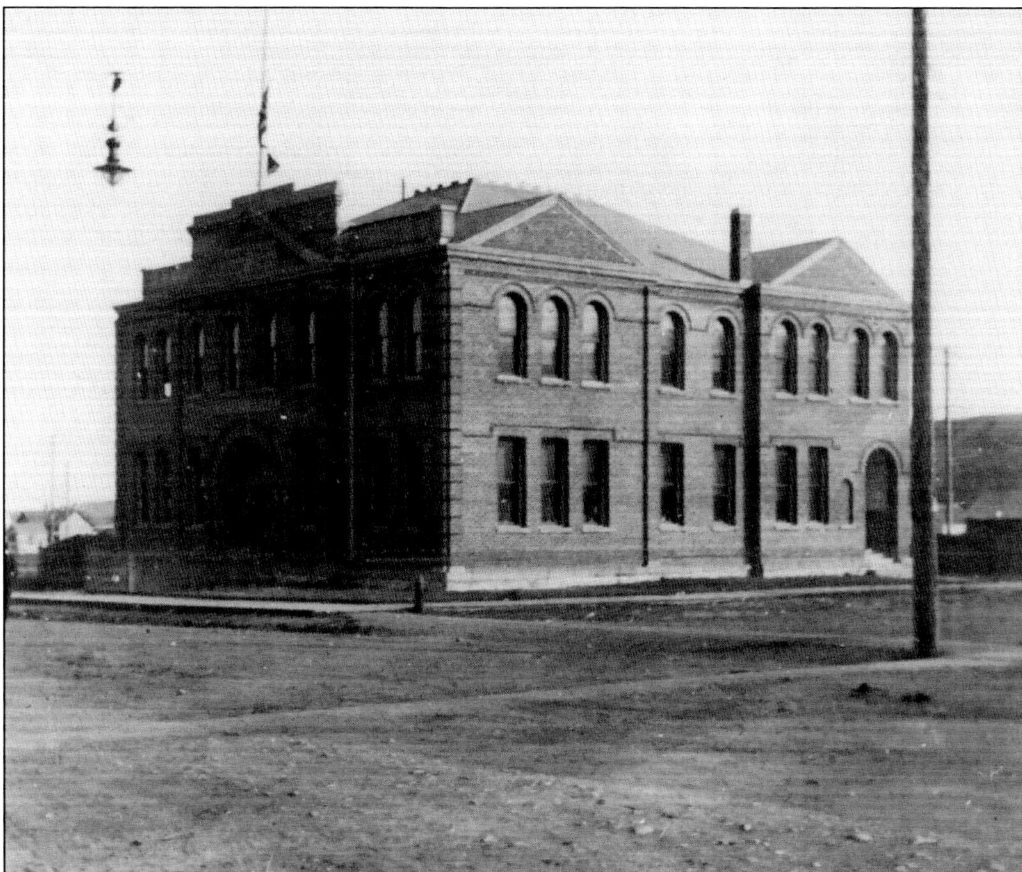

Seen here in 1900, a year after its construction, the Carbon County Courthouse stands on the corner of Tenth Street and Broadway in Red Lodge. The two-story brick structure cost $8,927 to build. Today, the building still houses the courts and the county attorney and sheriff's offices. (CCHS.)

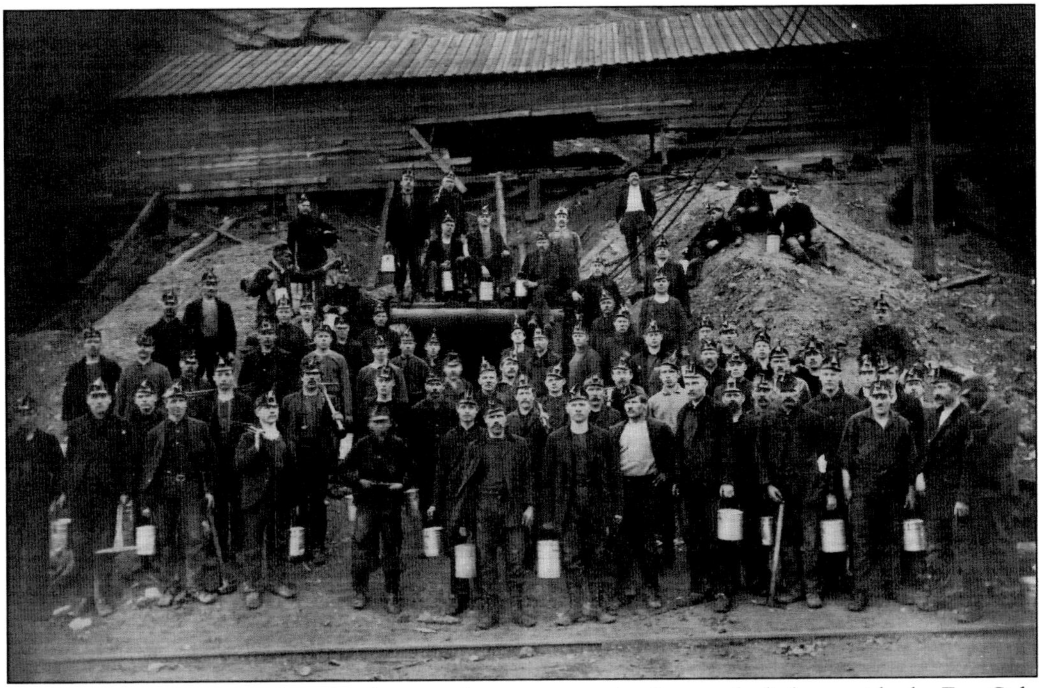

Miners representing a multitude of nationalities once again glimpse daylight outside the East Side mine in 1913. The mine bored into Red Lodge's east bench at the end of Thirteenth Street. By 1900, over 1,600 men worked in the Red Lodge mines out of a total population of over 5,000—double the city's current population. Between 1913 and 1917, Red Lodge mines produced more than one million tons of coal annually. (CCHS.)

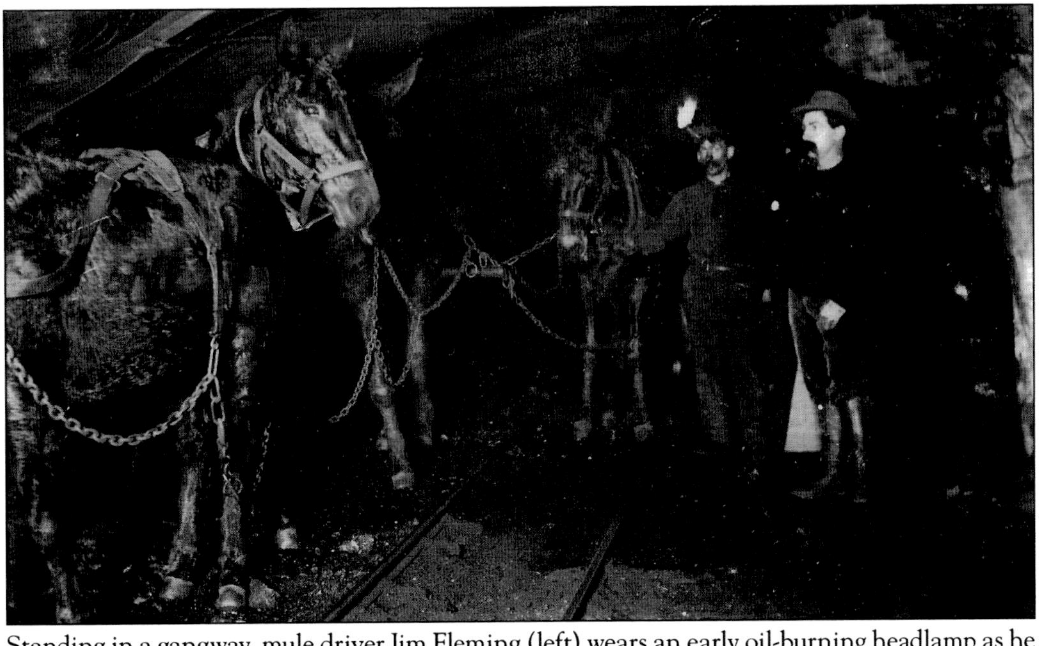

Standing in a gangway, mule driver Jim Fleming (left) wears an early oil-burning headlamp as he confers with L.F. Johnston. In the early years, most of the coal in the Rock Creek Valley was hauled to the surface by mules, some of which lived virtually their entire lives underground. (CCHS.)

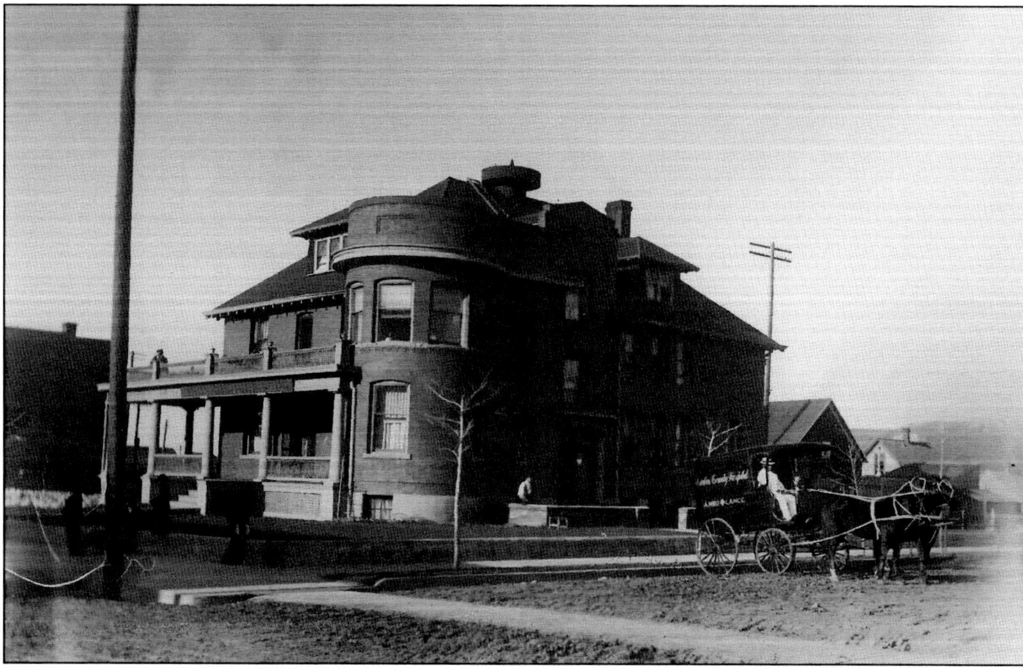

Mount Maurice Hospital was built in 1909 by Dr. S.M. Souders, who came to Red Lodge in 1901 as an assistant surgeon for the Northwestern Improvement Company. The four-story hospital featured white-tiled operating suites and a ward for patients, as well as private rooms, nurses' quarters on the fourth floor, and a black, horse-drawn ambulance. (Flash.)

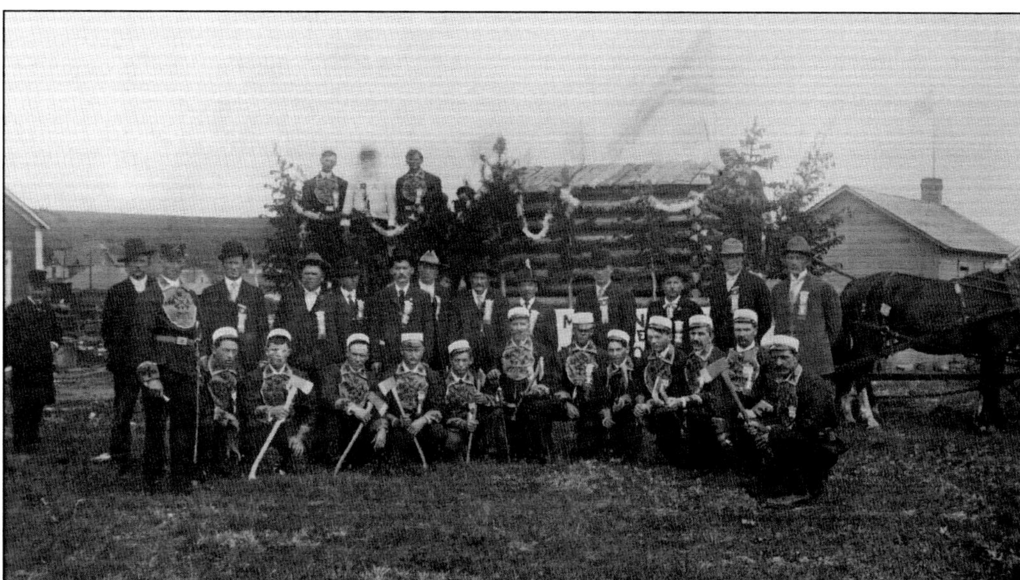

After a fire in the business block owned by the Red Lodge Improvement Company on March 23, 1900, caused $100,000 in damages, volunteers, seen in this 1900 photograph, formed a hook and ladder company and two hose companies. B.E. Vaill served as the volunteer fire department's first president, and William Larkin was its first chief. (CCHS.)

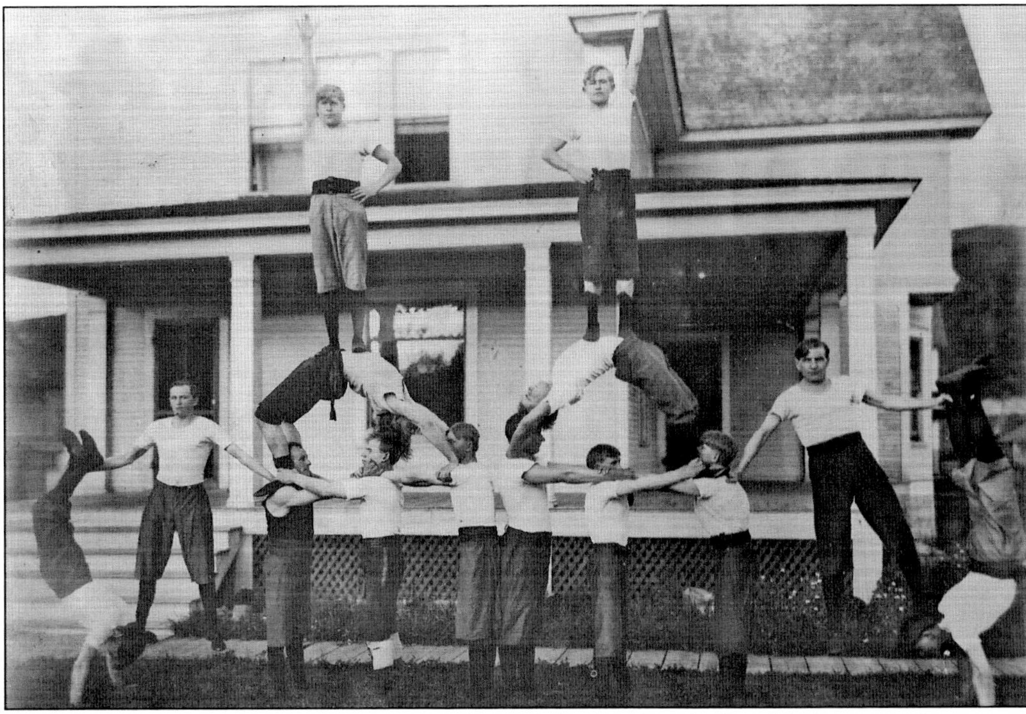

Gymnasts from the Finnish-American Athletic Club of Red Lodge bend, balance, and contort to form a twin-peaked human pyramid in front of the home of Miiko and Fiina Mero around 1930. The club formed in the late 1920s and held a series of dances to raise funds to purchase basketball and gymnasium equipment. (Redli.)

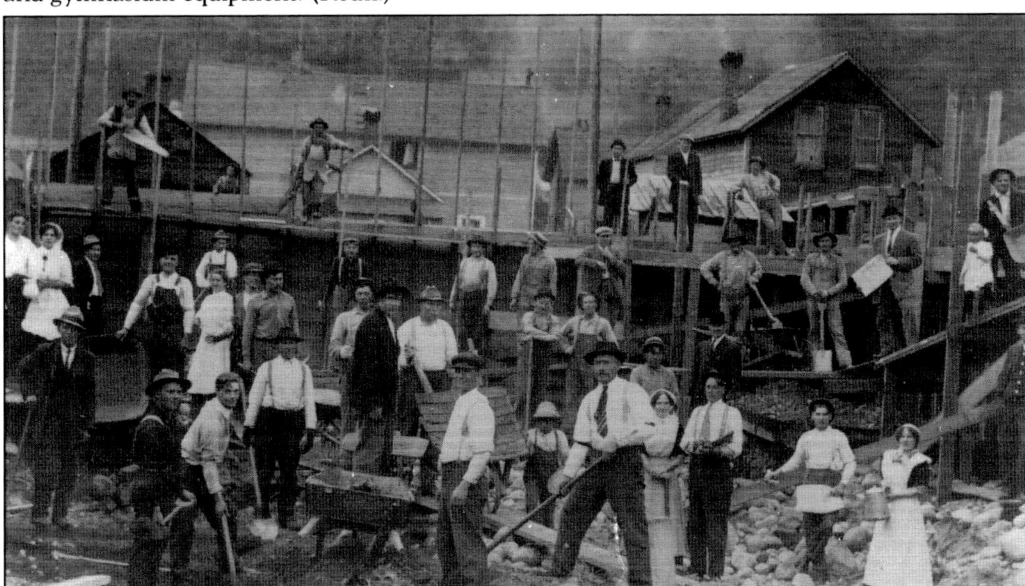

After working their shift in the mines, Finnish immigrants would clean up and don dress clothes before donating their labor to construct the Finnish Worker's Hall. Built in 1912, it was on Platt Avenue between Thirteenth and Fourteenth Streets and contained an auditorium, a kitchen, a dining room, and meeting rooms for Sunday school and a literature club. (CCHS.)

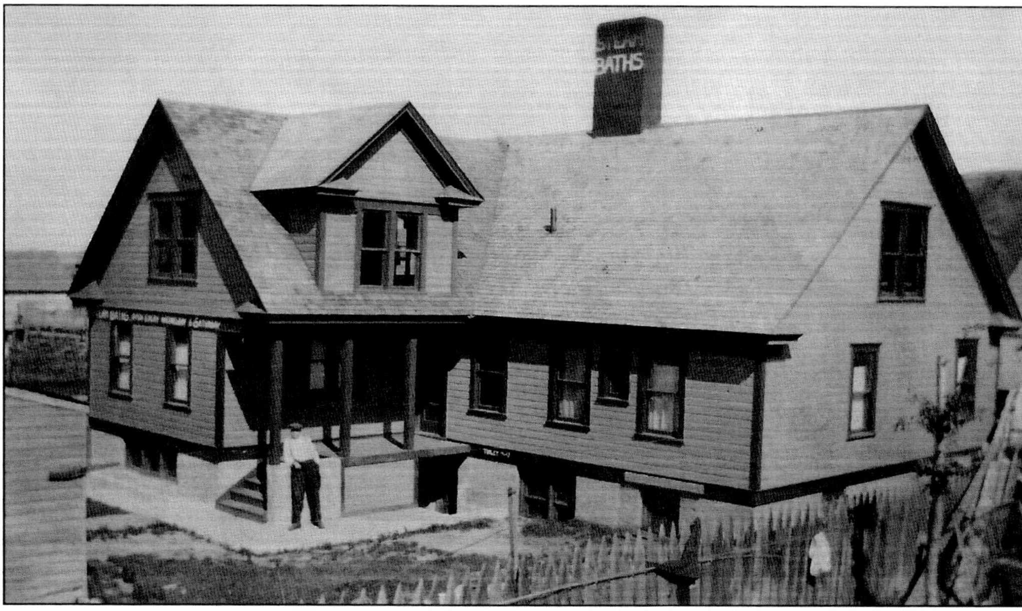

With its variety of ethnic and economic classes, Red Lodge developed as a city of distinct neighborhoods. There was Finn Town on the southeast side, where the Honkala Steam Baths (above) were a popular draw for muscle-sore Finnish miners. Little Italy lay on the northeast side, while Davisville included a large population of Austrian miners. Home to mine superintendents, railroad executives, and the city's most prosperous residents, the Hi Bug District, on Red Lodge's northwest side, was typified by neat rows of large, ornate Victorian houses set on large lawns bordered by picket fences, as seen in the 1908 photograph below. It remains the heart of Red Lodge's historic district today. (Both, CCHS.)

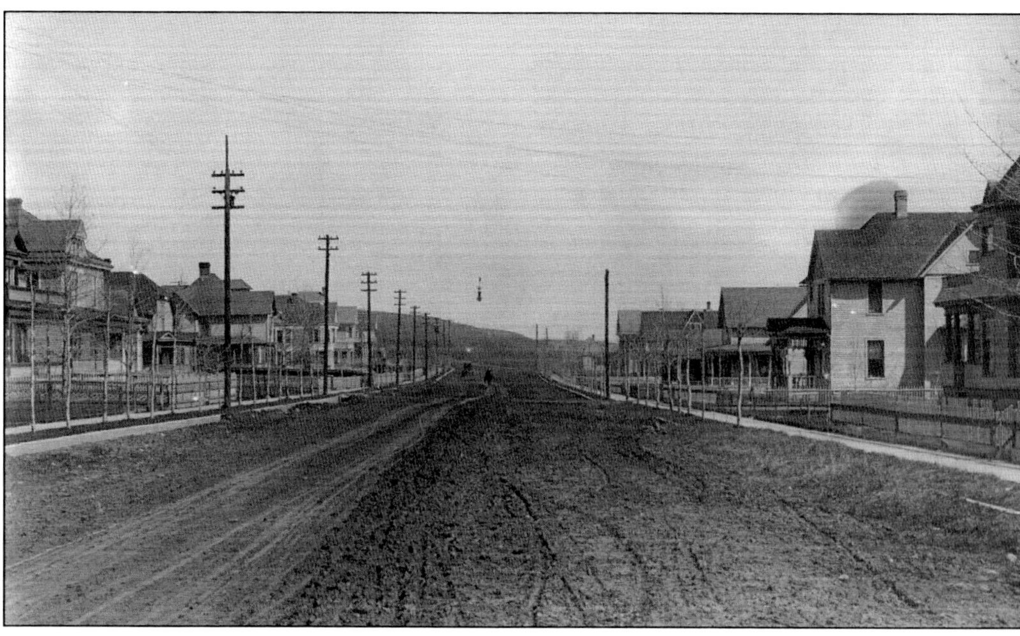

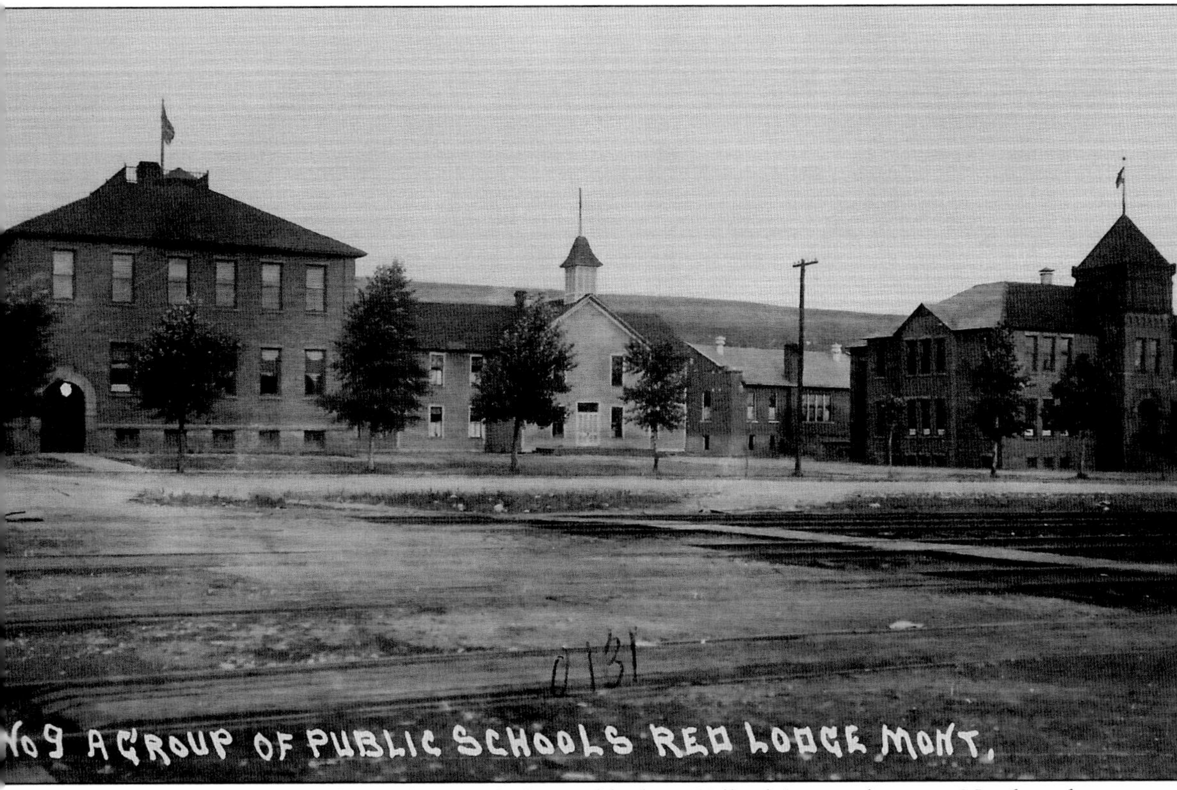

By 1910, schools in Red Lodge took up a whole city block on Villard Avenue between Ninth and Tenth Streets. The Field School (left) was built in 1908. Named for children's poet Eugene Field, it was used until 1952. Central School (middle) was the first frame school in Red Lodge, built in 1891 to replace the original log schoolhouse. The four-room building, which held two grades in each room, was later converted to an administration building. It was abandoned in 1921 after the Roosevelt School was built on Broadway. Carbon County High School (far right), also known as Washington Hall, was built in 1905. The high school's curriculum included three courses: Classical, English, and Commercial. Between the Central School and Carbon County High School is the Manual Arts Building, which was used as a relief office during the Depression. (CCHS.)

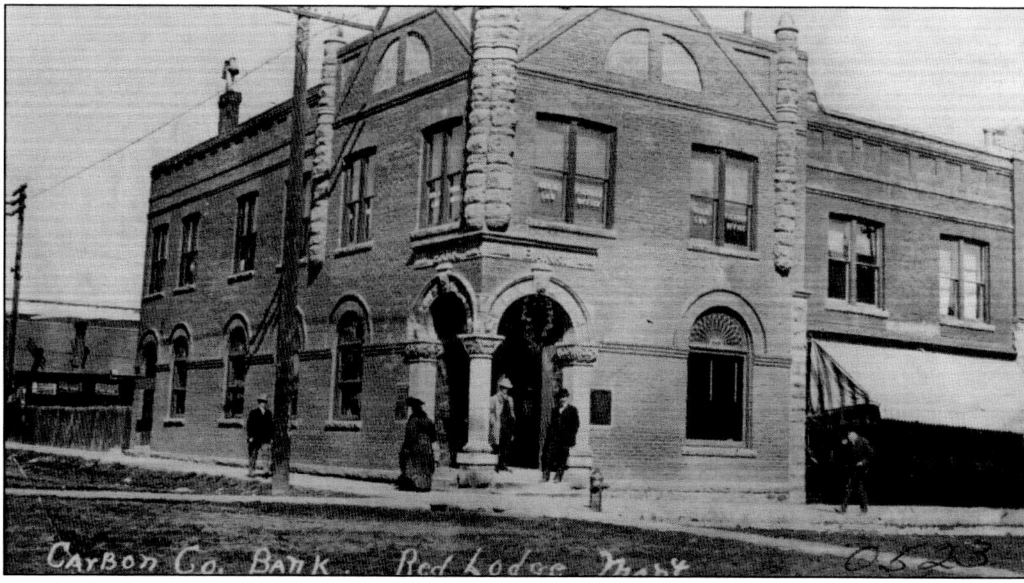

On September 18, 1897, Harry Longabaugh "Sundance Kid," "Kid Curry," and the "Wild Bunch" botched a robbery of the Carbon County Bank, seen here. Sheriff John Dunn and his posse chased the outlaws 80 miles before capturing them near Lavina, Montana. The outlaws were returned to jail in Deadwood, South Dakota, from which they promptly escaped. (CCHS.)

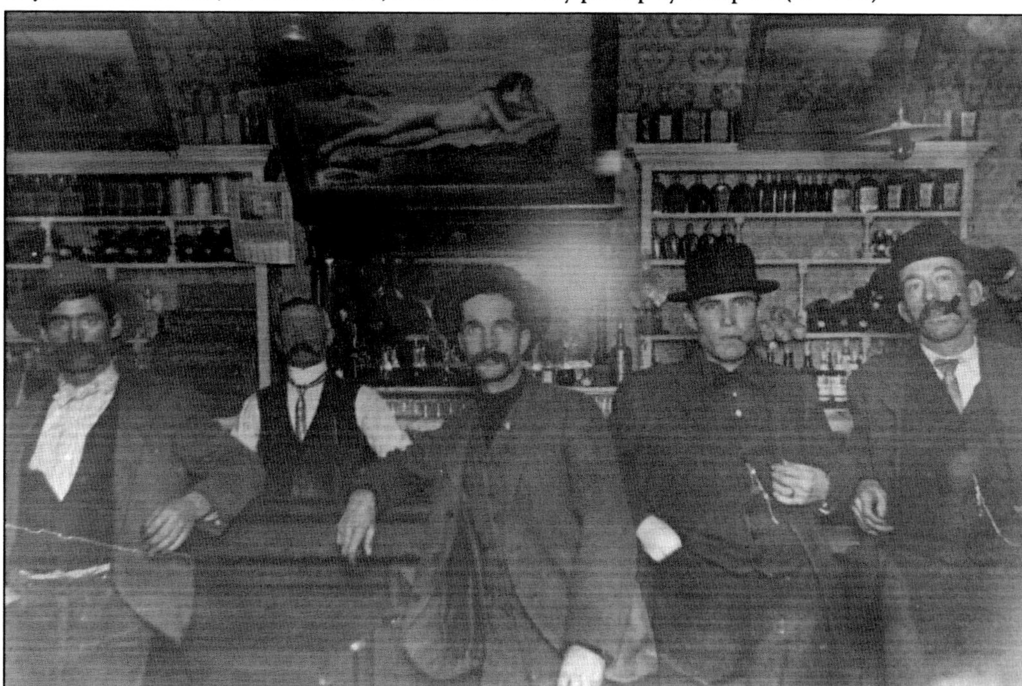

Taft's Hold Up Saloon, seen here around 1900, was a favorite watering hole of Martha Jane Canary, better known as Calamity Jane. A frequent visitor to Red Lodge, Jane was not one to shy away from saloons displaying risqué artwork like the piece hanging behind the bar. Proprietor George Taft is standing behind the bar, and his patrons are, from left to right, Jim Virtue, unidentified, Mina Minar, and Charlie Aiken. (CCHS.)

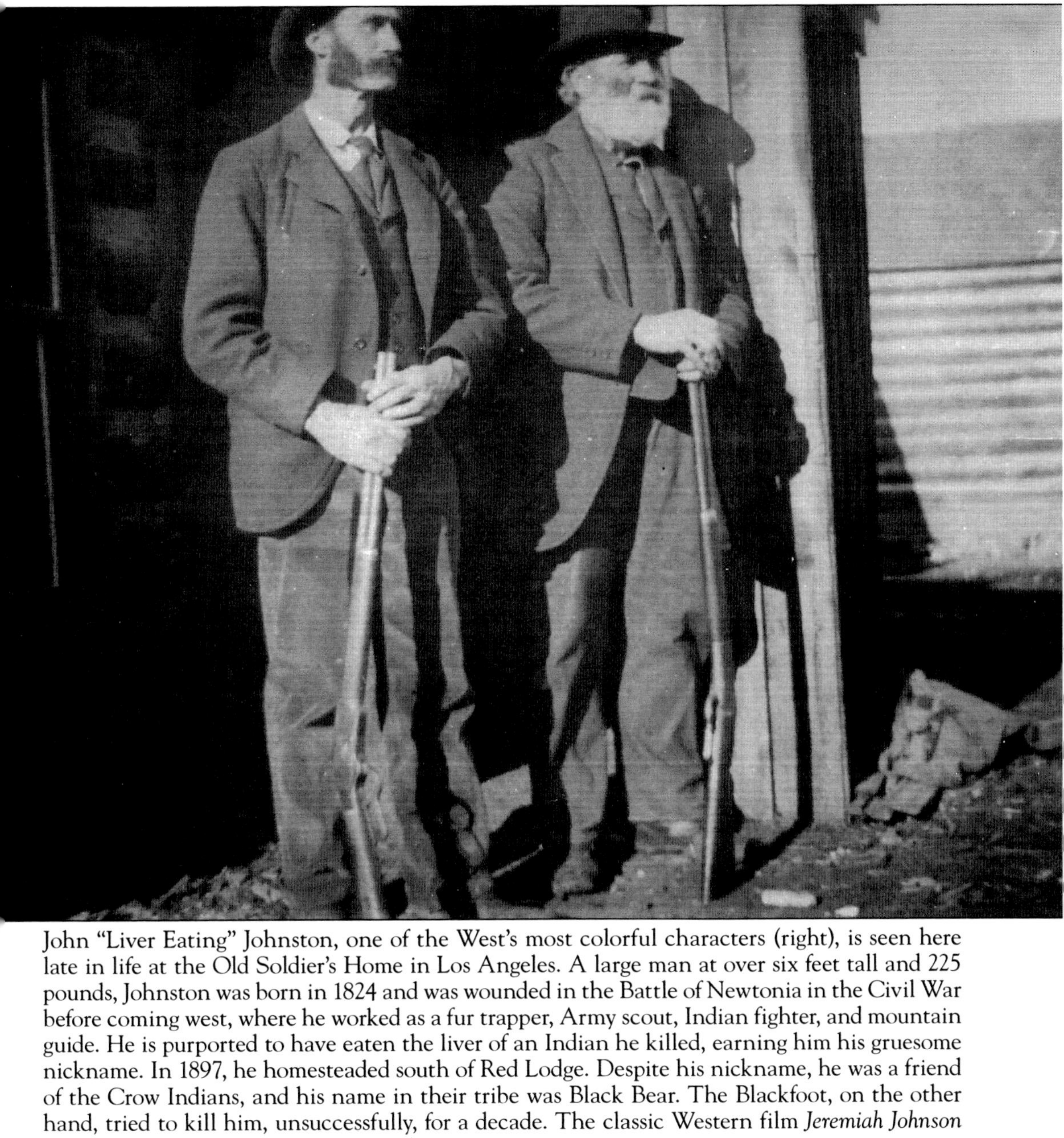

John "Liver Eating" Johnston, one of the West's most colorful characters (right), is seen here late in life at the Old Soldier's Home in Los Angeles. A large man at over six feet tall and 225 pounds, Johnston was born in 1824 and was wounded in the Battle of Newtonia in the Civil War before coming west, where he worked as a fur trapper, Army scout, Indian fighter, and mountain guide. He is purported to have eaten the liver of an Indian he killed, earning him his gruesome nickname. In 1897, he homesteaded south of Red Lodge. Despite his nickname, he was a friend of the Crow Indians, and his name in their tribe was Black Bear. The Blackfoot, on the other hand, tried to kill him, unsuccessfully, for a decade. The classic Western film *Jeremiah Johnson* was based roughly on his life. (CCHS.)

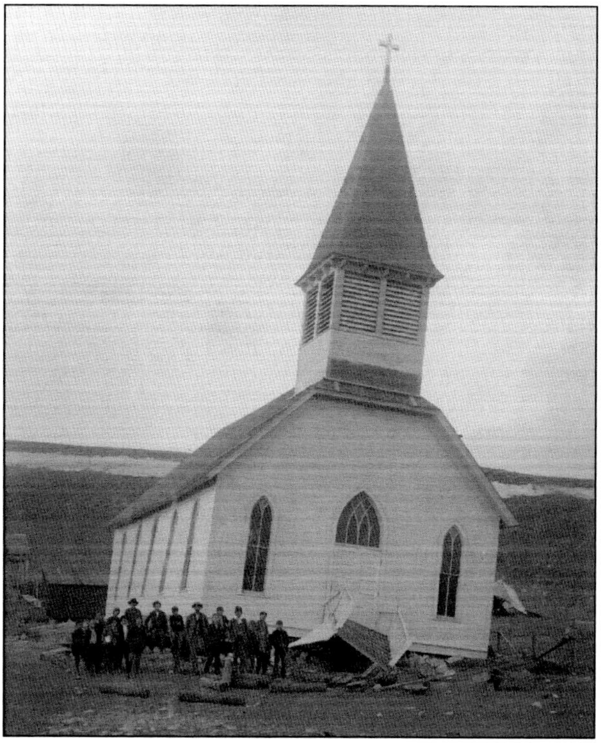

In November 1894, cyclonic winds destroyed several buildings, ripped the roofs from others, and moved the Catholic church two feet off its foundation (left). The "Big Wind of '94", which the storm became known as, "blew haystacks out of the county," according to local weather observer I.A. Draper, who worked in Red Lodge for the US Weather Bureau from 1902 until his death in 1961. His tenure was one of the longest in the bureau's history, and he witnessed many blizzards, including the March 22, 1934, storm that dumped between four and six feet of snow on the area. There was so much snow in town that tunnels had to be dug between businesses like Coleman's Grocery (below) on Broadway. (Both, CCHS.)

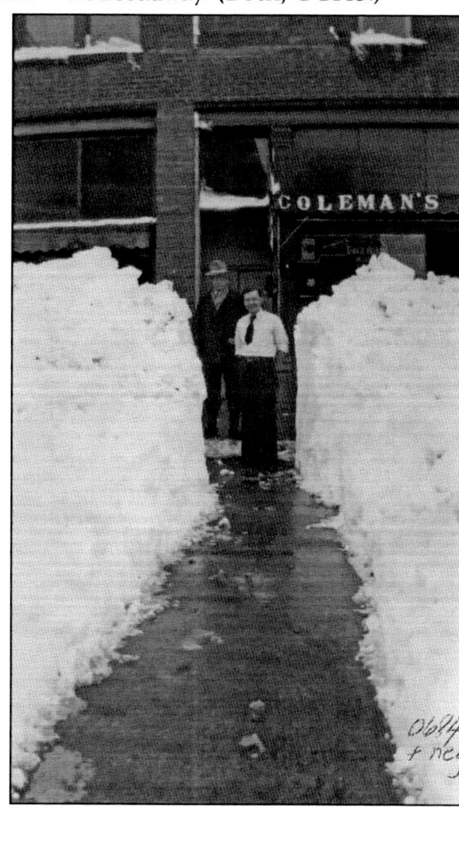

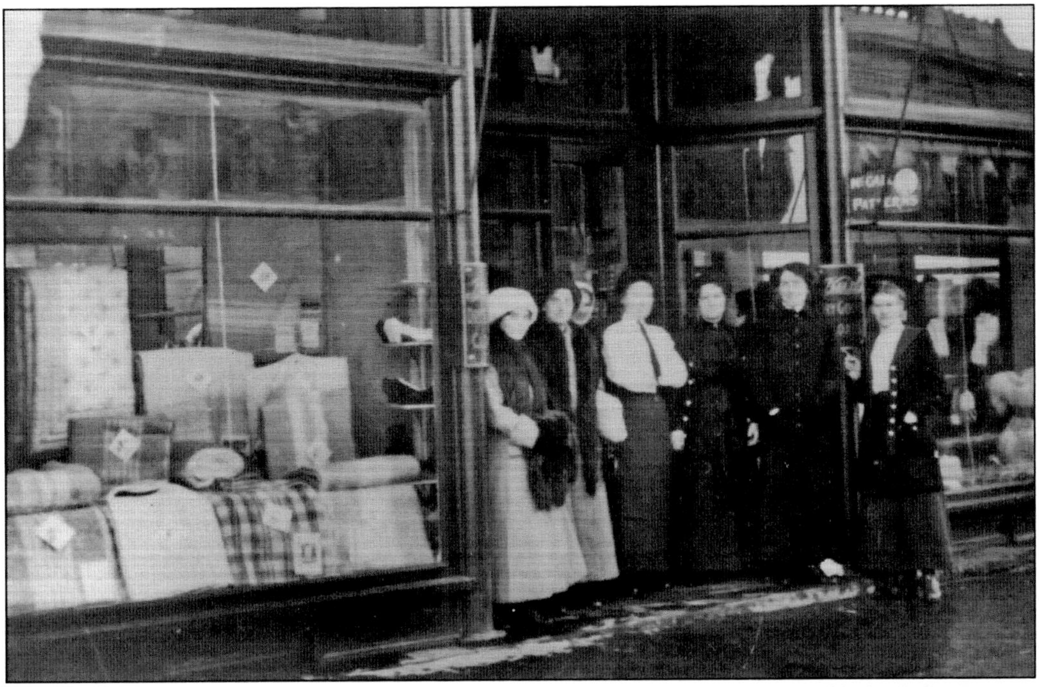

After the closing of his Carbonado store in 1902, Alfred Croonquist established the Boston Store, later renamed Croonquist Mercantile, at 13 North Broadway. Standing in front of Karl Dry Goods wearing the latest in 1914 fashions are, from left to right, Laura (Curry) Croonquist, the wife of Alfred's son Gus; four unidentified people; and Senia (Pollari) Croonquist, the wife of Alfred's son Alfred Jr. (CCHS.)

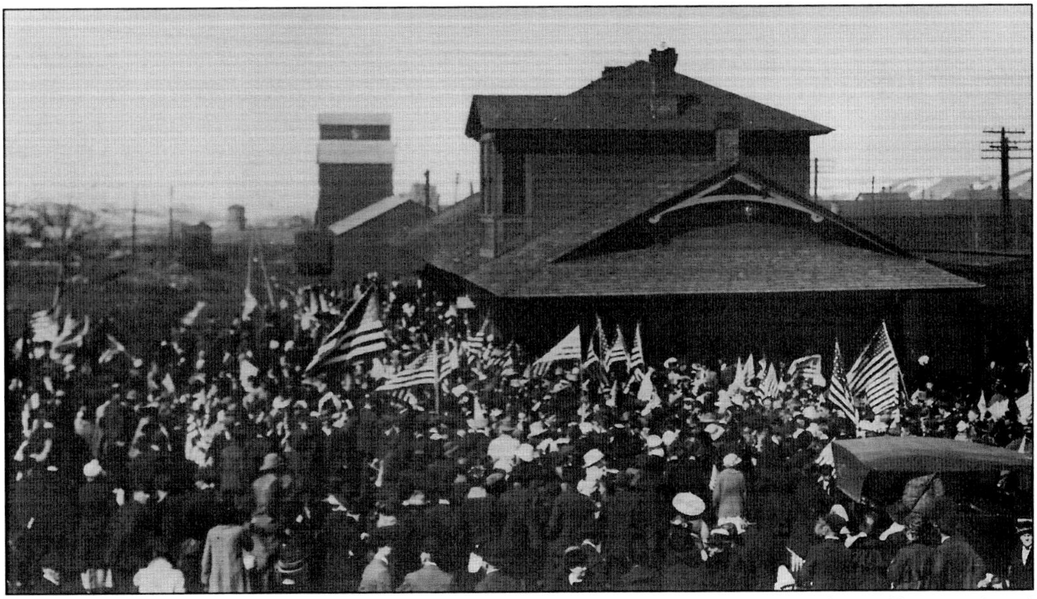

Within 48 hours of the United States declaring war against Germany and its allies on April 6, 1917, a total of 16 men from Red Lodge had already joined the Navy. A crowd of over 3,000 gathered at the Red Lodge depot to bid the naval recruits farewell. Prior to their departure, town dignitaries held a banquet in their honor. (CCHS.)

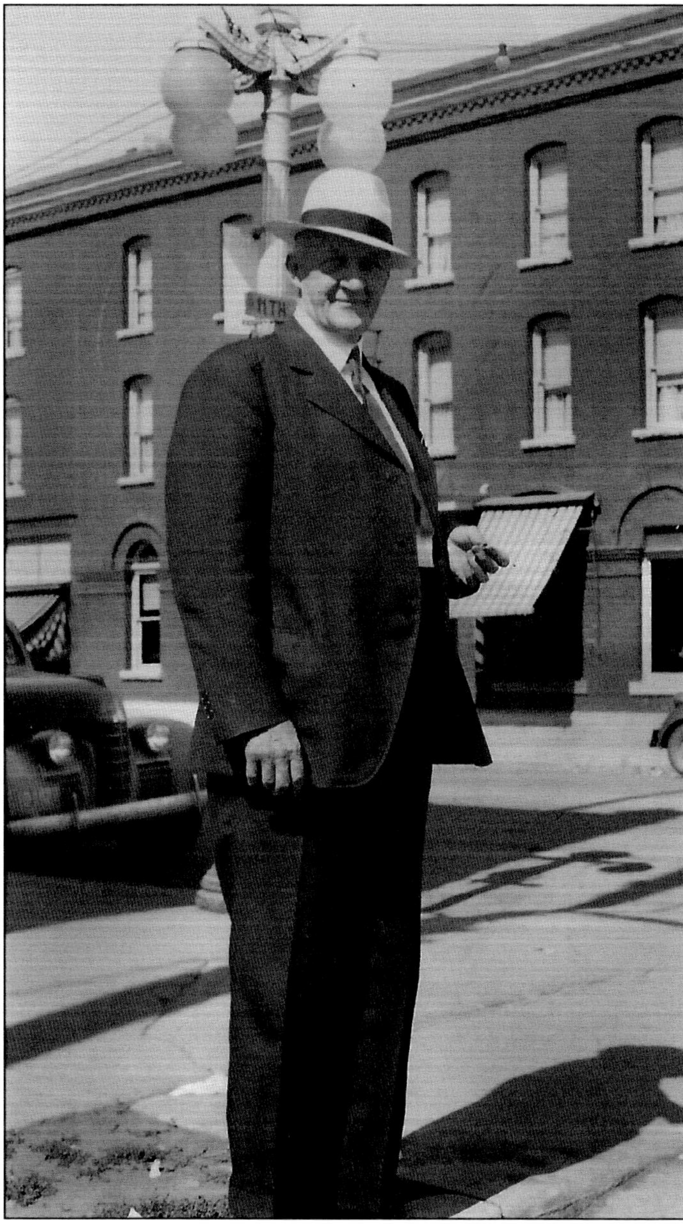

A towering man in both stature and status, Dr. John Charles Frederich Siegfriedt is widely considered to have been the county's biggest civic booster—a driving force in developing Red Lodge into a tourist destination. Dr. Siegfriedt, whom everyone called Doc, came to the region in 1906 as a mining company doctor in Bearcreek, five miles east of Red Lodge. He built a two-story hospital there before moving to Red Lodge in 1930. As a doctor, he tirelessly served the public, but he also engaged in paleontology and geology studies, inviting scholars from around the world to study the rocks of the Beartooth Mountains, some of which date back four billion years. He is one of the first to dream of a road over the Beartooth Plateau to Cooke City and Yellowstone. His vision for a road, which he called the Black and White Trail, led him to Washington, DC, where he helped lobby congress to pass the Park Approach Act, which led to the construction of the Beartooth Highway. (CCHS.)

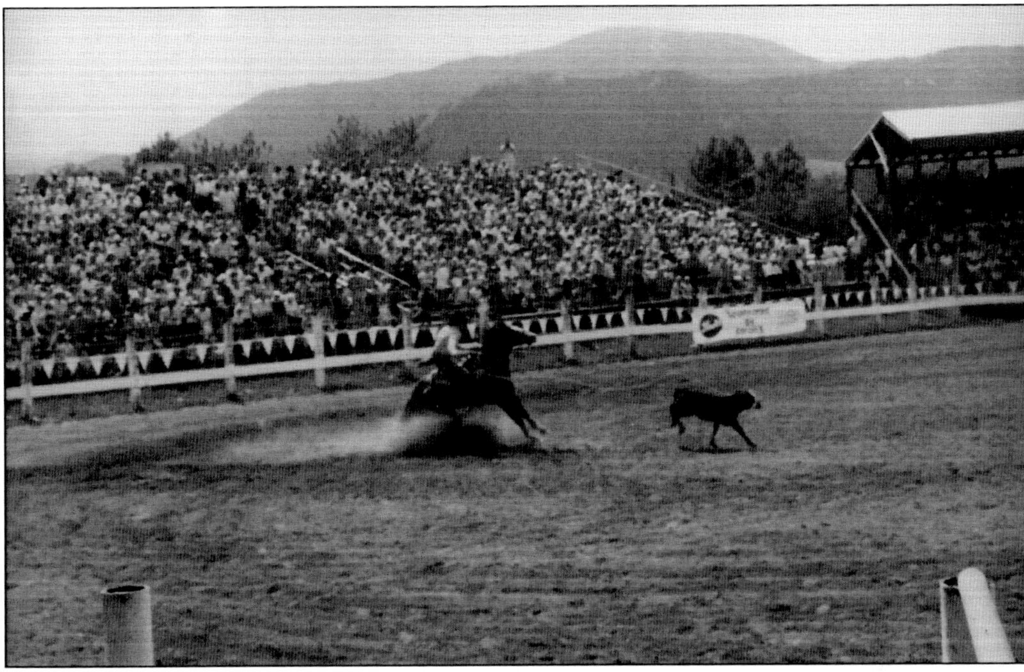

Above, a calf-roper takes his go-round at the Red Lodge Home of Champions Rodeo in the 1930s. Many Carbon County cowboys and cowgirls began their rodeo careers at the Home of Champions Rodeo, the centerpiece of Red Lodge's Fourth of July festivities. Per capita, the county has produced an inordinate number of rodeo legends. The Riding Greenoughs (Ben, Alice, Turk, Margaret, Bill, and Deb) were all raised in the Rock Creek Valley, and the Linderman family (Doug, Bill, and Bud) homesteaded in the Clark's Fork Valley and the Pryor Mountains. At right, Bill Greenough rides the bucking horse Frisco in the 1941 Home of Champions Rodeo. (Both, CCHS.)

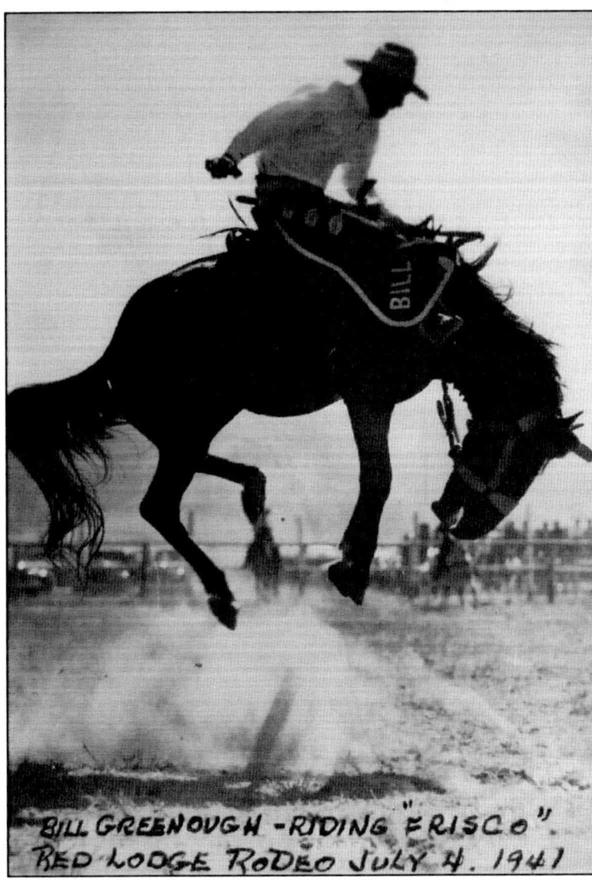

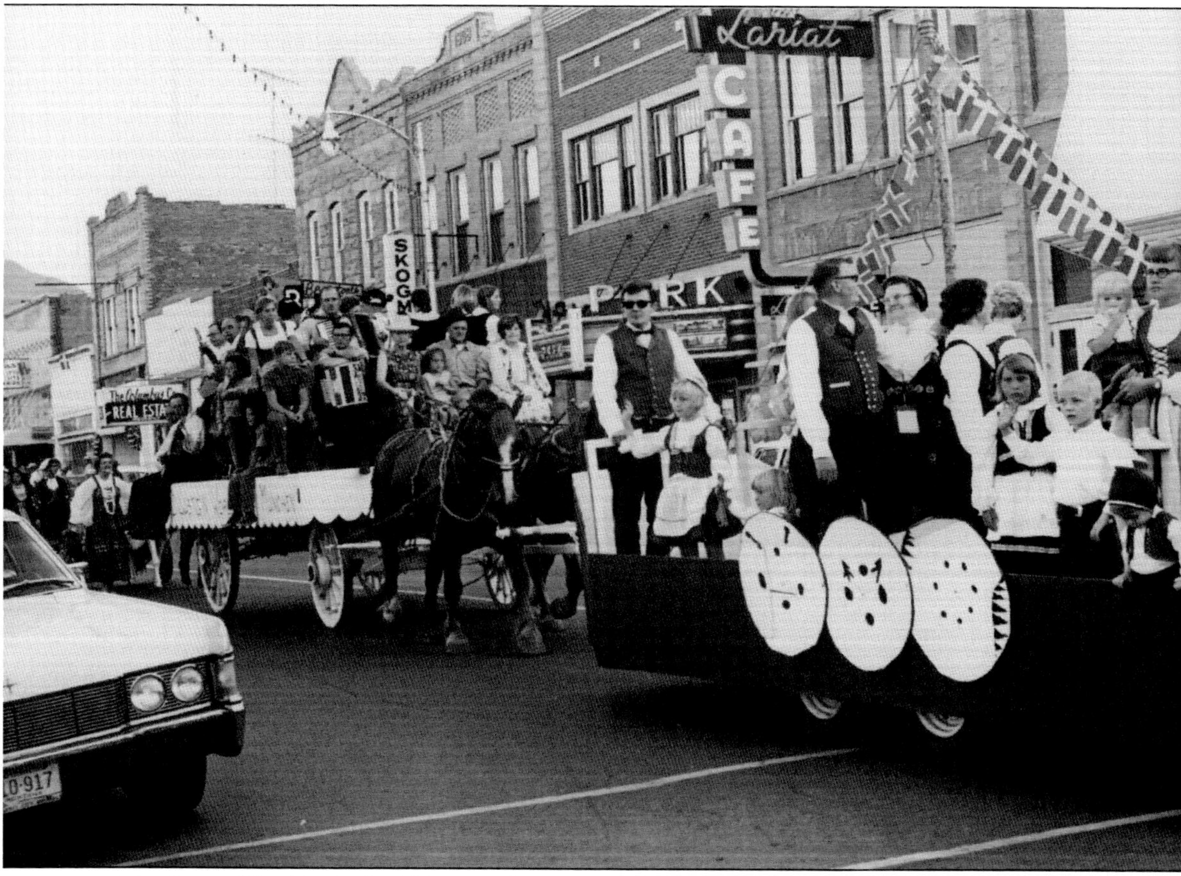

Members of Red Lodge's different ethnic communities, wearing traditional dress, parade down Broadway in 1970 as part of the Festival of Nations. World War II helped melt old ethnic dividing lines in Red Lodge, as second- and third-generation descendants of immigrants stepped increasingly into the forefront of community life. In 1951, Lucille Ralson suggested an art exhibit be set up as an annual fair celebrating the town's cultural diversity, and the Festival of Nations was born. It became an instant tourist favorite; its first year, 1952, brought visitors from 33 states, 39 Montana communities, and Canada. The festival continued to grow through the 1950s and 1960s, with newspapers from New York and Boston to Spokane and San Francisco including it in their annual travel sections. By 1970, the event had expanded into a weeklong festival that included Scottish bagpipers, Finnish dance, Slovakian handwoven lace, Italian bocce ball, German drinking songs, Croatian sausage, and traditional sourdough pancakes of the American West. Despite waning attendance in recent years, the festival is still held on the first weekend in August every year. (CCHS.)

Ten

Rock Creek Canyon

Three miles south of Red Lodge, the main branch of Rock Creek flows through the deep, narrow Rock Creek Canyon. The steep, jagged sides of the Beartooth Plateau to the south, Line Creek Plateau to the east, and Hellroaring Plateau to the west rise thousands of feet around Rock Creek. The narrow floodplain has been home to logging enterprises, cattle ranches, campgrounds, resort hotels, and dude ranches.

Since time immemorial, Rock Creek Canyon has acted as a gateway to the wonders of Yellowstone, which lies beyond the Beartooths. Paleo-Indians used it as a corridor between summer hunting grounds in the high country and winter lodging in the lower Rock Creek Valley. In more recent times, fur trappers and, later, dude ranch excursions followed Rock Creek Canyon into the Beartooths, one of the most remote areas in the lower 48 states—home to grizzly bears, moose, elk, wolves, mountain lions, bison, wolverines, and thousands of lakes fed by glacial runoff and heavy snowfall.

In 1936, the Beartooth Highway opened between Red Lodge and Yellowstone National Park. Open from late May to October, the scenic highway was called the "most beautiful road in America" by roaming CBS correspondent Charles Kuralt. Rock Creek flows from the icy waters of Glacier Lake, high in the canyon on the Montana-Wyoming state line, where peaks rise to over 12,000 feet above sea level, including Montana's highest mountain, Granite Peak, at 12,799 feet.

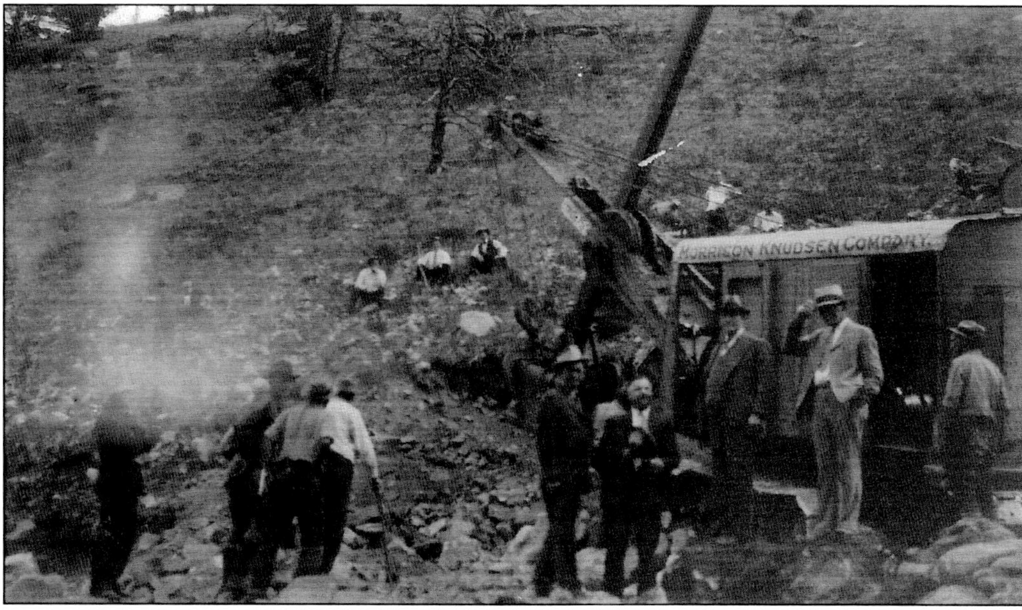

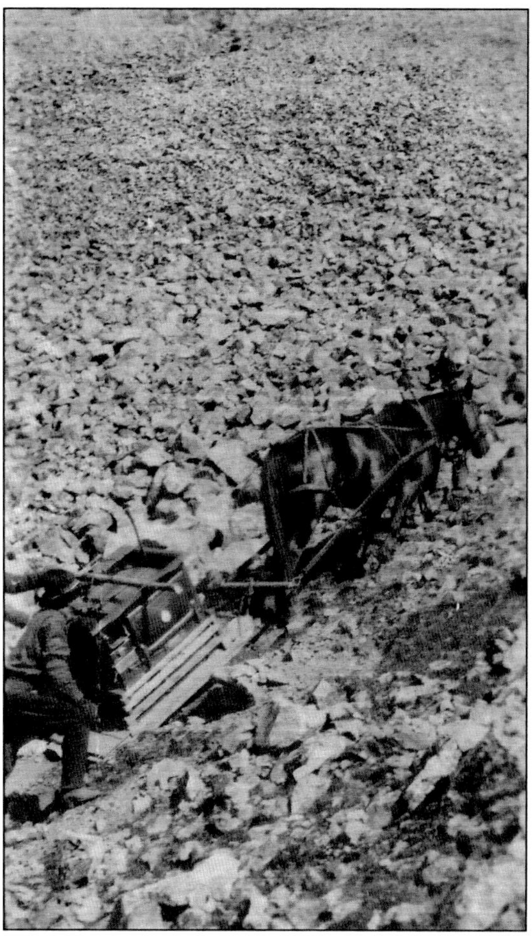

Above, near Quad Creek in 1935, Red Lodge civic boosters Dr. J.C.F. Siegfriedt (third from right) and *Carbon County News* publisher O.P.H. Shelley (second from right) check in with Morris Knudsen officials about the construction of the Beartooth Highway. Siegfriedt and Shelley presented plans to the forestry bureau for a road from Red Lodge to Cooke City in 1924. Their efforts resulted in the Park Approach Act and Amendment to the Federal Highway Act in 1931, which made financing and construction of the highway possible. The highway officially opened in June 1936, with Siegfriedt and Shelley leading the parade. Before the highway, taking pack mules up narrow trails and rocky slopes (left) was the only way to ship goods and materials to the remote ranches and logging and mining camps in the Beartooths. (Both, CCHS.)

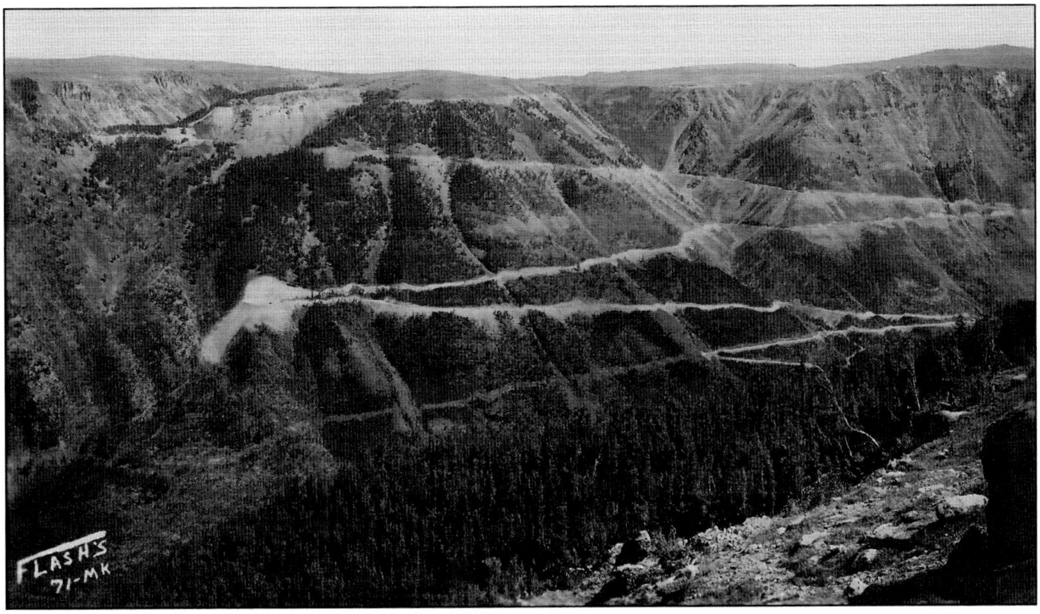

The Kay Egenes aerial photograph above shows how engineers constructed one of the most challenging parts of the Beartooth Highway, creating a series of switchbacks climbing up the east side of Rock Creek Canyon. The 64-mile-long road was built by three contractors: the Morris Knudsen Company built the switchbacks; McNutt & Pyle built the summit section; and S.J. Groves & Sons built the upper Clark's Fork Valley section to Cooke City. Workers from the Civilian Conservation Corps (CCC) also contributed labor. Each company had its own camp for workers. Morris Knudsen's was near where the M-K Campground now sits in Custer National Forest. Egenes also took the candid photograph below of workers from Morris Knudsen taking a break from their precarious perches on the side of Rock Creek Canyon to eat lunch. (Both, Flash.)

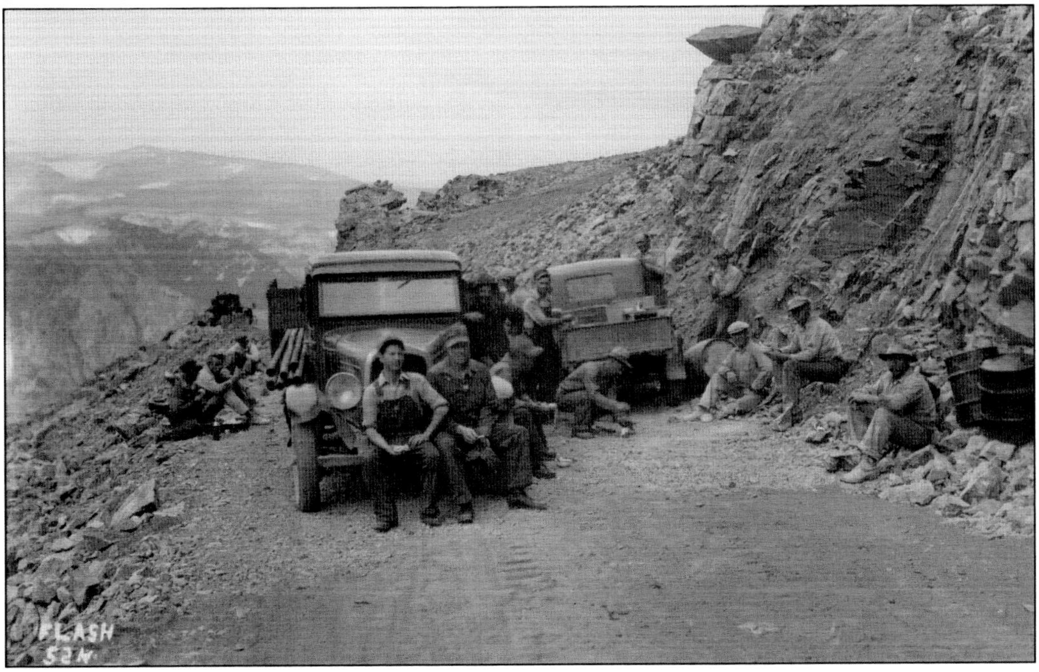

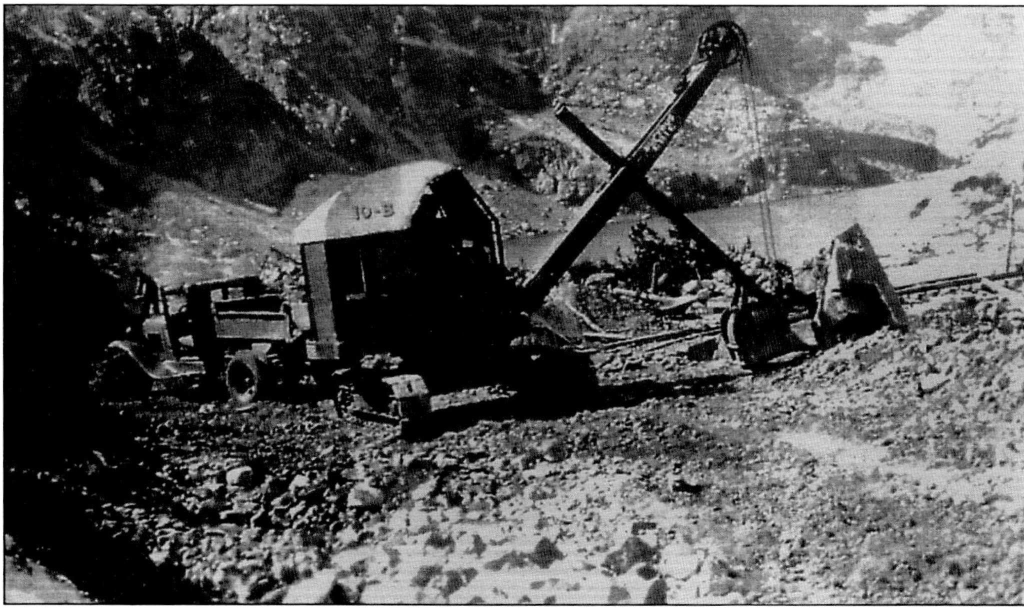

Glacier Lake, the headwaters of Rock Creek, is seen in the background as construction of the Glacier Lake Dam began in 1937. The lake sits at 9,700 feet above sea level and is situated at the bottom of a deep glacial bowl on the Montana-Wyoming state line. S.J. Groves & Sons, employing 64 workers, completed the dam project at a cost of $82,000. (CCHS.)

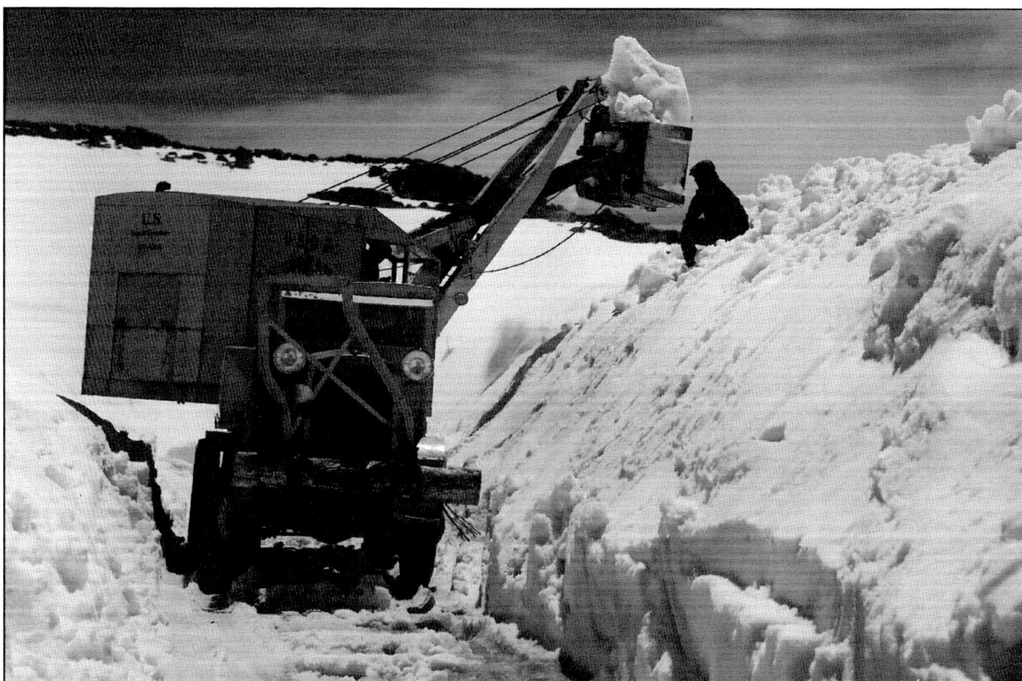

Snow can accumulate in drifts as deep as 20 feet or more on the Beartooth Highway. Workers like the ones seen here in the early 1950s typically start clearing the highway in late March or early April in hopes of having it cleared for the road's annual opening on Memorial Day weekend. However, the heavy, wet snows of March and April often hamper clearing efforts. (CCHS.)

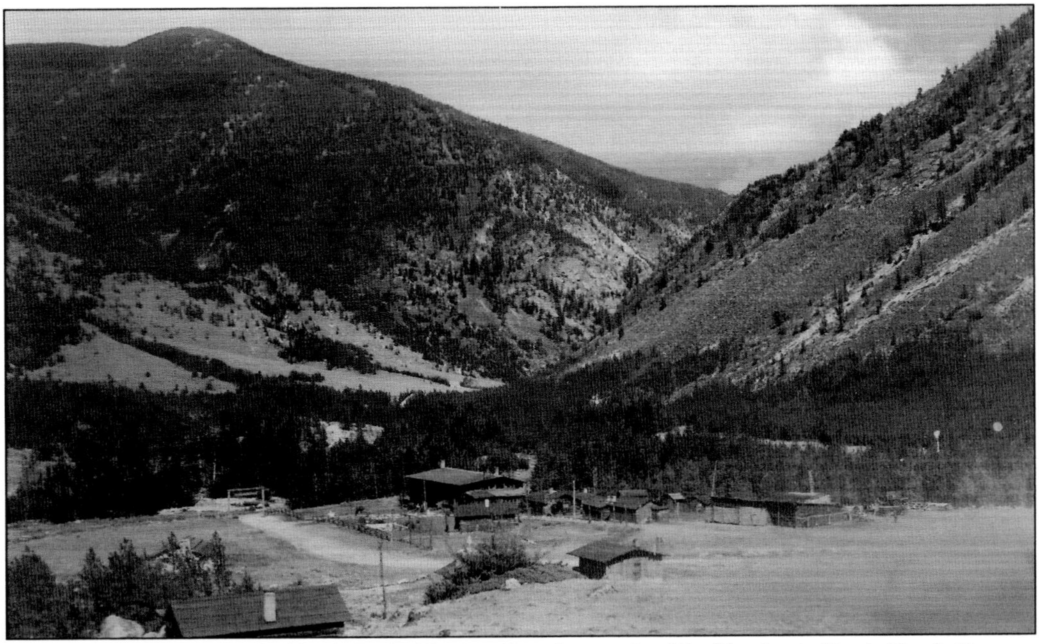

Herbert and Marion Richel built Richel Lodge 12 miles south of Red Lodge in Rock Creek Canyon at the junction of Lake Fork Creek. The Richels created a place where city people, especially children, could enjoy the simple pleasures of rural life, such as fishing, swimming, climbing, picnics, and camping trips. It attracted patrons from nearby Red Lodge as well as Easterners seeking a dude ranch experience. (CCHS.)

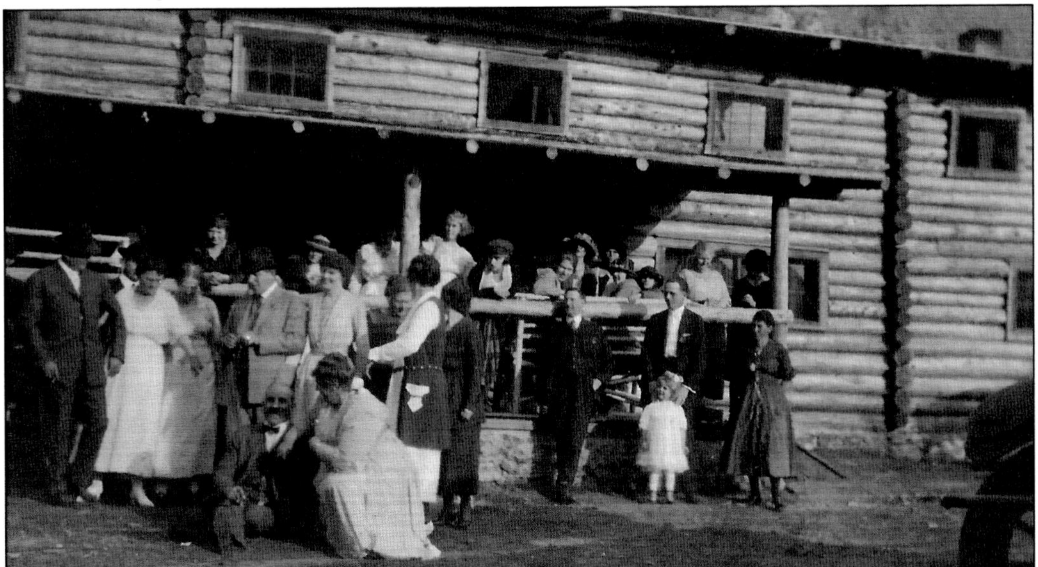

Over the years, Richel Lodge hosted concerts, conventions, political rallies, family reunions, and dances. This photograph shows a gathering of the neighborhood auction bridge at Richel Lodge in the 1930s. The group was entertained by Mr. and Mrs. B.M. Rogers. Identified in this photograph are, in no particular order, Mrs. Tom Pollard (Barbara), Emma Bradley, Jerry Montgomery, Mrs. Haggerty (Lola), Mrs. Luke Chapman (Nan), Mrs. Marian Adams, and Mrs. John Chapman (Alphia). (CCHS.)

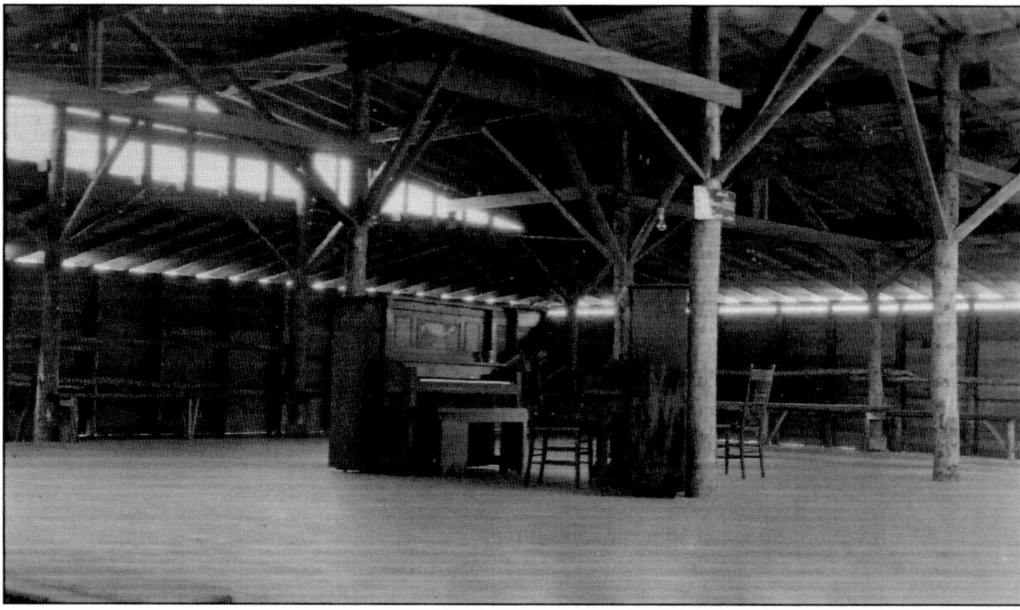

The cavernous hall at Richel Lodge (above) could hold up to 500 people. In addition to the hall, there was also a main lodge containing a living room, a lounge, fire pits, and a dining room (below). There were 11 guestrooms upstairs and 13 guest cabins outside. The lodge also had a pool and a waterwheel, which produced power for the lodge. The Richels made a complementary business team; Marion Richel financed its construction with money earned in her millinery store in Red Lodge, while Herbert Richel's construction skills kept the place running in top shape. The picturesque resort burned down in 1966. (Both, CCHS.)

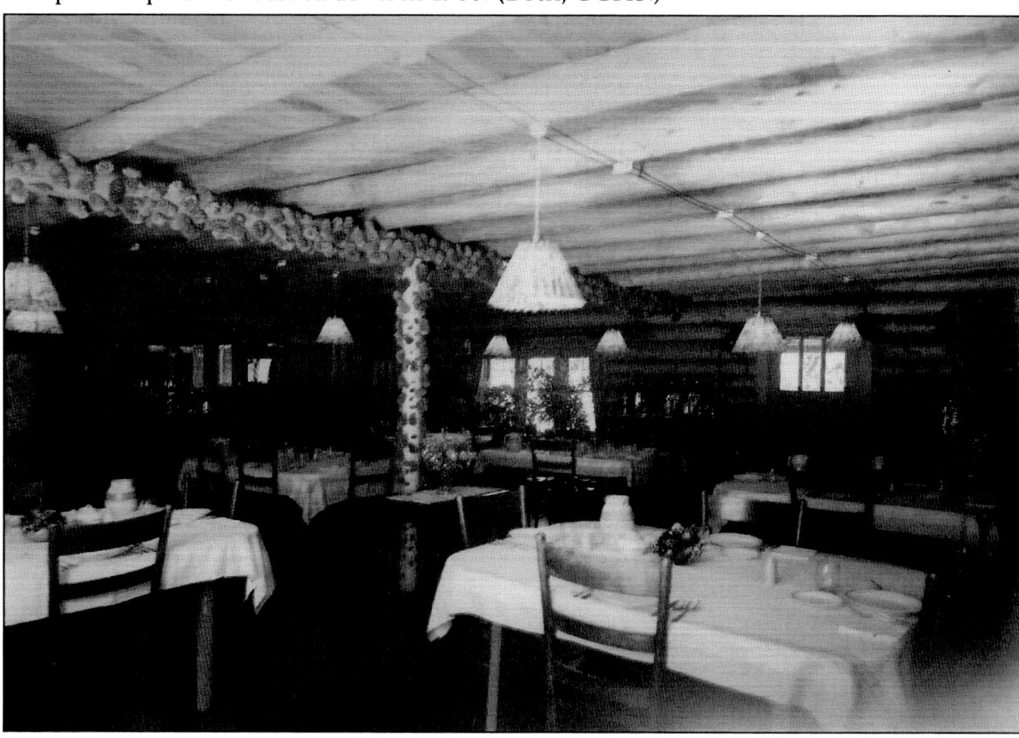

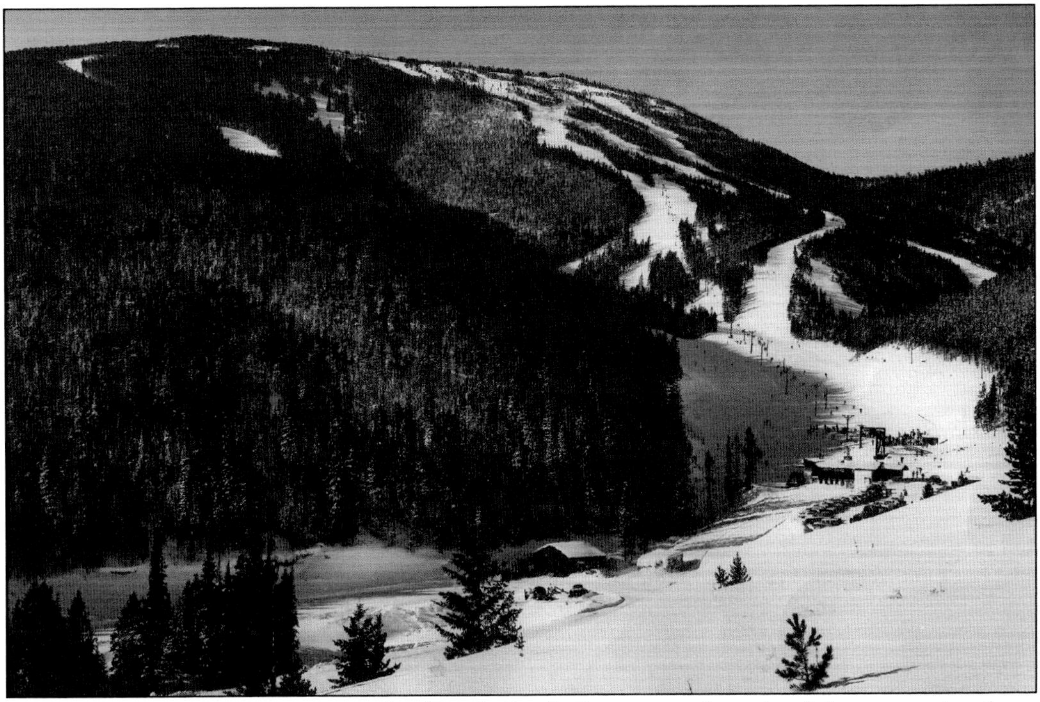

Nestled in a scenic ravine just north of Rock Creek Canyon on the side of the mountain whose name it bears is the Grizzly Peak Ski Area. Opened in 1960, it is the area's longest-running ski facility, now known as Red Lodge Mountain Resort. Daring locals, however, skied the backcountry for many decades before its construction. (CCHS.)

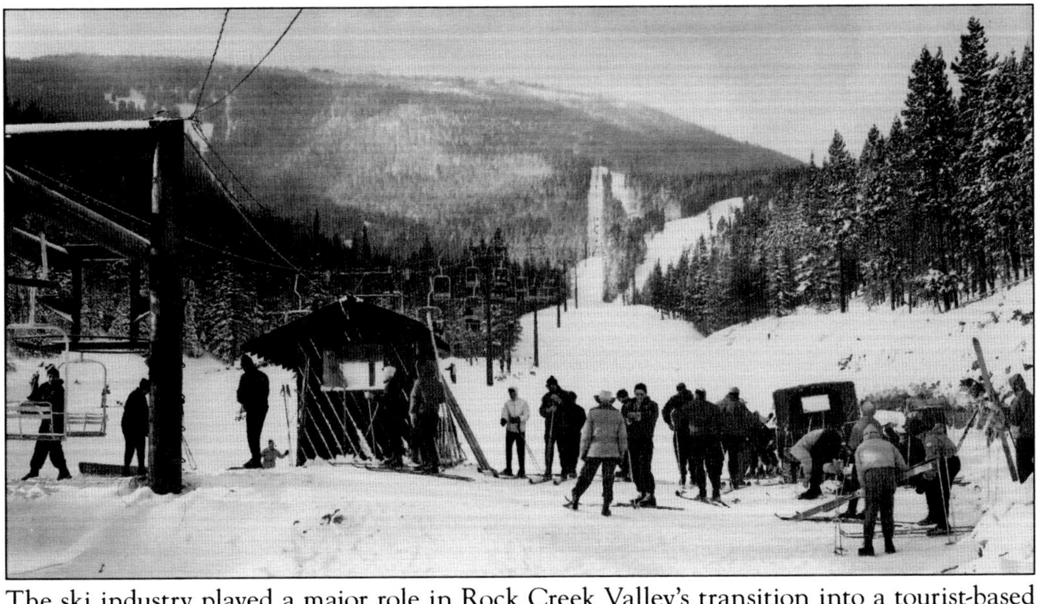

The ski industry played a major role in Rock Creek Valley's transition into a tourist-based economy. Here, skiers line up for the ski lift at Grizzly Peak Ski Area in the 1960s. Due to its unique geography—surrounded by mountains on three sides—Red Lodge and Rock Creek Canyon are subject to micro weather systems that cause heavy localized snowfall. Up to 250 inches fall annually in some areas. (CCHS.)

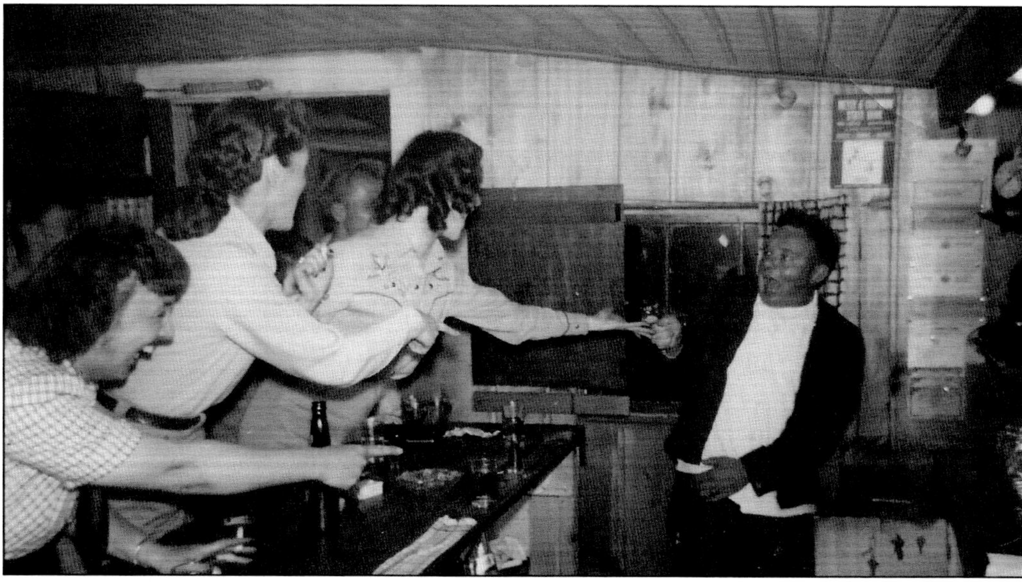

One person who did not like the fact that Red Lodge social establishments largely followed ethnic dividing lines was civic booster Dr. J.C.F. Siegfriedt. He remedied this by constructing Piney Dell Hall in Rock Creek Canyon, about three miles south of Red Lodge, with the idea that it would be used by all nationalities. No matter how cold it got outside, bartender Eddie Zan (above) had a warm smile and a joke for everyone. At the bar are, from left to right, unidentified, Fran Zupan, unidentified, and Bob Dupries. Below, one adventurous drinker takes on "the famous snifter for the brave and foolish." Piney Dell Hall still operates today as part of the Rock Creek Resort complex. (Both, CCHS.)

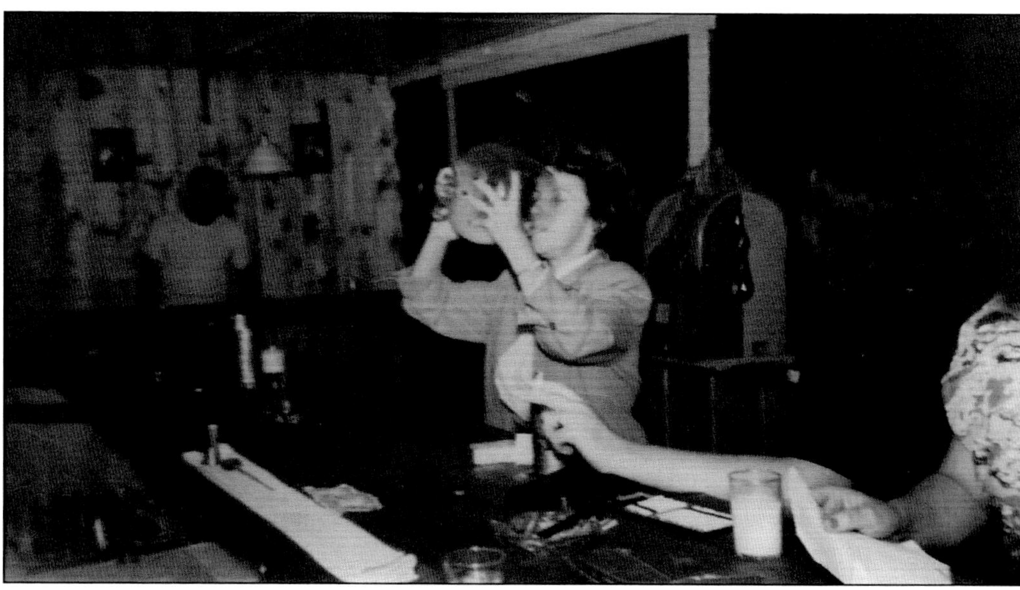

Bibliography

Clayton, John. Images of America: *Red Lodge*. Charleston, SC: Arcadia Publishing, 2008.

Gemmill, Mel and Edward Fenlason. *Roberts: The Agricultural Metropolis of Carbon County*. Joliet, MT: E&M Books, 2000.

Hooker, Patty. Images of America: *Beartooth Mountains*. Charleston, SC: Arcadia Publishing, 2012.

Lampi, Leona. *At the Foot of the Beartooth Mountains*. Coeur d'Alene, ID: Bookpage Press, 1998.

McNeish, Jeff. Images of America: *Clark's Fork Valley*. Charleston, SC: Arcadia Publishing, 2011.

Montana Tech of the University of Montana. *The Beartooth Highway*. Sun River, MT: Montana Litho & Bindery, 1995.

Oliver, Lt. Comdr. George A. (US Navy Ret.). *Joliet: Its Pioneers and Early Days*. Huntsville, AL: Monroe Printing Company, Inc., 1973.

Ringley, Tom. *When the Whistle Blows: The Turk Greenough Story*. Greybull, WY: Pronghorn Press, 2008.

Zupan, Shirley and Harry J. Owen. *Red Lodge: Saga of a Western Area*. Billings, MT: Carbon County Historical Society, 1979, 2000.